Petals of the Self-Formed
Antecedents of Travancore Kingdom

Petals of the Self-Formed
Antecedents of Travancore Kingdom

Raju S.

GYAN

ISBN: 978-81-212-6148-7

Published, 2022

Published by

Gyan Publishing House
5, Ansari Road
Daryaganj, New Delhi-110002
Phone: 011-47034999, 9811692060
www.gyanbooks.com
E-mail: books@gyanbooks.com

Printed at: Gyan Press, Delhi.

Contents

Foreword

Thiruvidamkod (Travancore) on the southern part of Kerala in the West Coast of the peninsular India was a matrilocal chiefdom of heterarchy governed under norms of the elder lineage and without headquarters and geographical delimits until the 18th century. However, historiography has represented it as a kingdom reigned by monarchs. Exposing the absence of any terms in the primary source (mainly the palm leaf records called the Matilakam *grandhavari*) in support of such a characterisation, the book makes a significant departure from the historiography that has entrenched the political past of the region as the history of the Travancore kingdom.

The central focus of the book is on the term *Swaroopam* that lexically denotes 'the self-formed', but connotes a socio-political and mutually interconnected entity. There are four *Swaroopams* — Threppappur, Deshinganadu, Chiruay and Attingal. In the *Matilakam Grandhavari* there is no mention of king and kingdom, which are historians' impositions, the outcome of their figures of speech forming part of the routinised language, used for characterising polity.

Another concept the source invokes along with that of the *Swaroopam* is *muppu* (the eldest among the heads of *Swaroopams*). Accordingly the author of the book points out two misnomers in the existing historiography of medieval Travancore — the 'over reading' and 'interpretational skidding'. This is best analysed in the second chapter through a deconstruction of the historiographical characterisation of the kingdom of medieval Travancore. The author distances the socio-political entity namely, *Swaroopam* from the kingdom and the *nadu* to unravel their intertwining in the historiography.

In the third chapter the author brings in the concept of *Mooppu vaazcha* (rule by the elder lineage) by distinguishing it from *raja bharanam* (the reign by the king). Unlike the king's reign, *Mooppu vaazcha* refers to the elderly lineage head's being in the world with distinction. How the minutely specified time of birth and intricate kinship among the members of *Swaroopam* (*swaroopikal*) play a decisive role in distributing members of *Swaroopam* in various positions of authority is shown in the chapter. Succession to the position and pattern of the four *Swaroopams* have been well brought out by the author. Patterns such as sequential succession, de-succession, multiple *Mooppu vaazcha* (one person becoming *mooppu* of more than one *Swaroopam*) are very well illustrated in the chapter.

One feature highlighted in the organisation of *Swaroopam* is that, even if one person becomes *mooppu* of more than one or two *Swaroopams* at the same time, *Swaroopams* do not get amalgamated. It has been shown that relinquishing the position of *mooppu* was quite frequent. Another feature prominently brought out is the institution namely, adoption of matured male and female members from outside the four *Swaroopams,* which was quite frequent. In the book adoption has been schematized into seven types. Both adults and children were adopted into the four *Swaroopams*. One or more *Swaroopams* could jointly adopt people from outside the *Swaroopams*. They may or may not become *mooppu*, but any way they are placed in positions of authority. Sometimes, conjugation happened to resolve dispute among the *swaroopikal* (the members of the *Swaroopam*). The practice of adoption was not just to fill the absence of any one to succeed to the position of *mooppu* but for a variety of other functions as well.

Adoption was customary and governed by specific rites (*aachaarams*), that were critical in the organisation and functioning of *Swaroopams*. The sixth chapter shows how the customs and rites were integral to relations of power and inter-subjectivity of the *swaroopikal*. They had much to do with the legitimacy of power not only of the prevailing time but of the future too. How they moulded and modulated subjectivity and inter-subjectivity are well illustrated in the chapter. Those written palm leaf documents (*grandhavari*) were functional in the everyday proceedings as well as exceptional on all times. Recalling of centuries old *grandhavaries* negotiated both intra *Swaroopam* as well as inter *Swaroopam* relations. The custom of archivalaisation or the role of customary power play is the central theme of the seventh chapter. Various specialised people such as *aachaarakkanakkar* (record keepers of customs and rites) were involved in the process of archivalaisation, which unfolds truth in the custom.

The book ends up with an afterward that explores new trajectories ahead rather than summarising the arguments in all the chapters. It deserves a special mention that the mode of analysis employed in this book is that of micro-history. Aggregate categories such as culture, politics, feudalism, society, domination, caste, class, society, state etc., are very sparingly used. If at all such categories figure anywhere, invariably they are exclusively in their generic and contextual semantics.

This book is a brilliant attempt at bypassing the methodologically flawed routine practice of characterising all polity as sovereignty by postulating state power everywhere. Although not overtly stated, the basic tenor of this book is poststructuralist. It is a different way of using the old sources, which helps discover strikingly new facets of the past, indeed at the micro level independent of the top down schema, and inevitably as part of the grounded, but not suggesting a flourish of the button up schema either. This precludes the scope of totalising as well as localising. It is a phenomenological search along the path it renders plausible in itself.

Thiruvananthapuram **Rajan Gurukkal**

Acknowledgements and Dedication

This book might not have come to print without Mr Jaiprakash Raghaviah. I do not know how to thank him. No words are adequate. I thank Mr Mano, Thrichur, for designing the cover page.

I dedicate this book to my mother S. Rugmini Amma.

Chapter - 1

Introduction

If the themes engaged in this book could be aggregated and generalised, it could be put as *how rulers were being ruled*. The tone of this assertion may appear as universalistic and pedantic. On the other hand, I do not propose to provide any universal or final answer to the general questions of kingship and dominating power. What is attempted in this book is a topical study of the discursively constituted relations of power in the late medieval Travancore (prior to the appearance of the Kingdom of Thiruvithamkur (Malayalam word)/ Travancore (English version) situated at the south-western tip of peninsular India. Although I use the proper names 'Thiruvananthapuram and 'Travancore', during the medieval period Travancore as a socio-territorial entity did not exist; but I am using it just to begin with. The *Swaroopam's* and *Nadu* were the main socio-territorial units in existence. Swaroopam's specificities which eventually got distorted and obfuscated under the traditional empiricist/positivist form of history writing have to be unravelled. Definitely the new type of historical thinking and reconstruction I undertake here is occurring across the world at present though its seminal inspiration derives from the poststructuralist thinking developed since the mid-1960's Europe.[1] Instead of any one methodology I use 'Conceptual constellation'. The 'conceptual constellation' of this book does not work with the concept 'stasis'. The term 'constellation' is used to allude to the multiplicity involved in going ahead with the subject matter. The concept 'constellation' persuades a researcher to maintain coherence and forestall falling into the pitfalls of self-contradictions and give primacy to coherence'[2]. I use conceptual constellation or conceptual complex without being eclectic. The word Kingdom does not appear in the core of this book, but only in the title. But then, it is the 'antecedents' which have freedom and high frequency in the Chapters to come.

I would also own up its influence to a great extent in my analysis; nonetheless, this intellectual stimulation is appropriately modified according to the logics of the discipline which is history and the context which is prior to the coming of Travancore kingdom. In short, content of this book is all about pre-Travancore kingdom; that is swaroopams.

The major analytical strands in the book are the organisation of co-existence of swaroopams and the relations of power within each of them and among them. I will be referring to events and activities that occurred during 14th to the beginning of 18th century AD. The historical studies about Travancore occurred mainly in the late 19th century onwards which is a mix of colonial cataloguing and ethnographic mapping to indigenous royalist adorations and crass empiricist reconstructions. The positions of power and representations are intertwined in a complex structure and therefore any attempt to clarify one part presupposes the rational analysis of the other part too. In my attempt here I give a tacit priority to the historiographic and representational part under the strong conviction that more than the lack of evidence or paucity of intellectual sources it is the distorted form of the so called modern historical writing that has created the grievous intellectual wedge in the continuum of history of pre-kingdom Travancore specifically the late medieval period. Definitely I do not point out any specific historian or school in this regard; nor do I fire aimlessly at the whole maze of historical writing on this period. It is more than simply an authorial or generic question. It spills out to the discourse of history at large and the sub-surface forces are at play here. In my analysis both contemporary narratives and future (19th and 20th century) historical re-constructions become equally important. More than factual truths, temporal identities or any specific work that I refer to is the genealogical linkages and conceptual mutations that occur in the discourse of the royal power in the period from 14th to the 18th centuries. Although I mention the historical period, I have strong awareness about the futility of historical reconstructions involving interpretation of origins and stages of transition in teleological perspective. The initial and terminal time points taken up for interpretations differ depending on the theme and variables that I will be concentrating on.

Coming to the strand of royal power, we find that most of the discursive representations-contemporary narratives, colonial constructions, empirical historiography etc, have distorted swaroopam's organisation and the modalities of the exercise of power. We may identify characteristic nuances at play here. The *genre* of the so-called indigenous history that emerged in the 19th century was written by historians commissioned by the royal office. Many of the works they produced became uncritical adulations of the royalty and its worldly being and functions. On the other side, the colonial manuals tried to locate royalty within the logics of a pragmatic civic-administrative discourse; the colonial interest was more on the hegemonic management of an alien population than the metaphysical or scientific understanding of kingship. A new form of history emerged by the 20th century which claimed to be scientific, secular, non-royalist, theoretical, and in some cases nationalist and cultural. Perhaps here more problems were galore than the previous two. The most important one is an illusionary trap into which this historical school fell in the name of scientific spirit and empirical precision. In the zest to write an absolutely objective and non-partisan history it not only incorporated western empiricist tenets, but also adopted a whole-cloth western paradigm of kingship itself.

The very figure of the authoritative head (not in a juridico-political sense) of swaroopams and the structure in which he was located got completely distorted. In the fervour to create a coherent image of kingship undue empiricist surgeries were carried out. The form of indigenous kingship with all its characteristic variations became monolithic and a simulacrum of the western model. The incumbent twisting that occurred here was not only methodological and conceptual but also political in some cases. The western model of kingship with its Romano-Christian undertones was sacred, dynastic, successional, and hierarchic. The paradigm was handy and formulaic and it was easy to enforce the indigenous material into this redundant structure. Once the kingship became fixed in such a structure, the reality over which the king ruled also could be explained using western theories. Models from political economy and empiricist sociology to Marxism and Positivism become handy for interpreting Travancore's history and its relation to kingship. Of course only a few such theories were applied here and a limited number of histories written as the facts stand. But we should be cognizant of the virtual potentiality of the western theories to spawn forth unrealistic histories of this land in the future. In the subsequent chapter, I will be detailing these aspects at length by taking up the existing works related to the subject matter of this book. Selection of texts does not exhaust the entire gamut, but they are selective exemplars.

In the western influenced histories of whatever theoretical persuasion, there has occurred far-reaching "Over-reading" and "Interpretational Skidding" (I will be explaining these two terms in the chapter two) in the understanding and representation of kingship in Travancore, especially from the late medieval period to the early modern times. This in turn resulted from the fundamental misunderstanding of the nature of ruling power, the familial structure in which royalty was embedded, the specific notion of the sacred that accrued to his office and the stratification and the ideological systems that ordered the social space. Contra the western model based on teleological temporality, dynastic succession and sacred hierarchy, the authoritative head in swaroopams was based on a complex structure of co-equal power positions, ascension by seniority and diagrammatic distribution of families. Genealogies, spatial distribution of families and seniority by age are utmost important in the organisation of positions of power. As already stated, the territory of the 'head' is represented with an indigenous term '*swaroopam*'. Its meaning and implications are far different from the semantically fixed and unified notion of Roman 'Rex' that has influenced the western concept of kingship. The western notion tied to territoriality, sovereignty, non-violability and sacrality is clearly distinct from the swaroopam and *muppu* (authoritative head or still better the most distinguished position within a swaroopam, tribe, clan, family etc) position of power whose protocol was based on a variant set of indigenous attributes. Only muppu of swaroopams are dealt in this book. The conventional historical analysis bypassed this theoretical nuance and trimmed the indigenous kingship or better *muppuvaazcha* of swaroopams to the western size. These points will be taken up for detailing in the second chapter.

Therefore, our task becomes more prodigious and challenging. First we have to clear off the discursive cobwebs that have swallowed up the figure of the muppu beyond recognition, mainly in the historical works, traditional narratives and the royalist paeans. 'Over-Reading' and 'Interpretational Skidding' have transformed muppu into king and swaroopam into kingdom. Secondly, once these patinas are rubbed off we may be able to deconstruct the historiographically constructed royal figure, his office and his realm of pre-Travancore kingdom of late medieval period and anchor under a more realistic historical light. If this latter task can be undertaken successfully it will open up a more creative theoretical trajectory that may be applicable to similar historical situations both within and outside India; in short, towards a much better understanding of 'how rulers were being ruled' with which we began this introductory chapter. Nevertheless, till the last chapter I do not use concepts such as state, society, people and domination and so on. As I emphasised earlier, the second chapter onwards analyse interiority of swaroopams and their co-existence premised on the deconstruction of the discourses that have emerged out of the notion of kingship and state. I shall turn to this aspect in more detail in the chapters to come.

I should beforehand ward off probable queries of potential readers of this book by stating that I am not concerned with the origins of swaroopams and their transition to kingdoms. Besides, any one searching for 'what is swaroopam' will be disappointed. This is because the central concern of this book is the customary practices, cultural patterns and inter-positional relations that enabled different swaroopams to co-exist without subsuming one another. To be specific, this book focuses on a period when Travancore had not become what it eventually came to be by the first quarter of eighteenth century. In other words, Travancore is a *post festum* construct of nineteenth century. While addressing the questions posed in this book, I attempt to demonstrate the philosophically grounded contention that historical writings at this juncture of poststructuralism and probabilistic sciences cannot be deterministic and assertive about the findings. Deterministic enquiries cannot capture the contingent, negotiated, momentary and yet structural character of the swaroopams. This book is at the same time about select aspects of swaroopam but it is not about what it was. I have mentioned earlier that if the questions posed in this book are summed up and generalised then the question is 'how rulers were being ruled'. I am posing the question 'how' and not 'why' purposively. In this book nowhere, the 'why' question is posited because of the conviction that the answers given to it linearly or non-linearly lead to some or other originary moment or event or condition. Addressing question of 'why' is a search for origin and the subsequent transformations. Whichever way qualified search for origin will be invariably, I have the conviction, tantamount to either metaphysics or theology. The Rankeian question of 'what' really happened is also deferred in this text. I have omitted this question from my interpretation and analysis. Instead the question 'how' is posited in the central court of the book.

Possible readers may get disappointed if they look for the answer to the question 'what is/was *swaroopam*'. Nowhere in this book I attempted to raise this question and therefore reached nowhere near the answer. This ontological question is partially dealt with by way of detailing nuanced relations that are included in the second to the sixth chapters. Some of my well wishers asked me whether or not I can define '*swaroopam*'. The answer was in negative tone. Defining it will involve reductionism as I will have to reduce the complex phenomenon into a complicated one whose variables can be explained or reduced to few.

Can the history of *Swaroopams* be portrayed in the conceptual framework of 'little kingdom' or its variants? The *Swaroopams* used to derive legitimacy and authority from their relation to the tutelary deity Sri Padmanabha Swamy. The devotion of the members of swaroopam and authoritative head (*muppu*) was such that he adopted the title *Padmanabha Padadasa*. I use the term 'authoritative head' for muppu in the absence of a better phrase in English. The temple of Padmanabha was administered by a Brahminical body known as *Ettarayogam* (hereafter *Yogam*) at least since 13th century and before that it was administered by a body known as *Sabha*. Skirmishes and contestations between authoritative heads of the swaroopam and yogam were frequent. This aspect is well known to historians. But none of such conflicting relations between them ended up in physical violence but resolved through 'customary practices' and their manipulations. How customs functioned in the relations of significance in the organisation of Swaroopams is elaborated in the fifth chapter of this book. Following Galey's model of little kingdom, Uwe Skoda in her article[3] argues that such a relation between the authoritative head and the tutelary deity as a condition of little kingdom. But then in the case of *Swaroopams*, it is true that the authoritative heads or *muppu* and other members of his family had outmost devotion to this temple of Padmanabha. Several others such as yogam and feudatories had special relation with this temple. In the matters of the temple, except material practices, yogam had a upper hand than muppu. In short, it is difficult to portray swaroopam had a space created by its relation with the temple of Padmanabha which lend legitimacy to swaroopam. It is most probable that swaroopam family had devotional and administrative aspects in relation to various temples and it in turn lent legitimacy to them. But in the case of this temple yogam and its *yogakkar* (members of the Ettarayogam) had superior role in comparison with the swaroopam families or muppu. Yogam had authority to prevent, prohibit, stop, any of the muppu's from performing rituals and ceremonies including reopening of the temple after closing down the temple for certain years. Yogam did so accusing the muppu for non-accomplishment of certain customary activities in the temple. The power relation between muppu and yogam was sensitive and specific to conjecture, time, occasion, condition, situation, context and so on. The strategic notion of power which resembles that of Foucault's 'power relations' help to make sense of such moments of irreducible power relations. This implies that although the special space created between muppu and the temple had legitimising power to control 'people', this special relation between muppu and the temple was decisively connected to his relation with yogam and his legitimacy among the *yogakkar*. I do not elaborate the relation between muppu and the yogam in this book although in the alignment between them it was critical in the organisation of *swaroopam*. The muppu had special relation with this temple but *Yogam* had super-special relation with this temple. Royal legitimation through the special relation to tutelary deity took place only after the formation of Travancore kingdom during the first half of eighteenth century or with the ritual of *Hiranyagarbham* performed in the temple and self proclamation of King Marthanda Varma as *Padmanabha Dasa* (Servent of the god Padmanabha). When concerned with the Padmanabha Swamy temple, devotion of the *muppu* to the deity was converted to strategic power relations since then.

Another aspect of 'little kingdom' is specific relation of a kingdom to a greater kingdom for its legitimacy as George Berkemer (2015) states in his article 'Little Kings or Kingdoms? In the instance of *Swaroopams* such a feature is absent. In any case there were no Kingdoms or any of its variants during the period under consideration; there were only *Swaroopams* and *Nadus*. In short, *swaroopam* cannot be imagined in the framework of the Little Kingdom.

If I situate the substance of this book in the plane of inter-disciplinarity, then what comes first to my mind is the convergence of anthropology and history. Ethno history[4] or historical anthropology comes to the proximity of the 'conceptual constellation' that I follow. But then the substance and methodology of this book cannot be qualified as ethno history. I have not engaged in any field work. I have not invoked Bronislaw Kasper Malinowski, Victor Turner or Clifford Geertz either for raising questions or for interpreting historical data. Among different methodologies and disciplinary combines, ethno history as a framework comes close to what is carried out in this book, but there is still something to be filled or the substance of the book spills over ethno history.

So far, I have been writing what this book is not. It is not to undermine the fields from which this book differs. By way of stating what this book is not, I am inadvertently alluding to what it is. It is also not to state that those theories, methodologies and disciplines are inferior to capture my object of interpretation and analysis. This exercise is to situate this book in the matrix of the existing literature to which it has proximity. I could have distanced this book from social history or total history, or regional history or local history and so on. But I do not venture to do this because the differences between the content of this book and those types of histories that I have just mentioned are self-evident.

Subject matter of this book could at best be a 'micro history'. My object of study is the interactions of small groups and individuals, isolating power relations among them, customary practices, writing culture, archivalisation and so on. The 'conventional' histories do not make them visible with clarity and thus remain unknown. I do emphasise the unique forces in operation within and among swaroopams without relying on universal principles. Even when I state that micro history is the suitable statement of this book, what is done is a selective choice of concepts and categories and imagines a constellation of them or analytical grid with which I as a writer go about. So, I work with this conceptual constellation/complex. However, as I mentioned earlier, I would be keen to avoid pluralism and eclecticism, and give importance to internal coherence. Following Richard Rorty, the relevance of epistemology also stands problematic in this text[5]. In any case I do not want to end up this book with any deterministic answer; rather the study is exploratory in nature and conscious of the tentative nature of the subject matter, history. Micro history is not the binary opposite of 'macro history'. In fact, micro history cannot be differentiated from macro history for it has no referential relation to macro history or general history. What goes in micro history is tracing of subtle and apparently unimportant patterns. It presupposes that even a small perturbation can lead to catastrophic and unpredictable effects. This aspect will become clearer only at the end of this book.

It is well known that during the period under consideration, Portuguese and Dutch were making their presence felt in the region. However, I make no reference to them. I would have mentioned them if my questions are related to the historical/social condition of existence of swaroopams. I confine myself to the interior of swaroopam and their co-existence. Therefore I have not invoked these two significant forces in the regions of Swaroopams. Nevertheless, I admit that these forces did influence the relations internal to swaroopams, yet I have taken note of only the interiority. One can level criticism against such a purposive omission. It is only conventional among the historians to seek the conditions that enabled the course of history and events that they trace. I admit that such a search is important, but that could not find a place in this book. This book confines itself to the internal dynamics of particular Swaroopams and co-existence and mutual relations of four different swaroopams known as Threppappur, Chiravay, Deshinganad and Kunnummel Ilayetam.

This book culminates with the period of erasure of swaroopams and the process of becoming Travancore kingdom. All the history texts mark emergence of Travancore Kingdom as the bench marker of modern Kerala. That is why medieval Kerala history is often characterised as pre-modern. The historiography of swaroopam days is therefore pre-modern in the postmodern times.

The Documents

> ...history now organizes the document, divides it up, distributes it, orders it, arranges it in levels, establishes series, distinguishes between what is relevant and what is not, discovers elements, defines unities, describes relations. (Foucault M., *The Archaeology of Knowledge*: Pantheon Books, New York, 1972: 6-7)

We may start with an observation about the relationship between the historian or the knowing subject and the 'documents' that are consulted to substantiate historical arguments and explication. The 'documents' that are invoked in this book forms a small fraction of palm leaf scripts which is known as Mathilakam Grandhavari. The mathilakam refers to the fortress within which the temple of Padmanabha Swamy, palaces and mansions of importance and other built up spaces were located. During the time of *Swaroopams*, from sixteenth century onwards there was an exclusive building, adjoining to the temple of Sri Padmanabha Swamy, where these *Grandhavaries/*

palm leaf documents were preserved. There were about three million inscribed leaves bundled into two hundred volumes. Now they are kept in the modern archives of government of Kerala located within the fort at the capital city of Thiruvananthapuram or Trivandrum. Out of the total number of palm leaves, few selected ones are compiled and published in print as books. About these compilations I will be mentioning in the subsequent chapters contextually. Some of the palm leaf scripts are published in the texts on the history of Travancore/ Venad. Once again, I selected and brought into this book only few 'documents' from the set of already published *grandhavari*. It shows that there is no dearth for 'documents' but only abundance of them. This selection is not a random process but purposive. These documents are purposively chosen mainly not for substantiation but for contextualised narration.

I am convinced that all the 'documents' are already interpreted. The interpretations undergo several stages. The grandhavaries were written (written when and where events mentioned in them were taking place or proclamations made) in language, this involves interpretation because language is not value free. Further, not everything can be captured in written language. There has been a realisation that what can be said with 'conformity' and what cannot be said are equally bounded by the 'language game'. The second stage is 'selection'. When the grandhavaries are scripted, what to be inscribed on palm leaves and what to be omitted depended on the 'importance' attributed to what is inscribed at the time of inscribing. When some grandhavaries are selected for publication a second stage of selection takes place. From this selected set of grandhavari, I ferret out few with a purpose in mind which is not context free. This is the third stage of selection or interpretation.

When I underscore that the 'documents' are already interpretations, that does not undermine the importance of them as without them many statements and propositions could not have been written by the historians. The grandhavaries are 'monuments' which are transformed into 'documents' by the historians or writers belonging to the present. The documents are not inert substances, but something that undergoes metamorphosis through writing and speaking about them. There is a reverse process in the present day world. That is, documents are transformed into monuments by memorising the past. Given my intention in writing history, what is more important is to interpret representations and interpretations than 'things'. In general, the relationship between the historical documents and the historian's craft, in the present, remains widely differentiated from that of the pre-mid-twentieth century historiography. So historian proceeds with documents to interpret what is already interpreted. Documents are not value free; each document has multiple signifieds. Even if one were to believe that documents can lead us to a representation of the past as it really took place, any claim to objectivity/universality of one's representation or interpretation would hardly be maintainable. This recognition has broader and far reaching implications to writing history.

Documents are enabling as much as they disable or generate entrenchment. Documents reveal as much as they omit information. Documents bring forth and foreclose. Documents permit and at the same time deny. These are all because of selections that I mentioned above. There is no stasis in the case of documents. They are in their becoming as interpretations have no limit or their limits tends to infinity depending on time, space and *dispositif* (a certain physical, intellectual, institutional, discursive way of understanding or schematising within a certain field possible. It is a condition of possibility, not a cause). As paradigm and *episteme* (the body of ideas that determine the knowledge that is intellectually established at any given time point) change and shift as time pass by, a particular document releases new visibility and appear as if it is a new one. Finding the epistemology that centralises and provide fixity to the transcendental 'subject' and 'object' is not persuasive enough. Poststructuralist theoretical circles stressed the importance to historical rules governing knowledge and discourse. In the present state of theoretical thinking, it can be said that history of a culture or of a 'thing' can be equated to a continuous chain of ever new interpretations. The notion of historical objects devoid of changing meaning and significance is metaphysical. Documents help us not only to understand the past and present but also enables us to constitute objects of analysis or transform already existing objects into something that has no semblance of already existing ones. That is why instead of kingdom I have swaroopam.

The Design

A self-reflexive analysis of the existing historiography texts in which the primary unit of description is Travancore kingdom of the late medieval Keralam is taken up in the second chapter. Only select or few texts are referred as exemplars to elucidate my points. The attempt is to lay bare the literary devises and tropes that enabled imagining a homogenous and coherent 'medieval Travancore' and its 'kings'. It was found that figures of speech gave visibility to medieval Travancore and constituted and perpetuated it as a taken-for-granted entity in historiography. My appeal is not to exorcise figures of speech from historiography; although I am aware of the fact that hidden and unjustified *a priori* assumptions find a place and position in it. That is why a self-reflexive analysis of textual strategies is taken up in the beginning itself. The intention is not to find fault with any authors for the metaphorical character of their conclusions. No inter-textual comparison is attempted but highlights internal contradictions within the texts. Verification and falsification of the truth-value of the texts find no space in this chapter. How 'language thinks for us' as Samuel Taylor Coleridge had felicitously phrased, is quite vivid in many of the texts referred to. This chapter clears way to trek towards swaroopam by dislodging the taken-for-granted entities.

In the third chapter the primary unit swaroopam and the most distinguished position within it namely muppu are introduced. In this chapter the internal dynamics are analysed. It is argued that neither is the swaroopam reducible to the schema of kingdom nor is muppu identifiable with the king. The muppu's identification with the Swaroopam is through his *vaazcha* (being in the world with distinction). It is in contra distinction with what king does within his territory that is *bharanam*. The acts of *vaazcha* and *bharanam* are distinguished. The seniority in terms of 'age' factor is brought in.

How minutely divided time is employed to distribute individuals across various positions of authority in the organisation of Swaroopams is delineated in this chapter. Some of the assumptions and conclusions about kingship and succession are called into question by introducing the concept of *kuuru-mura* schemata. In this scheme inter-subjective relations within the swaroopam families and time of birth are combined to place individuals in the hierarchy of power positions. Inter-subjective relation suggests that *muppus* of the four swaroopams were drawn from the eldest sons of the Attingal family. The female members of the swaroopam family were residing at this place known even now as Attingal which is north of Thiruvananthapuram or northern part of Threppappur Swaroopam. The principle of scales of seniority that determines which eldest son becomes the muppu of a particular swaroopam is not searched here. This remains as an open ended question.

I am convinced that by concentrating on the swaroopam as a micro-unit one cannot arrive at generalisations about macro-South India or Keralam. Conversely, in understanding micro-unit deduction of macro-unit's characteristics to the former is also not in place. This is one of the specificities of the swaroopam.

The relationships between the muppu and the ruled are outside the purview of this book. This chapter is to search how the so-called authorial positions were themselves embedded in power relations in such a way that they were bound by the 'present' necessity of perpetuating the past or *aachaaram*. Since the sixth chapter is on aachaaram, I am not detailing it here. Both the ruler and the ruled are embedded in the web of relations of power in varied ways. They are to be situated as subjects implicated in manifold relations of power and subject positions. Therefore, changes and shifts in historical process need not necessarily be narrowed down to the actions and reactions of the ruler and the ruled. That is subject-centered history is not attempted here. In general, the juridico-political conceptions of power and sovereignty models[6] have to be set aside in conceiving power relations in swaroopams. While this chapter deals with the internal aspects of swaroopam, the next one focuses on the inter-swaroopam relations.

Assume that there are two kingdoms, say 'X' and 'Y' with respective kings for each of them. Then, if the king of 'X' becomes the king of 'Y' or the other way round, then there is no more two kingdoms and two kings. There is only one kingdom and only one king. That is there is no more 'X' and 'Y', but only 'Z'. Several expressions are used to describe such an occurrence; annexation or incorporation or subjugation, subsuming or any of their synonyms. But in the case of swaroopams no such instances take place. This is the specificity of *muppuvaazcha* and co-existence of swaroopams. This aspect lends luminance to the fourth chapter of this book. The key phrase is *multiple muppu vaazcha*. Even if a muppu becomes muppu of one or more swaroopams, they remain as self-formed entities during and after multiple muppu vaazcha.

What are traced in the fourth chapter are manifold patterns peculiar to the ways in which one succeeds to a swaroopam muppu position and in turn becomes muppu of more than one swaroopam. In this chapter I also trace patterns of de-succession from a swaroopam and sequential succession to the position of muppu of another swaroopam.

The sequential succession occurs when one person becomes muppu of a swaroopam after another one. In this sequence one may either forgo the previous position or may retain it or terminate it after the lapse of some time. Therefore, we get patterns that involve discontinuity and overlap in muppuvaazcha. Instead of treating them as exceptional or complicated and at the end omitting them as external to the descriptive field, such patterns of succession are highlighted in this chapter. The multiple muppu vaazcha made possible co-existence of different swaroopams without one infringing upon the integrity of others. It is possible to propose that multiple muppuvaazcha existed in Swaroopams and at the same time it is also possible to propose that multiple muppuvaazcha enabled Swaroopams to co-exist. The *swaroopams* towards the end of this chapter, how multiple muppuvaazcha was functionalised in the strategy to erase the self-identification of *swaroopams* to establish a kingdom is abbreviated. swaroopams and several naadus together were made into a kingdom and muppus were reconstituted as *raajavu*/ king by the first half of the eighteenth century.

The fifth chapter traces patterns of *dathetukkal* or conjugation and its effects on *muppuvaazcha* and inter-subjective relations among *swaroopikal*. The practice of dathetukkal or adoption was regular in swaroopams, in spite of the possibility of multiple muppu vaazcha. That is lack persons to occupy positions of distinction is not the condition for adoption. Indeterminacy is brought into the diagrammatic ordering of persons of distinction. Although the Malayalam word dathetukkal can be translated as adoption, in our context it is not tenable. Dathetukkal as an act does not seem to satisfy the context for adoption. Adoption becomes tenable only by the middle of eighteenth century. Therefore, I will be using the term 'conjugate' for dathetukkal. Many of the *muppus* of *swaroopams* were conjugants. There were situations in which elderly persons or bearers of important positions in *muppuvaazcha* got exchanged between two *Swaroopams*. Some of the patterns in dathetukkal are traced in this chapter. The practice of conjugation could redraw the diagram of succession as well as the composition of Attingal family of women and children. Both female and male members were conjugated. Persons of distinction of a swaroopam were conjugated to another swaroopam. Mutual conjugation of persons of importance between swaroopams also took place. But then, when a swaroopam conjugate a person from another one to erase or dilute any dispute between them and to realign their mutual relations, a mutual transposition between them without having any positioning of the conjugant in the muppuvaazcha of the receiving swaroopams occurs.

When someone is transposed to a swaroopam where there is sufficient number of successors, then the phenomenon of dathetukkal becomes overtly political as it reorders the existing kuuru-mura and inter-subjective relations among the members. In the case of persons of distinction of two swaroopams become conjugaters and conjugants at the same time, the conjugaters do not involve in the organisation of the receiving swaroopam. Such an act seems to be a part of history dissimilar from the generally known history of adoption in kingdoms and thus dathetukkal demands problematisation.

When two or more swaroopams engage in the act of dathetukkal, the manner in which each of them defined it's interior and exterior *vis-a-vis* other swaroopams as well as within its sub-divisions is shown to be complex. The complexity is such that in this act, the unity and coherence of the concept of the swaroopam and the continuum between swaroopams in terms of kinship etc are found to be non-problematic.

The patterns of the exterior and the interior of *Swaroopams* are traced from the interaction and co-action of the swaroopams as in the dathetukkal are different from those found in the kinship/blood relations in the multiple muppuvaazcha. What gets real and primary is the persistence of the swaroopams. But then, instance of the coherence of the interior of swaroopam could be found in the act of dathedukkal. The dathetukkal when analysed, reveals the interface between swaroopam (family) and *Swaroopam* (socio-territorial unit), the manner in which both the identities become, at times, one and the same and the modalities by which they were separated. Although the subjectivity of the actors involved in dathetukkal had been grounded firmly on Swaroopam than swaroopam, there were instances when the coherence of Swaroopam and swaroopam were overlooked. Such instances exemplify exteriorisation of a part of the interior of the swaroopam. That is the *thaivazhi* of a swaroopam was sometimes posited as another unit or *swaroopam* and *dathetukkal* took place between swaroopam and *thaivazhi*. Such *Dathetukkal* was carried out with norms and customs or *aachaarams*. In fact, *aachaaram* (literally it means custom) means something that does not change, something to be abided etc. But for different castes, different temples, different households at different situations or moments different persons in distinguished positions had to follow different aachaarams. The sixth chapter deals with how aachaaram was intricately related to relations of power, relations with other corporeal and non-corporeal world and inter-subjectivity. The question of legitimacy is shown to be grounded in the manner in which different groups and individuals relate within a shared *aaachaarakramam* (literally, it means the order of custom). An analysis of aachaaram has significance in terms of legal history as well as political and cultural analysis. The aachaaram becomes extremely sensitive in the relations with the temple of Padmanabha and other temples of importance to swaroopams. Therefore, the relations among the *muppu*, *swaroopam* temple and y*ogam* are decisive. It should be admitted that no detailed description of *ettarayogam* could be conducted in this book.

The multiple muppuvaazcha and the intricate relations involved in the practice of dathetukkal persisted within an aachaarakramam that displayed its potential to perpetuate the swaroopam*s* as a constellation. The manner in which the aachaarakramam functioned is analysed indirectly by explicating the relations among swaroopams, muppus of swaroopam*s* and yogam. After this analysis, a detailed analysis of the event known as *padiyettam* (the literal meaning is ascending the steps of a temple) is provided. Padiyettam marks succession of a muppu position. This exemplary event, when analysed, shed light upon the intricate and complex ways in which aachaaram functioned or affected. This event can be viewed as an aachaaram that involves a set of procedures having symbolic and material implications.

Aachaaram is not embodied by any individual or collective as in the logo-centric conception of law and power that foist these things on the Lord or God. At the same time, it is something that is never to be wilfully flouted and something to be perpetuated. It is flexible with environment and time; yet it was something that cannot be changed by anyone, if at all changes are made, it happens through consensus of positions of importance in the *swaroopikal* and *ettarayogam*.

Aachaaram is heterogeneous in the sense that groups can be differentiated in terms of *aachaaram* that they follow. Each unit entity identifies itself with a set of *aachaaram* and their relation with oneself and others and with the world out there are conditioned by it. The aachaaram at the same time individualises unit entities with respect to date of *janmam* (birth) and *kuuru*. The differentiation of 'one' from 'other' on the basis of aachaaram is not fixed, there is possibility that there existed other aachaarams which made possible their union and wherein the 'you' and 'I' become merged in a collective 'we'. The question of how the inter-actions between the muppu positions, ettarayogam and their mutual relations as it took place within a field of *aachaarakramam* is detailed in this chapter. One is obliged to observe one's aachaaram and one cannot compel or influence others to deviate from it without committing *duraachaaram* (antinomy of aachaaram). There was no monolithic aachaaram, but it was specific to context and being at a moment. That is aachaaram in a specific moment can be duraachaaram and the other way round. For instance any one of significance could over-rule muppu, especially yogam, for breaching aachaaram. Aachaaram was general, in the sense that every one were to abide aachaaram that they are supposed to follow. In principle, aacharam was a-temporal as its referentials are in the past. Rulers were ruled in the name of the aachaaram and duraachaaram. Aachaarams were written as well as transmitted orally; one of the examples is the codifications of *aachaarakarams* into a written text known as *Vyavaharamala* (garlands of rules) compiled during the second part of the sixteenth or fifteenth century. Aachaarams were also gleaned from grandhavari. Aachaara*ms* were so central in the organisation of swaroopams; it validated and disapproved action and reactions of everyone in the swaroopams. Aachakramams were applicable to the plebeians to the most distinguished persons. Idea of aachaaram enframed individuals and set of people into two sets: followers of aachaaram, and those engaged in duraachaaram (antonym of aachaaram). In the history of Swaroopams, aachaaram could turn the power relations upside down. For instance, *yogam* could overdetermine the muppu and the other way around. Written or orally transmitted, aachaaram was at the same time effective as well as affective. Aachaaram by definition is not something which can be changed by the whims and fancies of those in the position of power, but it can be altered by following the norms implicit in aachaarakramam.

The seventh chapter deals with how events and proceedings becomes aachaaram of writing them down and recall them from time to time; that is writing the present forever. But at the same time both the written documents and orally transmitted truths were treated equally valid. In the context of, disapproval, dispute and legitimisation of certain acts are ratified by reading documents/grandhavaries written centuries ago. Some aachaarams were written some others are not. What was left out and what was included in writing is not clear. Whatever it may be, aachaaram that was to be followed by 'X' need not be followed by 'Y'. Yet 'Y' can question non-compliance of aachaaram that was to be abided by the 'X' and *vice versa*. Aachaaram was constitutive of individual subjectivity as well as inter-individual subjectivities. Writing down what has been happening in the Yogam which was read out contextually over a period of time was critical in the organisation and programmes of Swaroopams. This chapter is all about writing/documenting and reading/re-reading those documents with effects of power. Therefore, its title is 'Custom of Archivalisation: Documenting the Present for the Future'. It is said that the total number of grandhavari amounts to about three million even after decay of palm leaves and negligence over time.

This chapter takes up writing and reading of aachaarams, as events of past and present are archivelised. Representation of past and present in written form was quite substantial. The implications of which were manifold. This aspect is taken up for detailed discussion in this chapter. The archivalisation shows the need for recording and amassing a mass of written documents. These documents were not inert substances, but they were perpetually recalled in the assembly of *sabha* or *ettarayogam* in which muppu was supposed to be present or in his absence his representatives, who were customarily accepted, were to be present. Some of the conclusions of this chapter would question the general belief that the 'Orient' had no written law as also the notion that it had been far removed from any kind of 'writing culture'.

This chapter demonstrates how recording, writing and recalling what were written got recognised as an aachaaram. Aachaarams were written down, as well as there was an aachaaram of writing what was thought as important. As these documents were written on palm leaves prone to decay, they were intermittently re-written. This shows the significance of the aachaaram of writing and documenting.

The extent as well as the complex ways of documentation will be shown in this chapter. Grandhavaries are classified, attributed different names; this itself constitute a long list. Similarly scribes were also classified and have different powers and names. The documents, especially *aachaarakanakke*, describe the way people inter-acted and related with the material and spiritual worlds. Practice of extensive recall of documents generated new documents that refer to the manner in which people related with documents; written documents generate documents about themselves as and when they were recalled. There were several positions of writers with specific names and taxonomy of documents. This aspect will be elaborated in this chapter. The comprehensive term that I use for such documentative processes is 'archivalisation'. In part this chapter focuses on the power effects that are generated along with the process of documenting and its repeated invocation. The act of invocation of the already written documents is also written down. The way power affects individuals could be seen in the manner in which the written material is converted to documents. This is archivalisation. Archives were not merely abode of documents, they were stock of materials which could effect and affect 'people'. Archivalisation process also brings forth how people related to themselves as well as the truth that is attributed to written material. Archivalisation aided judging the present and also formalised actions that have a bearing upon future. Archive was not only a place where documents are preserved. It enabled recall of past documents to the needs of present organisation of swaroopams. Consulting or recalling old documents (*Karanam*) was a regular feature. The earliest grandhavari is said to belong to AD 1304. The recall of old grandhavari took place in 1810-11; and it appears that probably it was the last instance of this kind of recall. But then, by that time only vestiges of swaroopams existed.

In the last chapter, I will take up this recall of the grandhavari to show the strategic cunningness involved in British rule in Travancore. This chapter differentiates swaroopam from kingdom-imperialism. In other words how knowledge about the former is significant in understanding the latter combine. This last chapter brings forth the crevice between swaroopam and kingdom. The implications of micro history or micro analysis will become clearer when one reads this chapter. This chapter distinguishes 'culture of politics' of swaroopams from 'political culture' of kingdom and the Princely State.

It is time to break the habit of overestimating philosophy and of thereby asking too much of it. What is needed in the present world crisis is less philosophy, but more attentiveness in thinking; less literature, but more cultivation of the letter. (Heidegger, M. 1947:308)[7]

Notes

1. Foucault, M. (1977). "Nietzsche Genealogy History".In *Language Counter-memory, Practice: Selected Essays and Interviews,* edited by Bouchard, DF. Ithaca: Cornell University Press.

   Lyotard, Francois-Jean, (1984), *The Postmodern Condition: A Report on Knowledge*, University of Minnesota Press, UK.

   Deleuze, G. (1988), *Foucault,* Athlone Press, London.
2. Alcoff, Linda, (1993), 'Foucault as Epistemologist', *The Philosophical Forum A Quarterly*, New York.
3. Frenz Marget and Berkemer, G. (eds), (2015), *Sharing Sovereignty*, Primus, New Delhi.
4. Dirks, B. Nicholas, (1989), *The Hollow Crown: Ethnohistory of an Indian Kingdom*, Cambridge University Press, Bombay.
5. Significance of epistemology as a befitting endeavor in itself has been abandoned in the recent times. Further those in the theoretical and epistemological circles have been moving towards what Richard Rorty has termed as 'pragmatism'. Richard Rorty, 1991, 'Solidarity or Objectivity?', *Relativism and Truth* : Philosophical Papers, Vol. 1, Cambridge University Press.

   Richard Rorty, (1979), *Philosophy and the Mirror of Nature*, Prinston University Press, Prinston.
6. Foucault, M, (1977), *Discipline and Punish: Birth of the Prison*, London, Penguin Books.
7. Heidegger, Martin, (1996), 'Letters on Humanism', in Cahoone, L.E. (ed) *From Modernism to Postmodernism: An Anthology*, Oxford: Blackwell Publishers.

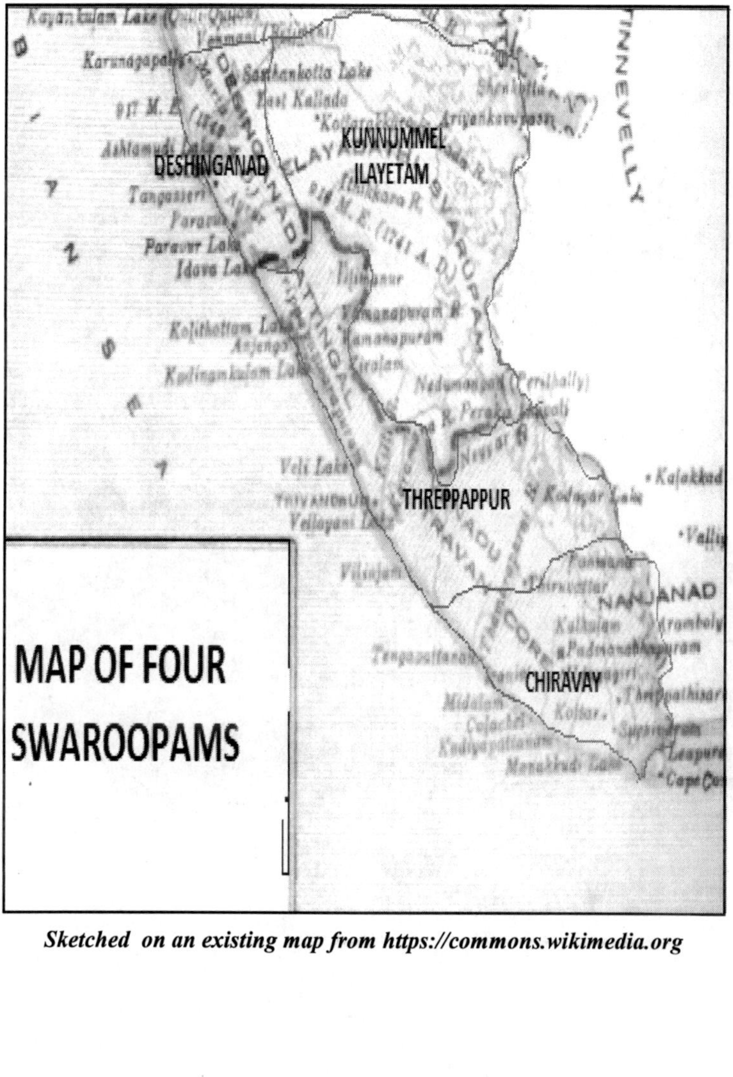

Sketched on an existing map from https://commons.wikimedia.org

Padmanabha Swamy Temple (New photographs)

Chapter - 2

A Search for the Travancore Kingdom and its Kings Ends Up in Vain

If one is concerned with the late medieval history and the search for the Travancore kingdom and its kings, there is no doubt that existing historical writings are replete with them. Historical references to them are based on documents, primarily the *Mathilakam Grandhavari*. I have searched for the kingdom and kings with more or less the same documents that enabled the writing of a history of the Travancore kingdom and its kings. I could not find any information about the Travancore kingdom or kings in these documents. This is perplexing because existing historiographies have taken for granted the existence of the Travancore kingdom and a long genealogy of kings from medieval period onwards; and in some cases from the ancient period. Given this, one is prompted to take another look at the existing historical texts. I have referred to a few of them among many which claim to have both coherence and objectivity. Only a few among the many texts have been chosen because my objective is limited to shed light on the incongruousness implicit in written histories and the figures of speech involved in them.

The texts referred to are only exemplars to carry out my purpose; and in this sense the choice of the texts referred to are purposive. My objective is related to another one, which is to bring forth the idea of swaroopam more vividly into historiography. Moreover, my objective is to distance the subsequent chapters from certain 'taken-for-granted' ideas that have been persistent in historiographies, and in turn have gained wide circulation as if it were true. I would like to state that the motive of writing this chapter is confined to provide the historiographical scene from where I depart. I am not claiming that there can be any historiographical truths or for that matter, any universal truth or final judgement. This has already been accepted by thinkers for several decades or even centuries ago.

I am not arguing that the statements that are invoked from the existing historiography are sophistry but they certainly amount to it in their effects. If I were to exaggerate, they are hyperboles. In other terms, such historiographies could be considered as an espousal of the Orientalist discourse of kingdom or kingship, by employing figures of speech or stylistic devises such as 'tree', 'branch', and other comprehensive names. To repeat, I engage in this exercise because it is important to limelight the idea of the swaroopam and downplay the relics of a bygone 'tree', 'branch' and other such metaphors. The metaphorically derived kingdom of Travancore/Venad may amount to a hyperbole. My intention, however, is not to highlight the hyperbolic nature of this kingdom but to stress on giving greater importance to the co-existence of swaroopams in historical writing.

While the question of how incongruous statements found in texts claiming coherence is addressed, no attempt has been made to evaluate them critically by setting them alongside some 'real history' or newly found 'historical evidences'. I have not taken up the issue of the authenticity of the 'documents', nor do I question the historically or socially conditioned intentionality of the authors referred to. These questions definitely need to be addressed, but then, I do not take them up here. Only the textual strategies and rhetorical/stylistic devises that have gone into the construction of a unified Travancore and its kings have been taken into consideration. This is only to underscore the need to pay attention to the distinctiveness of swaroopam and their co-existence. This chapter exemplifies how to engage with the existing historiographies and also how to differ from them. Since I am concerned with the historiographic devising of the kingdom of Travancore and its kings in this chapter, let me begin with the figure of the 'king'.

Over-reading and Figuration of the King

The conviction and longing that an existing kingdom ought to have a long and continuous historical past had been prevalent for several decades, and the social conditions that encoded it is well known to historians. During the formative period of historiography in Travancore (from the third quarter of the nineteenth century), a projection of the present onto the past was never seen as a problem. The legitimacy of the present kingdom and kingship were anchored on a glorious past; and a long continuum from the ancient past was formed[1]. By now it has become well known that such historiography has to do with *rajabhakthi* (devotion to the king) and *rajyabhakthi (devotion to the kingdom)* or combination of both. The Travancore State Manuals[2], which appeared in the first half of the twentieth century, criticised those histories mentioned above as inaccurate on account of subjectivity and a lack of document-based substantiation. But a king-centred historicisation also appeared in these Manuals with different 'shades'. Hence, a search is made on how the late medieval Travancore and its kings got devised in historiography. First, the search is for kings in history texts.

The king-centred representations un-problematically affirm that kings ruled over the territory of Travancore from ancient times or at least throughout the medieval period.[3] The Travancore State Manuals are considered as authentic texts and sometimes as documents even by the present day historians and administrators. Before these Manuals appeared, the word 'sovereign' was used instead of 'king' without any conceptual differentiation.[4] In another example, the king was not juxtaposed with the kingdom but with the dynasty[5]. All these texts display different shades of positivism[6] the credo of modern scientific inquiries. In these texts, conclusions are made with the authority of the documents or evidences to claim objectivity.[7]

These historical accounts consulted 'primary documents' known as the *Mathilakam Grandhavari* to come out with the history of the Travancore kings. I have searched for the word 'king' in the same 'documents'. However, I could not find such a word in them. The grandhavaries that the above-mentioned historical accounts take up as documents refer to a position called muppu or *muuthathiruvadi*, which does not lend itself to the English translation as 'king'. Moreover, the word raja or raajavu which can be translated as king or sovereign has no mention in the documents. I should emphasise that none of the documents which lend support to the existence of a king use the word raajavu or raja. In literary works, idioms with such words appear as part of a long honorific which may include 'lord/ruler of the world' and so on. Instead of raja/raajavu, the word muppu had been repeatedly employed in the documents. Undermining the dictums of objectivity that prevailed, the *raajavu* or king is central even in the so-called document-based histories; this is despite the fact that, such an idiom with such a word is absent in the documents. It is particularly important to note that the term *raajavu,* though commonly found in literary texts, had been carefully kept out of the documents as though it is figurative. Instead, the term used to refer to the highest position within a swaroopam is 'muppu'. The distinction between the two terms, muppu and raajavu, is not, after all, unsubstantial one. Muppu can at best be translated as the 'seniormost and distinguished'[8]. Despite this, in historical accounts there is a tendency to identify a king or sovereign wherever they located the term muppu. Indeed, it is difficult to find out an appropriate English word for muppu, and yet we discern an issue which is far more serious than the problems involved in translation.

The word muppu was first displaced or transposed into raajavu, another Malayalam word, before being translated it into English as 'king'. The critical issue here is not so much with the translation problems of muppu as 'king' but rather its transposition. The erasure of the distinction between raajavu and muppu enables projection of the term 'king' onto muppu. There is definitely a rhetorical move which can be phrased as 'over-reading'. It is the over-reading of documents that enabled the identification of muppu as raajavu. Over-reading need not be understood as resulting from purposive rational tactics of the author or limitations of the author due to individual or historiographical context. Rather, it is the *dispositif* that enabled such an over-reading. *Dispositif* indicates ensembles of discourses, various mechanisms (institutional, physical, architectural forms, and administrative) and knowledge structures, which enhance and maintain the exercise of power within social relations.[9] This is only a proposition that I float for future historians to address. Since the main attention is not the history of systems of thought or the history of ideas, I return in search of kings in different guises.

The absent, if not non-existent kings were glorified, and the notion of their continuous succession was sanctified; thereby the centrality of the rajavamsham was legitimized. For instance, those who find authority localised in the king would make use of phrases like "those who ruled over Travancore"[10]. There are those who accept into their discourse the entity, the medieval kings, as if it cannot be otherwise.[11] The following phrases are other examples of the manner in which reference is made to the thirteenth and fourteenth centuries: "Ravi Varma, the king of Travancore and the suzerain of Kerala"[12], and "the sovereign of Venad"[13]. Such figurative statements might have been determined by adherence to some English 'model' which is inappropriate in describing or conceptualising muppu. There are other examples wherein the king in his singularity is not considered as central, but his dynastic lineage is so, as can be seen in the usage of the phrase "Travancore royal dynasty"[14]. Another one: "records relating to the chronology of the sovereigns of *Travancore* for the period 15441677"[15] and "Travancore dynastic records"[16]. Such phraseology would be enough to exemplify how over-reading enables the concoction of 'kings' with the help of medieval documents. As I stated earlier, the word raajavu king is absent in these documents, yet historians whom I invoked here and who claim objectivity find it in the documents, thereby the idea of a 'document' itself gets complicated. This is what over-reading does.

Interpretational Skidding and the Chief/Ruler

Another mode of formulating kingship circumvents the explicit problems of over-reading but commits an 'interpretational skidding'. In some accounts, the elimination of the distinction between muppu and raajavu is not to be found and 'king' is not an inevitable category in them[17]. At times they retain the term i.e., muppu, as it is in the documents. Both the texts advertently recognize the difference between muppu and raajavu.

Nevertheless, it is possible to find the usage of the term 'kings' who ruled Venad till the turn of the fourteenth century in those texts. At the same time in the same text we find that after the fourteenth century, there were no Venad rajas until the close of the medieval period[18]. But the self-contradiction is that same text retains phrases like *Deshinganadu rajavamsham* (Deshinganadu dynasty) for the description of Venad between the fifteenth and seventeenth century[19]. When it is classificatory schemes, categories like *raajavu* and *rajavamsham* become indispensable.[20] The co-existence of raajavu or king and muppu in the text give the impression that they are mutually transposable, even though they are not. Such interpretational skidding leads to constant tensions between the two that is, between muppu and raajavu. For instance, there is a statement that "there is an accurate genealogy available for the *Thiruvithamkur kings* who were the *Chiravay muppu*" (translated) between 1532 and 1758[21]. The conceptual tension between muppu and king is self-evident as the statement specifies them as entirely different and at the same time fused together as identical.

In some texts muppu is translated as the 'eldest' and then it is conceptualised as the 'chief' or 'ruler' of Venad[22]. Here the tension is not so much between muppu and king but between muppu and 'chief'/ 'ruler'[23]. Now let us see how the figure of the chief or ruler is portrayed. The way in which the term muppu is centralised, as if muppu is a metonym for king, is self-evident in the statements like, "The elders of swaroopams thus held *political and economic rights* over the *entire area* under their *control*[24]."[25] This representation of the 'elder'/ 'chief'/ 'ruler' and of his relation to what he controls resembles the relation between king and his subjects/kingdom. The elders are attributed with the political and economic rights over the entire area under their control. Even when the term king is not used, the chief/ruler is portrayed with kingly political attire. The synonymous use of muppu and chief/ruler/elder, and attributions together take place at the moment of 'interpretational skidding'. Shades of sovereignty model haunt the conceptualisation of muppu as chief/ruler. Preference for the terms 'chief'/ 'ruler', 'the eldest', instead of king or sovereign is tantamount to substitution of these terms for king. The outcome is self-contradiction. Elsewhere we find that a muppu has control only over a restricted 'region' within the territory of Venad, as if some others could possess control over the entire Venad[26] interpretational skidding can be found elsewhere as well.

Coming to terms with the 'ruler' as the 'eldest' or the 'eldest' as the 'ruler' results in congruity.[27] Compare the two statements of this text. First, "The muppan of the Trippappur, Deshinganad and Chiravay Swaroopam could lay claim to being the ruler of Venad."[28] Second, "[Thus] accession to eldership (*muppumura*) signified the position occupied within the family and privileges associated with it, rather than the extent of territorial authority acquired"[29]. The first excerpt pitches the authority of the 'ruler' within the territorial domain and combines three swaroopams as the territory of Venad. The second excerpt finds the elder's position within kinship relations and undermines the first statement. In the first, muppu is attributed with the function of ruling, in the second it is merely given a position within family; hence the distinction between the function of ruling and the position within the family is ambiguous, although the ruler and eldership are separated. This clearly creates ambivalence because there is separation as well as a fusion of these two terms. The search is for the presence and absence of the Travancore/Venad kingdom and its kings. The metaphysics of both presence and absence is one of the unsaid features of these excerpts. Once the indispensability of any single figure possessing authority and power is at least at the vicinity of the conception, then it may lead to internal contradictions of the following kind. It is said that conventionally the muppu of Chiravay Swaroopam was the elder/ruler of Venad[30]. But in the same text there is a statement that Chiravay muppu was only a title assumed by the senior princes of the family which merely claimed a share of the income of a portion of the territory. The self-contradiction is clearly obvious. Such a transfiguration of muppu involves interpretational skidding.

Once the elder is distinguished from the ruler, there is an attempt to depict the precondition for the accession to eldership. There are texts in which the presence of a sovereign figure with absolute authority is not needed to historicise 'medieval Travancore'. They concentrate on the preconditions on becoming the elder as if it was not hereditary. The legitimacy given by other political and economic elite, and rituals conducted in the temple becomes preconditions. For example, there is such an argument:

> Becoming an elder involved two major requirements. One, the acceptance of services from the landlords, (*madampikuur*) and the militia (*arisipadijanam*) attached to the *swarupam*.... The other requirement was the benediction of the tutelary deity of the elder. (Ganesh K.N, 1990:19, *emphasis added*)

There is a clear recognition of the event of succession and the preconditions to become the eldest.[31] The interpretational skidding mentioned above reappears in a different tenor. There is power not merely localised on an individual but differentially distributed. Otherwise, there is no need of 'requirements' because succession to the position of an elder at the instance of demise of the existing elder is hereditary. This shows that an 'elder' is not just an 'elder'of the family alone but more than that. It is obvious that the 'elder' and the 'ruler' are not interchangeable as it is mentioned in the text of Ganesh K.N. Legitimisation is required because the elder is also located within the existed power relations, that is why becoming an elder requires 'acceptance' and 'benediction'. At the same time, power is centralised even when extra-kinship legitimisations are brought into the depiction.

Why search for a position where power is most centralised or localised on a person, as if it were, there ought to be such a position? The texts that we have taken up so far could be broadly classified as the socio-political history of the medieval period of modern Travancore. Apart from the differences among the texts, one could find several similarities in the conceptualisation of the 'king/raajavu' and 'ruler'. According to them, the power of the king/chief and his rule over the kingdom is necessary and has to exist, and it is both legitimate and desirable. The 'longing'of a patriot is to perpetuate it. The model that is employed here is to devise a king/ruler/elder advertently, while inadvertently assuming indivisible sovereignty of the king/chief as an imperative.[32] The need for and naturalness of someone at the apex with power over the entire domain/territory, be it the kingdom, raajyam, naadu, swaroopam or family, is taken for granted. Now let me move on to diverse ways of devising the late medieval Travancore kingdom in the existing historiographies.

The Travancore Kingdom and Figures of Speech

We come across the Travancore/Venad kingdom in existing historiographies; in fact, it is so conspicuous so that there is no need to search for it. In this section, an attempt is made to dislodge this concept by showing the figures of speech that devised the existence of such a kingdom. That is, it is not so much the documents that the historians invoke which revealed the kingdom. Rather, it is the stylistic devises that constituted it primarily. In the existent historiographies, there is a tendency to project a unified Travancore, as if it existed and after a lapse of time it got branched off. The historiographic issue here is that the presence of a 'unified' Travancore during medieval period underplays the co-existence of different swaroopams.[33] An exemplary excerpt referring to the second half of the fourteenth century says that: "Travancore at that time was dispersed as five branches. Their names are Venad, Tiruvitamkode, Trippappur, Chiravay and Jayasimhanadu."[34]

One thing that comes to prominence is the usage of the 'branch' simile. It is this simile which gives presence to a trunk which got branched off, as only a trunk can branch off. The 'dispersed branches' belong to Travancore. Although the branches have their proper names, they are overshadowed by the trunk, that is, Travancore. The organising metaphor 'tree' comes to the aid of undermining the existence of the branches namely Venad, Tiruvitamkode, Trippappur, Chiravay and Jayasimhanadu. Periodicity is overlooked through the use of the metaphor of the tree and by overplaying the trunk, but bracketing out the existed branches. Instead of the history of the branches and the branching, the bygone trunk is taken up as an entity to be historicised. The tree that organised the historical imagination and devised the primary unit Travancore collapses the moment the branches are captured in the frame. In other words, the history of the branches is left to the imagination of the readers and what is talked about is the bygone trunk, so that it is possible to talk about a unified kingdom of Travancore, a hyperbole.

The tree metaphor reappears in other texts as well; an exemplary statement:

> Ravi Varma's successors ruled over Kerala south of Kollam, and were known as the 'Thiruvadis', the ruler being the eldest member among the five collateral (matrilineal) branches, into which the amalgamated royalty of Venad and Jayasimhanaad was apparently split up, at .. the ruler being the eldest member among the five collateral (matrilineal) branches, into which the amalgamated royalties of Venad and Jayasimhanad was apparently split up, at least from 1375 AD onwards. (Raghunandana Menon, 1939, reprint 1980:21)

Here we encounter a medieval Kerala! Instead of Travancore, as mentioned in the previous quote, here we have Kerala. More importantly, it appears that the south of Kollam had rulers who belonged to collateral matrilineal 'branches'. The eldest among the 'branches' were the rulers or '*Thiruvadies*'. Apart from the collateral family, there were 'royalties' such as Venad and Jayasimhanad which were amalgamated. This obviously implies that they were separated at some time point but got amalgamated eventually. There occurred an amalgamation of royalties and a subsequent splitting into five branches. The unity of branches is achieved with the aid of kinship relations. This implies that politically, they were two royalties. Whether this split existence was political or territorial splitting of the royal family is not clearly decipherable. But yet, a common origin[35] and a continuous genealogy are urged upon us as if those branches were united within the singularity of the trunk or that of the eldest. The ambivalence in the description is pronounced despite the 'branch' simile.

Yet another model of devising kingdom is by introducing the stylistic devise such as the "comprehensive name" besides the branch-simile. In this case, the kingdom is not Travancore or Kerala, as in previous instances, but Venad.

> Venad is a *comprehensive name* which included the territories ruled by all the branches of the Vanchi dynasty. ... The legitimate conclusion which arises from the foregoing facts is that the several

> branches were looking after the affairs of portions of territory, the eldest, and perhaps the fittest of all, assuming the title of the king of Venad and exercising a general authority over all. (Velu Pillai, T.K, 1940:130-31, Vol. I, *italics added*)

Here there are two unifying themes; one being a "comprehensive name" and the other, a dynasty. The comprehensive name alludes to territories ruled by the branches of the dynasty. Here the trunk is not the kingdom but the Vanchi dynasty. There are territorial branches and dynastic branches at the same time. The unsurpassable question that arises here is whether a comprehensive name can be taken as a unifying structure or boundary condition of different territorialities. Moreover, what is the rightness of attributing a name to a set of rulers of the territorial branches? What is the criterion to discern the elements within a set of branched off territories labelled as Venad? These questions are posed here not with an intention of seeking answer. What comes to light is the idea/concept/theory of a unified and coherent kingdom due to a comprehensive name and a continuously ruling dynasty. What takes place in this statement quoted is construction of a bygone trunk as if it is alive.

The distinctiveness of territorial branches is downplayed by an enframing "comprehensive name" and with the aid of an imagined figure of Venad. The recurrent simulative function of the branch simile is clear by now. Territorial distinction, though accepted, is metaphorically reduced to dynastic unity. On one hand, the territorial unity is achieved through kinship, and on the other through language, by attributing a proper name without any (specifically obvious) criterion.

'Branching' has taken place in the Vanchi dynasty, and yet the Vanchi dynasty retained the unity of the 'branches' as a well-bounded totality of the kingdom because there existed a "general authority over all". What is meant by the usage of terms such as "general authority" and "over all" is not clear. Nevertheless, it is clear that while the comprehensive name unites the territorial divisions, the 'rulers' are united as members of a dynasty. The relative seniority due to being the "senior most" of Vanchi (in relation to rulers of branches) draws adherence from the territorial rulers because he is 'fittest of all'. But how the 'eldest' can be the fittest of all is a question that is not taken up in the text. Whether the eldest has been the fittest of all in terms of kingship or kinship is also overlooked. In such historical representation, a territorially united Venad along with a dynastically united Vanchi turns out as a grand narrative devising the kingdom of Venad and its rulers on the throne.

The branches fused into a unified whole takes place differently. An example: instead of the Vanchi dynasty and its branches, there surfaces the Threppappur royal family and its branches[36]. Further, in this text Venad is only one among the five branches of the Threppappur royal family, not of the Vanchi dynasty. This also implies that Venad cannot be a 'comprehensive name' because it is only one among the branches. The incompatibilities abound.

If a comprehensive name can combine all the particular territories, then the most crucial question for historians is how one can decipher the authority structure in terms of a 'comprehensive name'. Does a comprehensive name, which is obviously a *post festum* term, justify or legitimise the exercise of sovereignty over either the 'rulers' of each territory or over 'territories and things'? How did this name guarantee the sovereignty of the king over the entire territory? The answers to these questions may help us verify the validity of using the comprehensive name 'Venad' or treating Travancore/Venad as a unified entity.

Now let us see how the swaroopam[37] enter into the history texts in difference to the unifying narratives of kingdom. Generally, these swaroopams appear in historiography as unities that are contained in a well-defined universe named Travancore/Venad. The swaroopams, which are taken as territorial and juridical entities exhaust the universe. The problem is to find space for Travancore to exercise of authority over territory. In historical accounts, there are instances where the unity of Travancore is interpreted in terms of the relations between the swaroopams. It is then represented as a "confederation"[38]. But for this to be true, it should emerge from the relations among the swaroopams through some or other active force of consensus or contestations among them. Then what is primary is not the confederation, or the unity, but the will of each swaroopam with its historic specificity (something that is absent in the text under reference). In that case what would have been more glaring is the distinctiveness of the swaroopam in comparison with the 'unity' named Travancore. Incongruousness appears when we find that in some texts that the mutual relationship of the swaroopams are characterised by perpetual conflicts as against confederate situation[39].

During the search for the kingdom of Travancore, what I could find is that in some of the texts[40] *Swaroopam* is recognised as the basic unit. But the way in which it is conceptualised reveals that the 'trunk' or the comprehensive name is still indispensable. "In Venad, Threppappur, Deshinganad, Chiravay and later Elayadam were called *swaroopams*." (Ganesh, K.N, 1990:18, *emphasis added*). Here Venad is portrayed as the container of the *swaroopams*. The *Swaroopams* are said to be in 'Venad' as if it defines them or puts the outer bounds. Despite the acceptance of *Swaroopams* with individual names, the primary category, namely Venad, remains the same, because it contains the *Swaroopams*. *Swaroopams* are referred to only as elements belonging to this generalised set. This implies that the trace of the comprehensive name/term has been inadvertently retained.

The question of how the unity of Venad itself had come into being in the first place has been omitted. What is the semantic and ontological status of Venad in relation to the swaroopam identities? How did these swaroopams exist in the region of Venad? These questions are easily deferred by finding recourse in the name Venad as an *a priori* ontic entity, while the swaroopams are treated as its constituents.

There is recurrence of Historiographic skidding which is implicit in the descriptions of swaroopams in the language of the variants of the sovereignty models. Had the term swaroopam been subjected to the above questions before being accorded a place in historiography, conceptual confusions and internal inconsistencies[41] could have been avoided. It seems that terms or names like Venad and Travancore are used as though they are defensible in any period and any historical process without anachronism. This shows that periodicity is overlooked.

The figure of the 'branch' can be seen even in the texts in which *swaroopams* and their specificity are recognised[42]. There is a struggle to escape the grip of the kingdom model and to also avoid the problem of historiographic skidding. Yet, the unity of the branches is conceived differently. It is a religious sphere that unites the branches; and this is neither kinship nor political. The common devotion of the branches towards Lord Padmanabha is said to maintain unity after branching[43]. Whatever be the specifics, we find the unavoidable presence of unified, homogenised entities such as 'kingdom', 'Travancore', 'Venad' and so on.

I could find in historiography, a figuratively and metaphorically devised late medieval Travancore. A kind of unity among the branches is simulated. Evoking an allegorically unified Travancore and giving it 'fixity' from the ancient to the modern period is not a value neutral textual practice.[44] The figurative language that has been used has succeeded in drawing the readers into its magic circle and generates consent. I only suggest that such metaphorical representations are inextricably linked to the *dispositif* that existed during the beginning of historiography. Much after power relations changed the figure of the medieval king and the Travancore kingdom became incredulous. I do not intend to continue with this thread here.

If Travancore cannot be the primary unit of analysis and the concept of a 'kingdom' unsuitable as a comprehensive category, then the swaroopams and relationships among them become more important than Travancore or Venad. The political and territorial unity of Travancore during its medieval days adheres to the imagined figure of a kingdom with its metaphysical unity and fixity. Such adherence encodes the early nineteenth and twentieth century historian's identification of the object for description. The textual strategy is a metaphorical reduction that entails unity. The unity that is particular to the metaphor is imposed on the object of analysis that resists this unity. That is how the incongruence, pointed out above, is born and recognition of it is deferred. Or one can seek refuge in the ambiguities of figurative language and leave the metaphors to think for us.

The King and the Kingdom

In this section I concentrate on the tensions between kings, kingdoms, dynasties, and territorial divides. For this purpose, the ironical situation of the appearance of two kings for a kingdom is brought in. Once a king or sovereign is required for historiographic purposes, then there is a search for proper names which are most suitable to be considered as 'king'. Such searches often come up against several dead ends such as the difficulty in finding proper names, the appearance of more than one proper name for a 'king', the unavailability of the initial and terminal years of 'rule', and the appearance of mutually contradicting documents and so on.

The history of kingdoms usually expects the present king's genealogy to stretch back into antiquity. The historian is persuaded to interpret the available documents with *a priori* assumptions and over-read them by attributing meanings that are hardly permitted by the 'evidence' to arrive at definitive statements about the identity of medieval kings. Further, they are led to take recourse to principles and norms that exist outside the document to isolate 'one' from the jumble of names that are available. This phenomenon is well exemplified by the two "Travancore State Manuals". When induction fails, they resort to deductive systems that do not have any foundation that is required of it. Such methodological problems lead to other inconsistencies like differences in the proper names that different texts identify for a given period and the overlapping of the periods of different kings and, most importantly, differences in broader conclusions. At times, the documents that are found to be inconsistent with the assumptions/conclusions get overlooked. All this becomes imperative to fabricate medieval kings and to visualise an unbroken genealogical continuity stretching to antiquity for the king concerned. These observations are elaborated in the following sub-section.

Once a Travancore kingdom is metaphorically arrived at, then there is compulsive requirement to concoct an authority that is localised on a person or dynasty, not merely a centre of authority. The requirement that is consistent with the kingdom model is an individual king or chief for the 'entire' Travancore who wields authority 'all over'. The requirements of a central figure which can be 'generalisable' at the same time had to be met. I shall now proceed to the presence of two kings for a kingdom in historiography and how it creates incongruence.

More Than One King for a Kingdom

Sometimes we come across ironical themes. If one finds two kings for a kingdom, what can be done with such a predicament? One finds two proper names as the kings of one kingdom during the same duration (co-kings, as it is portrayed); let us pay attention to two ways of tackling such an unusual scenario. The problem for me is not whether co-kings existed or not. Rather, the issues taken up here is the rhetorical devising of the 'co-kings problem', and ways to overcome it. It is an exemplar that brings forth rhetorical tactics and ways of attribution.

> Adithya Varma and Rama Varma Maharaja Varma Kulasekhara Perumal might have been co-kings, i.e., members of the same family in charge of different portions of the country, ruling on behalf of the head of the family under his authority. It is equally probable that Venad and Jayasimhanad which became one kingdom in the reigns of Ravi Varma Kulasekhara and his successors were again separated into two kingdoms ruled respectively by Marthanda Varma and Adithya Varma who according to the inscriptions belong to Threppapur (Jayasimhanad) and the Chiravay (Attingal and Venad) dynasties respectively. (Nagam Aiya. V, 1906, Vol. I:277)

It is assumed without doubt that there were kings and a kingdom. In this excerpt there is no conclusiveness, and two alternative possibilities are opened up. The first possibility is that there were co-kings in the kingdom and they ruled two different territories in it. This possibility maintains that the co-kings were separated by their respective 'portions of the country'. It also assumes that there is an overarching authority identified as the head of the family who binds both the kings from above. The separation of the kingdom in terms of rule and kinship-based unification takes place at the same time. The overarching authority is localised in 'someone' who was the head of the family, under whose authority the kings rule, and hence the possibility of co-kings comes in. There is an overarching authority but the proper name is missing.[45]

Kings are under the authority of the head of the family. So if a king could rule on behalf of another mortal within his territory, what would Kingship mean in terms of authority? What prevents one from depicting the head of the family as the King or the King of Kings? We know very well by now that the concept of the 'king of Kings' and the 'Great King' existed in several parts of the world[46]. It is also said that the idea of the 'Great King' existed in Malabar as a mode of legitimisation of rule, by genealogically linking with Cheraman Perumal.[47] But the question here is not that. The question here is about the forms of power that relate the head of the family with the kings. What could be the power relations between the head of the family and the subjects? Is it different from the relations between the kings and their subjects? How were different kings mutually related when it came to power relations? Such a maze of questions is baffling.

The second possibility that can be opened up is that the two kings were absolutely independent of each other without any common superior authority above them. Their territories were clearly divided into two kingdoms ruled by—instead of one— two different dynasties. They were respectively ruling Threppapur (Jayathunganad) and Chiravay (Attingal and Venad). Here the paradox is that *explanans* dissolves the *'explanandum'* initial object identified for explanation, namely the existence of co-kings is made to disappear. No more is there a presence of co-kings but kings with their respective territories, which constitute two different kingdoms. The unity of both the kingdom and dynasty are given up but the sovereignty of the kings over their respective territories is retained.

When we read the two alternative explanations together, it is surprising to see that the statement includes possibilities which are so divergent and oppose each other in such a way that they are incommensurable. In one case, the *explanandum* consists of two mutually independent kings with their respective kingdoms. In the other there is coexistence of two kings and only one kingdom. Further, it could be said that such mutually exclusive reasoning is the outcome of both over-reading and historiographic skidding. Another Manual writer overlooks the 'co-kings problem' so that the unity of Venad is defended.

> Venad is a comprehensive name which included the territories ruled by all the branches of the Vanchi dynasty. We also find out in addition to Rama Marthanda Varma of Jayasimhanad succeeding to the sovereignty of Venad, Adithya Varma describing himself as an ornament to the family of Jayasimha, the Lord of Chirava and the king of Vanchi. The legitimate conclusion which arises from the foregoing facts is that the several branches were looking after the affairs of portions of territory, the eldest, and perhaps the fittest of all, assuming the title of the king of Venad and exercising a general authority over all. (Velu Pillai, T.K, 1940, Vol. II:130-31).

Here the possibility of 'co-kings situation' does not directly appear. At the same time there are two references to kings; the 'king of the Vanchi dynasty' and the 'king of Venad'. Thus, it can be said that there existed two 'kingly positions' or 'kingly functions' within the 'dynasty'. Both the unifying terms, whether it is Venad or Vanchi, which is the comprehensive name of the territories (or the dynasty) have their respective kings. Alleging that the co-king situation is 'unsustainable', the author[48] had *prima facie* rejected it. Yet we find the concept of co-kings entering obliquely into the very statement that had so diligently attempted to keep it out of historical descriptions. But the nature of the co-kings that emerges is different from that in the passage cited before. Ironically, there is a king for Venad and another one for the Vanchi. The authority relations between these two kings are evasively stated as "the eldest, and perhaps the fittest of all, assuming the title of the king of Venad and exercising a general authority over all". The criterion for being considered the 'fittest' are left to the imagination of readers. Apart from this, a unified kingdom is asserted.

The kinship relation between the king and the rulers cannot legitimize the authority relations between the 'rulers' of branches of the dynasty and also their relations with the respective 'subjects'. This is so as these two relations constitute different fields in the relations of power. Besides this, the "king of Venad" is only a "title assumed" by "the seniormost member of all the branches taken together"[49]. All branches have their own 'rulers' and seniormost ("or perhaps the fittest of all") among them has the 'title' of king, but is not the king. In spite of the 'title' that the kinship structure allows, he is given a function that goes beyond the title and kinship network as he exercises 'general authority overall'. The 'title' is linked to the exercise of authority within the field of symbolic relations. The mode way in which the title was attributed to the function of wielding authority over the rulers of the branches and, in turn, their subjects (general authority) seem to contradict the characterisation of kingship as a mere title. Further, it may be possible that the period under consideration had a politico juridical space which was primarily conditioned by symbolic relations. In other words, within the descriptive matrix using the concept of kingdom, the discovery that kingship is only a title is untenable. A king who wields general authority over the rulers of the territories and the entire universe of Venad cannot be thought of as functioning within the symbolic relations alone. Kingship combines the maximum focal points of power relations within the kingdom. The portrayal of the king as a mere 'title' holder takes place in the absence of a king in the sovereignty model.

The same problems occur even when one accepts that each of the swaroopams was ruled by a muppu/chief. Here also, the *muppu* is again considered as a mere "position occupied within the family"[50]. If historical descriptions of political organisation and its character revolve around such a position within kinship/family domain, then political and power relations cannot be described in terms of the *muppu*. I return to an earlier point.

The portrait of kings having 'general authority overall' may have two different connotations. While the 'rulers' of the branches have authority over their own respective territories, the king of Vanchi or the king of Venad would have authority over them. The second possible connotation could be that the authority of the "king of Venad" extends directly over not only the other rulers but also on their territory and subjects. The vague and fluid nature of the descriptions and the rhetorical or stylistic devices in the representations is found to be repeated in several other phrases and representations as well. Formulations such as "rights over the entire area under their control"[51] are quite typical. Such formulations tend to evade the entire realm of political and power relations, by shrouding it with semantic ambiguity and projecting the position of a ruler or king as if they really existed. In the ambiguity of such usages, the singular figure of the ruling king, whatever the boundary may be is what is given visibility, whether it is kingdom or *swaroopam*, or 'trunk' or 'branches'.

An attempt has been made to lay bare the textual strategies that have given rise to Travancore/Venad kingdom and kings in historiography. Further, historians have attributed unity and fixity to the kingdom.[52] We have looked into the slippery conceptual foundations of and the assumptions behind the historiographic portrayal of Travancore/Venad and its kings as though they existed during the medieval period. The metaphors and other figures of speech that are involved in devising the unities and the localised authority centres have been demonstrated. We also see how this has been repeated without much change in diverse historical representations.[53] The luminescence of Travancore and its kings has made the *Swaroopams* and its *muppu* get eclipsed (partially) in historiography. For a greater clarity of the analysis, it would be better to start with *Swaroopams* with their uniqueness and differentials, rather than attempting a conceptualisation of Travancore as a kingdom with a continuous successions of kings. The *Swaroopams* should be viewed in their singularity and relations to one another instead of merely regarding them as an entity within Venad or Travancore[54]. Otherwise, the analysis would sound like a fable of a king without a kingdom or a kingdom without a king. The search for the Travancore kingdom and kings led to a rendezvous with the non-existence of them except in historiography. It reveals the futility of retaining them in historiography of late medieval period. Instead, the retention of the term *Swaroopam* and its *muppu*, and their co-existence appears to be speaking a lot more at the present state of historiography. This is clearly evident in the 'documents' which are replete with the terms *Swaroopam* and *muppu* and not '*raajyam*'/kingdom and *raajavu*/king. Let me proceed to reinterpret the already interpreted documents.

Notes

1. Pachumuthathu, (1986) and Shangoony Menon, (1878, 1983).
2. Nagam Aiya, V, (1906, 1951) and Velu Pillai T. K. (1940, 1996).
3. For details, See, the Chapter VI in, Nagam Aiya.V, (Vol: I, 1906: I, 1906), reprint (1989): 209-332 and Chapter III of the same text and Velu Pillai. T.K, Vol. II, (1940): 95-261.
4. Sundaram Pillai P., (1894).
5. Rajaraja Varma Raja, (1928-1933): Series I, III, VI, VIII (Kerala Society Papers).
6. One of the interesting ways to characterize positivism, which may appeal to historical sensibility, is to say that: knowledge is to be modelled on the early twentieth century's understanding of certain pieces of the nineteenth century and especially seventeenth century physics (Macloskey, D.N, 1996: 5).
7. These Manual writers were the earliest subjects of Modern Rationality who in turn also became the bearers of that rationality.
8. I shall return to this point in the subsequent chapters.
9. The word '*dispositif*' has been translated as 'apparatus'. See, for a definition of it by Foucault M. "The Confession of the Flesh" (1977), In Power/Knowledge Selected Interviews and Other Writings (ed. Colin Gordon), (1980): 194–228.
10. Nagam Aiya V, Vol. I, (1906, 1989): chapter VI.
11. Rajaraja Varma, M., (1941)
12. Velu Pillai, T. K, (1940), Vol. II: 95.
13. Velu Pillai, T. K, (1940), Vol. II: 127.
14. Sundaram Pillai, (1894), reprint, 1943:10.
15. Rajaraja Varma, (S.1, 1928: 1-29).
16. Rajaraja Varma, (S.1, 1928: 1-29).
17. Ganesh, K.N., 1990 and Shivashankaran Nair, K, (1993).
18. Shivashankaran, Nair K, (1993).
19. Shivashankaran, Nair K, (1993:8397).
20. One of the examples would be that there are references to *rajas* twice in consecutive paragraphs of Shivashankaran Nair, K, (1993: 1067) as if they really existed during the fifteenth century.
21. Shivashankaran, Nair K., (1993:110), (*emphasis added*).
22. Ganesh, K.N, (1990:18).
23. In the text, the terms 'chief', 'eldest' and 'ruler' are used more or less synonymously and conceptual differences, if any, are not recognizable.

24. Ganesh, K.N, (1990:20); (*emphasis added*).
25. Here 'right' gets characterised and conceptualised as political and economic as against symbolic, or ritualistic, or kinship-based or religious rights etc. The range of this right spreads over the "entire area under control", which means that the right is over the territory, and authority is territorialised. This suggests that the right is all inclusive in the sense that it leaves no area un-territorialised; thus the *entire* territory is the domain for the rule of *muppu*.
26. Ganesh, K.N, (1990:17), The *swaroopam muppu*, referred to here (*Chiravay muppu*), is portrayed as having only partial and restricted control. But, note that the same author states the following: "Conventionally the *muppu* of *Chiravay* was the elder of Venad." There is an apparent inconsistency between this and what was said above.
27. Ganesh, K.N, (1990:15-33).
28. Ganesh, K.N, (1990:18).
29. Ganesh, K.N, (1990:18).
30. Ganesh, K.N, (1990:18).
31. If the above conditions are prerequisites, how can the same text maintain that "Venad chiefs exercised hereditary authority over their territory from Chera times." (Ganesh, K.N. 1990)?. When one conceives succession of a ruler as hereditarily transformed, then the argument that succession is bounded on extra-hereditary aspects like ceremonies conducted at the temple and the consent of feudatories appears to be anachronistic. This is because the distinction between the 'right of one to be the elder' and the 'right of one to exercise authority over the territory and things' is overlooked. This could also be another instance of interpretational skidding.
32. I am particularly alluding to the Travancore State Manuals.
33. In the subsequent chapters I will elaborate about the co-existence of *Swaroopams*.
34. Parameshwara, Aiyer S, (1941, 1961:124).
35. It is quite surprising how one can decipher origins, for it is not even clear whether patriliny or matriliny existed during the period under reference. I have argued in one of the subsequent chapters that what existed was 'matrilocal' lineage.
36. Panicker, K.M. (1957:254).
37. Although I equate *Swaroopam* and branch here, this is not to be taken as the actual situation. In fact, *Swaroopam* should be conceptualised without the aid of the tree metaphor branch-allegory.
38. Velu Pillai, T.K, Vol. II, (1940).

39. Another example is the argument, which locates general authority in Jayathunganadand its *muppu* till the seventeenth century or so, and then attributes it to Chiravay for the period till the eighteenth century. There is yet another characterisation wherein it is stated that "[c] onventionally the *muppan* of *Ciravay swaroopam* was the elder of Venad." (Ganesh, K.N, 1990:18).
40. Ganesh, K.N, (1990).
41. Apart from these problems it also leads to internal inconsistencies. For example, compare the following sentences:
    (1) "The elders of *swaroopam* thus held political and economic rights over the entire area under their control."
    (2) "Thus accession to eldership (*muppumura*) signified the position occupied within the family and privileges associated with it...." (Ganesh, K.N, (1990:21), *emphasis added*).

    If in the first statement the position of the elder is primarily in the field of political and economic powers, in the second, the same position is located in the family and distanced from political field. (It is only a privileged position within the family). They evidently contradict each other.
42. Shivashankaran Nair, K. (1993).
43. Shivashankaran Nair, K. (1993:81).
44. It is not that value-neutrality is possible in historiography or any social sciences, but impossibility of it has to be self-reflexively recognised.
45. In general, kings make their presence felt by inscribing and leaving documentary proof of their acts, which in turn become historical documents and monuments. Keeping this in mind, it is very difficult to comprehend how the *superking's* traces remain un-discovered even though the proper names of kings are available in inscriptions. This appears as a riddle.
46. George Berkermer, (2015:241-251).
47. Margret Frenz, (2015).
48. Velu Pillai, T.K, (1940, Vol. II:130).
49. Velu Pillai, T.K, Vol.II, (1940:130).
50. Ganesh, K.N, (1990:21).
51. Ganesh, K.N, (1990:20).
52. I do not argue that Travancore/Venad is a general unit, and therefore more disaggregate analysis is needed. This argument should not be interpreted as a stand for not losing specificities within the aggregated unit. Instead, the emphasis is in avoiding the totalising and centralising

of categories. It should also be noted that while delving into texts, I have included only those that directly refer to Travancore/Venad.

53. It should be stated that the attempt is not empirical verification or falsification of the statements in the texts referred to, but to deconstruct and lay bare the assumptions, premises and encoding effects of metaphors which lead to self-contradictions and ungrounded conclusions. My purpose is not to counter-pose one statement of a text against another statement of some other text but to analyse texts essentially from within. Also, we have moved towards new objects and relations that seem to be more appropriate units of analysis.
54. There are intersections of *Swaroopams,* but at the same time they were relatively autonomous so that they could be differentiated and had respective proper names.

Chapter - 3

Swaroopam, Age and Kinship

Let me begin with a near platitude. The past, as it took place, can neither be recalled in language nor represented in historiography. For the contemporary academic community, this proposition may not require any elaboration. The 'documents' that belong to the past can be interpreted even if the past 'as it took place' cannot be re-presented. Any document is already an interpretation or is an interpretation of what has already been interpreted; yet they can be re-interpreted. In this sense, documents have the potential to multiply. Written materials belonging to the past become historical documents only within an interpretative regime, and the history that is deciphered from such documents is primarily a discursive reality. This is a reality that is bound by the principles of justification/verification which prevail at the time of interpretation and the prevailing paradigm that guides the interpretation. The desired ability to convince and persuade stems from the interpretative procedure that come forth partially by choice and then by chance. These are some of the presuppositions implicit in this as well as in the chapters to follow. The strand cutting across different chapters till the end of this book employs an interpretative procedure that projects certain patterns which prevailed in a swaroopam. What a swaroopam means has never been addressed.

The elimination of the distinction between kingdom and pre-kingdom histories and historiography necessitates redundancy. The theme of the previous chapter was on how this distinction has been eliminated with the aid of the figures of speech. In this chapter, some of the patterns have been traced from the already interpreted documents that have a significant place in history texts. Once we accept the distinction between the 'Travancore kingdom' and 'pre-kingdom' and focus on the latter, then what becomes visible is the swaroopam. That is, the 'kingdom' is distinguished from swaroopam for writing history.

It is evident from the previous chapter that some form other than a kingdom existed till the first quarter of the eighteenth century. The existing evidence lends itself only to conceive of swaroopams till then. Therefore, the terms swaroopam and muppu are elaborated by providing an analytical framework that can shed light on different dimensions of the internal organisation of the swaroopam and the position and place of muppu within the swaroopam, rather than seeking to define or describe the history of swaroopams. The distinctiveness of these terms in comparison to the categories that appear in any of the variants of the history of 'kingdom' has to be demonstrated. But then, I will not make it explicit as the attempt here is not to trace the antecedents of the swaroopam at all[1]. As we move on, the distinctiveness mentioned above will become clearer.

It will be demonstrated that the process of determining the individual who occupies the position of the muppu of a swaroopam takes place through what can be called a hierarchy. This is determined not only by the successor's relationship with the predecessor, but also the age or a precisioned arrangement based on *janmasamayam* or the time of birth of the potential successor. What is suggested here is that it is not only the age of the successor alone but also that the age of the mother of different potential successors which matter in the exercise of power by a *muppu*.

It is possible to re-interpret the connotations of the terms swaroopam and muppu by distancing the swaroopam from the 'Travancore of the late-medieval' or 'Pre-modern Travancore' as it appears in the prevailing literature.[2] The attempt here is to trace how these terms are interrelated and to isolate the critical binding forces.

The most distinguished position which an individual could occupy within a swaroopam was muppu and not king, unlike in raajyam. Let me repeat, the terms swaroopam and muppu are elaborated by providing an analytical framework that can shed light on different patterns and interior specificities of swaroopams and the inter-positional relations among muppus within them, rather than seeking to define or describe what actually they were. The idea of Venad as centralised by some of the eminent historians[3] has already been shown to be a hyperbole. I have taken up the swaroopams in their own right and I also examine the interrelationships among them through the positional roles of muppu. It has to be said at the outset that I am not talking about the transition of the swaroopam from *naadu* as some scholarly historians has done.[4]

The Swaroopam Units

The terms swaroopam and muppu began to appear in the documents recurrently from the mid-fourteenth century onwards, along with intermittent references to another political entity, Venad, and its ruler (as in the phrase *venad vaazhntharulinra*). Although the name Venad and the phrase *venad vaazhntharulinra* existed even during the fourteenth century as the fag end of a trend, the references were becoming less frequent. Thereafter, a majority of the published documents have referred to only the swaroopam (prefixed with any of the proper names) and its muppu and not to Venad and '*venad vaazhntharulinra*'[5]. By the end of the fourteenth century, the terms swaroopam and muppu began to acquire prominence and the term Venad gradually fell into disuse in the *Mathilakam Grandhavari*. It disappeared completely by the turn of the fourteenth century[6]. By the beginning of the thirteenth century itself, two swaroopams, namely Chiravay and Threppappur, along with their respective muppu positions, began to be specified in the documents.[7] Deshinganad and Kunnummel Ilayetam, the other two swaroopams of the region in focus, are frequently used in the documents from the second quarter of the fourteenth century.[8] Thus, from the fourteenth century onwards, the swaroopams becomes more and more conspicuous in the documents. Representations of the swaroopam were proliferation, especially in the documents that are published and contemporarily available. As I mentioned in the introduction, the documents that are re-interpreted here are only those which found place in the already existing history texts.

The fourteenth century marks the beginning of a trend in the history of presentation of the swaroopams and their respective muppu positions. As stated above, in concomitance with this trend, the terms Venad and venad vaazhntharulinra disappeared from the documents. This trend is not just a matter of the substitution of terms or categories, but something more than that because the late medieval Swaroopam was an entirely different phenomenon. The appearance of the Swaroopam and the disappearance of Vanchinaadu show a discontinuity in history rather than a 'transition' as Ganesh K.N[9] puts forward.[10] Such a conceptualisation follows Darwinian evolutionism which has been well challenged by incorporating the concepts such as 'rupture' and 'discontinuity' in historiography. Besides, I propose that swaroopam cannot be conceptualised as a phenomenon that emerged from the changes in family formation alone. That is, it cannot be conceptualised that swaroopams emerged from *thayvashies* as Raghava Varier[11] did. To this author, joint families and the number of members in them multiplied over time, especially after the rule of Cheraman Perumals, and this led to *kuruvazcha* in *naadu vazhiswaroopams*'[12]. This implies that the multiplication and proliferation of joint families and their sub-divisions led to the emergence of swaroopams. The family-formation based conceptualisation of swaroopams was postulated by both of the authors mentioned above. Both of them conceive the concept of the swaroopam with aid of 'family'; however, they have carried it out differently.[13] These conceptions appears authentic, but not is sufficient as swaroopams had authority over 'territory' besides the landed property and 'things' of the family—however, blurred and shifting the boundaries were. The swaroopams also exercised power over the people who dwelt within the respective territories.[14]

It was stated that swaroopams were *naatutayavor* during the time of the Perumals.[15] The connection between the Perumal period and Swaroopams has been carried out by Ganesh K.N. as well. For instance, he states that "(S)ome of the features of medieval political structure could be seen in the Perumal period. Political authority over the naadu followed the form of *kuruvalcha* (which can be rendered as parcelled authority)."[16] If these propositions or arguments can be elaborated with details, not only we will gain fresh insights about the genealogy[17] of the *Swaroopams* but also about the 'Chera' way of organising exercise of authority.

There were sub-units of authority within swaroopams as well. These aspects made the swaroopam a swaroopam. Both the authors mentioned above accept the fact that naadu continued to exist even after the emergence of swaroopams. Therefore, it is very likely that both the swaroopam and naadu forms coexisted at different parts of pre-modern Thiruvithamkur. Relatively, naadus might have existed independent of the swaroopams or existed as sub-sets of them. The nature of each of them and patterns of relations between them are aspects yet to be elaborated.

From the fifteenth century onwards up to the mid-eighteenth century, the term Swaroopam was profusely suffixed with proper names such as Chiravay, Threppappur, Deshinganad and Kunnummel Ilayetathu. That is, by the fifteenth century, the presence of formalised Swaroopams with their respective muppu positions became quite luminescent. From the mid-eighteenth century, these terms became 'something of the past' and we find only the Travancore kingdom and *maharaja* or *raaja* with several honorific prefixes. Since I am not concerned here with the shift from Swaroopam to kingdom, I am leaving this issue to those who have already been concerned with it or to those yet to get concerned.

The Term Swaroopam

The term Swaroopam can be more closely examined and understood as a basic unit of referential category that extensively and intensely circulated among the privileged groups of the late medieval period in the present day Keralam and the eastern part of Kanyakumari of Tamil Nadu. This term circulated along with its close referentials such as *Koyikkal*, *Kovilakam*, *Illam*, *Naadu*, *Uru*, *Desham*, *Sanketham* and so on. Some of these terms were widely employed in other parts of the South India as well. But then, Kerala was the only region in India or elsewhere which had the concept of swaroopam. Of course, naadu was common in South India. swaroopam and naadu had maximum prominence as they had the biggest territorial coverage and relative concentration of authority in muppu, temple, Brahmins, sabha, yogam[18] etc.[19] swaroopam had a more or less formalised[20] and continuous existence for at least four to five centuries. This term swaroopam simultaneously implies its exclusive and relational existence.

To begin with, let us consider it from the semantic, etiological and etymological angles. In the most general sense, the swaroopam meant 'belonging to one's own' or 'one's own shape' or 'having one's own form' or 'the law which is identified with myself', 'self-form' etc[21] and refers directly to self-existence and self-form (as in 'self-formed' or 'self-forming'). In the semantic sense, it connotes a self-determining quality, a 'real' form that can be identified as 'internal' and natural to anything. So it has the potential for permanence and to regenerate itself. The concept of the Swaroopam exists without reference to any other form (for example, concepts like *pararoopam*; the supposed antinomy of the term swaroopam). The selfhood of the swaroopam is defined in terms of itself, as it is a 'self-form'. Therefore, as a concept it enables a fundamental unit for inquiry, unlike any 'comprehensive name'.

To repeat an argument that is in the previous chapter, a comprehensive name like Travancore is derived by aggregating constituent entities. Such an aggregation overshadows the constituent entities which had its own existence. Without such an aggregation, constituent entities could perhaps have gained more light. When the term swaroopam is conceived in itself, then the distracting and encoding effects of the comprehensive name can be beneficially avoided. From the analytical point of view, it is expected that it would be more advantageous to treat it as a unit of analysis in its own right, to seek for new possibilities of interpretative fields. There are other merits for paying attention to the swaroopam as well, which are discussed below.

Encountered in different semantic structures of speech, the term swaroopam also circulated as a referential word. For example, Threppappur, Deshinganad, Chiravay, Kunnummel etc, were recognised as swaroopams. Here, the swaroopam functions as a common noun, which by definition is a referential word. However, when the word swaroopam comes as a suffix to any one of them, as in the case of Threppappur Swaroopam, where it functions as a proper noun. So whenever any swaroopam is singled out in relation to others or employed to refer to any one or more individual swaroopams, say Threppappur or Chiravay, then it is invariably used as a referential word. In this case it as an object, the swaroopam refers to a subject and never assumes, in expressions, a subject position by itself.

Perhaps the term swaroopam is also an abstract noun, which makes it possible to use it as subject, object and appositive. This immense semantic richness of the word itself is an indication of the complexity of the swaroopam phenomena and opens up the vista for a heterological (having the potential to develop into different forms) inquiry. There appears to have been a heterogeneous use of the swaroopam in language itself, parallel to the co-existence of different swaroopams in the non-discursive terrain as well. The differentiated senses of the word suggest the co-existence of several 'self-formed' entities, something "that has presented itself to the eyes". In this context, one begins to realise the significance of focusing on the points of differentiation and the formation of the constellations of swaroopams. The term 'constellation' suggests the dynamic aspect involved in their co-existence as it is transient.

To add to the complexity, the term swaroopam denotes at the same time a family[22] in the anthropological sense and a more or less defined space (with people of different kind and things) in the exercise of authority. For instance, an expression such as the Chiravay Swaroopam simultaneously denotes the proper name of a family of individuals and households, and a given geographical and social space where the family could exercise authority over the people therein. Hereafter, when we use the term Swaroopam (with capital letter 'S') it denotes a given socio-territorial space (a 'territory' with blurred and overlapping boundaries) where muppu could exercise authority, and when it begins with lower case's' (swaroopam) it refers to the family. If the Swaroopam is an outcome of a superimposition of the family name over spatio-territorial spread, then one can assume that Swaroopam, as a concept, is inclusive of the swaroopam. This is indicative of the power relationships, or more fairly among different kinship and extra-kinship relations that existed. A sense of territoriality concomitant with the projection of the family name on a given geographical and socio-political space is at work here. In the conditions that permitted the projection of a family name over a given domain, one could find the foundations of exercise of authority of a swaroopam/muppu within a Swaroopam. A realisation of this would enable one to formulate a project of tracing how, and to what extent, the swaroopam was attached to the Swaroopam organisation in distinction to providing any account of Swaroopam organisation in itself or in terms of the authority 'prevailed' by swaroopam. That is, the Swaroopam cannot be conceived independent of swaroopam and muppu and *vice versa*. Here, muppu was a common factor both in the Swaroopam and swaroopam.

The fact is that several self-formed phenomenon (Swaroopams) co-existed with interstices as well as in relation with each other with intersections. It is not that one self-form or even a self-form in opposition to some other existed. The co-existence had both referential and non-referential implications. An analysis of the relations between Swaroopam and swaroopam has to traverse between their common noun and proper noun to grasp their power relations. Compared to the reliance on convenient 'comprehensive names', which are often found in the existing history books, the treatment of the Swaroopam as a descriptive and analytical term gives more scope for introspection and contemplation. The realisation of the semantic difference between the Swaroopam and kingdom will be made clearer in the next section. The differentiation of the word swaroopam as family and the Swaroopam as a generalised socio-political space testify the analytical potential of both of them.

When there are several autonomous and formalised entities having self-formativeness and self-determinacy, how are the differences and intersections among Swaroopams are to be traced? There were both integral and differential relations among Swaroopams since they coexisted. These relations had given rise to a certain set of practices that were manifest, and therefore perforce the inquiry to turn into a study of the enabling condition of these practices. In the course of our discussion it will be shown how the Swaroopam was organised outside the 'Swaroopam-pararoopam' antinomy. Perhaps, in determining the pattern of relations of inter-self-forms, there could be recognition of one's own form in another individual *Swaroopam* without losing one's own self-identification.

The Position of Muppu

In a S(s)waroopam, muppu is the most distinguished position and bears a unique presence. This is so at least from the fourteenth century to the early decades of the mid-eighteenth century. This is what can be gleaned from the documents that I have consulted. Next to muppu was *Ilamkuru* or junior muppu. Lexically, muppu meant the eldest among a given set of family members who were known as *swaroopikal,* when the unit entity referred to is the swaroopam. In a Swaroopam, the muppu was the most privileged position that had potential to exercise maximum power when compared to other positions of power. Only the muppu of a swaroopam can become muppu of a Swaroopam. In a S(s)waroopam the position of muppu was the most distinctive in the sense that he was not supposed to stand in front of anyone else. Standing in front of others and sitting along with others made a considerable difference. In other words, the positioning and self-placement of individuals bodies and the hierarchy of biological age mattered a lot. The eldest to youngest was a spectrum in which the muppus were distributed and it was known as muppumura. When several Swaroopams coexist, it is not the seniormost in the family alone who occupies the position of muppu. For instance, as in our case, if four Swaroopams coexist, then there would be at least four muppus who are placed in terms of hierarchy of age. The placement of muppus is not as simple but relatively complex. I will take up the complex modality of such placements in detail later. Besides, I should mention that the position of muppu was not confined to the S(s)waroopam unit alone; it was identifiable in other unit entities such as *thavazhi* (descent group), *kuttukutumbam* (joint family), clan, sect, tribe, family, and in several other transient groupings such as pilgrims and so on. There need not be any semblance among these muppu positions of these different units, yet, they are all men of distinction within the respective groupings. This implies that within each of these unit entities, there would be a unique and distinguished position designated as muppu.

In other words, muppu position was not exclusive to S(s)waroopam. Yet, the Swaroopam muppu was the most distinguished among all other muppus.

Although in several other unit-entities there were muppu positions occupied by various individuals, the muppu position of a Swaroopam is differentiable from those positions in other unit entities in terms of the respective activities and the functions that the position entailed. The muppu of a Swaroopam was the most distinguished among all other muppus. He had unique roles and he was positioned within manifold relations, thereby having a bearing on other muppus of the entities mentioned above. One should not lose sight of the play of distinction among the identical positional terms.

The word *muppathi* could refer to the wife (!) of a muppu but it does not appear in any of the documents. However, the word *amma* (the literal meaning of this word is mother, but it also signifies women of distinction belonging to certain elite families) had a distinctive position within the swaroopam. For *ammas* also there was a *muppumura* in terms of age and kinship relation. They used to reside at a place known as Attingal which lies at the north of Thiruvananthapuram. The ammas of Deshinganad used to reside at a place known as Kallada. Although they had their own territory, it was never known as a swaroopam. There were several occasions in which, in the absence of a muppu, the amma performed the roles of the muppu. There were well known instances of both Portuguese and the British negotiating trade related affairs with them.

What does the Swaroopam muppu position enable or what is it expected to do? The Swaroopam muppu position is actualised in the acts of *vaazhal* and thus the expression *muppuvaazhcha* or *vanaruli*.[23] Lexically, vaazhal or vaazhvu means 'being in the world', not in a simple sense of existing, but existing with a distinction. This distinctiveness is articulated by joining the expression with another one *aruli* (proclaimed) - hence the common phrase vaanaruli.[24] The word aruli does not refer to the act of speech alone, but invariably goes as the honorific suffix to the term vaazhal. It renders a distinctiveness both to the act of vaazhal and to the muppu as in the expression *muppuvaanearuli (*muppu-vaane-aruli). This expression implies the activity of the muppu; to be in the world with distinction. At a general semantic level, the term vaazhal refers to the individual's being in the world and the existential condition of the position as exemplified by the phrase *irunnaruli* (in the literal sense it means "sat and proclaimed"). The demise of the muppu is denoted by the term *mutinjaruli* (*mutinju* means ended). Vaazhal is distinct from mere existence, for it is the quality of being in the realm of happiness and prosperity. More than the functional connotation of the activity, the term refers to the modality of existence of a person occupying the position in the activity or role, and the human condition of the one in the position or *vanor*. The existence of vanor is defined by the human matrix and the distribution/ordering of positions within and between the swaroopams, not by the order of 'things' and territory as in the case of a king. This is one of the reasons why the translation of muppu as 'ruler' is conceptually a misnomer, for this would confuse between the existential aspect, and the positional and functional aspects of the term muppu. Nevertheless, there is ruling of humans and non-humans. This aspect will become clearer when the contrast between *vaazhal* of muppu and *bharanam* of the king will be explicated.

A feature that stands out is the concomitant occurrence of vaazhal in several other unit entities other than the swaroopam. For instance, there are expressions like *naatuvaazhi* and *deeshavaazhi* which are positions of two separate entities namely naadu and desham. Here, the positions are defined through the activity of vaazhal attached to the object of their function that is naadu or desham. However, one has to reckon that in such instances, the suffix *aruli* could not be found. It could be that aruli is not explicitly spelt out, but it is connoted through the activity that binds the position within the unit entities. Therefore, both muppu and vaazhal occur when referred to different unit entities, but only independently; the position of muppu and the act of vaanarulal get linked exclusively within the Swaroopams. There were several *deshavaazhzl* and *naaduvazhal* within a Swaroopam, but muppu-vaane-arulal was exclusive prerogative of the Swaroopam muppu.

One cannot generalise that wherever there is a muppu, the act of vaazhal accompanies. In the case of unit entities like family, *thaivazhi*, clan and so on, as noted above, there could be muppu positions but the term *vaanarulal* was never suffixed when referring to them. It is not that vaazhal gives distinctiveness to these positions, yet they had certain distinctiveness for they were muppu. Similarly, in the case of the unit entities like naadu and desham there is no muppu position although the term vaazhi appears. Therefore, the confluence of the position and activity as expressed in the phrase muppu vaanaruli was unique to the Swaroopam taken as a unit, although muppu and vaazhal occur independently in many other unit entities.

Another fact worth spelling out is that although the positional term muppu simultaneously occurs in the Swaroopam and swaroopam, the term vaanarulal appears only when referred to Swaroopam. The term S(s)waroopam is employed here to designate the unique combination of two entities, the family swaroopam and the supra-familial and territorial (protected space) Swaroopam. We get two different groupings here. In one group, what unifies is the position of muppu, let it be the swaroopam. In other group, the unifying factor is vaazhal, so let it be the Swaroopam or desham. In the former, the muppu position is placed within a kinship network or other familial relations among the swaroopikal or is internal to swaroopam. The latter bases itself on the activity of the muppu whose functional implications extend beyond the kinship relations to power and territorial space. Though they are two types of groupings, the swaroopam is internal to the Swaroopam, the entity where the position and activity are combined, and becomes visible as unique. The muppu vaazhcha gives us clues to the link between kinship relations and power relations involved in the organisation of the Swaroopam. The projection of a proper name of the swaroopam onto the Swaroopam is only one of the instances of power relations. The term muppu and vaazhal taken independently show the presence of interstices between the first and the second groupings (in other words, the possibility of identifying a separate existence) while the combined expression muppuvaazcha depicts the fusion which is operative in the Swaroopam.

The expression muppuvaazhcha and its distinctiveness with respect to territoriality can be clearly brought out by differentiating it from raaja-bharanam (rule of the king); bharanam often follows the term raaja (king) and thus the expression raaja-bharanam. But, the phrase 'muppu-bharanam' does not occur in any of the documents, moreover, such a usage appears incongruous to anyone interpreting these documents. The distinction could be elucidated in the following manner: the word raaja and the usage of the term raaja-bharanam were well known during the period of reference here. In spite of this, this usage was never treated as substitute for or synonym of muppu vaazhcha in any of the documents. It is important to mention here that the term raaja bharanam appears in the copper plate and rock inscriptions of Chera documents (9th to 11th centuries) as an honorific title, but not in any inscriptional or written evidences belonging to the historical period of our concern.

Often raaja-vazhcha and raaja bharanam were used interchangeably. But I have taken up only raaja-bharanam for discussion. This choice is not random, but purposive as my intention is to bring forth the distinction between vazcha and baranam with a view to shed more light on the function of muppu-vazcha. The term bharanam means 'to support', 'to carry' and implies 'to contain'. At one level, the difference between "to contain" and "to be with distinction" is self-evident. Historically however, it is useful to note that in the beginning of the eighteenth century, we see a shift from muppu vaazhcha to raaja-bharanam.[25] The term raaja was not repeatable when referring to any other unit entities, unlike the muppu position. For instance, for a family, there could be a muppu, but not a raaja. Likewise, for a clan there could be a muppu, but not a raaja. Further, the situation of two raaja positions within a kingdom is paradoxical. On the other hand, within a Swaroopam there could be muppu positions of different entities such as desham, naadu, family etc. This implies that within the Swaroopam organisation, the muppu position and the activity of vaazhcha could occur at several sub-units such as family, clan, tribe, thayvazhi and so on. In the case of raajyam or kingdom, the raaja cannot be a positional name in any of the unit entities. If there is a raaja, then there must invariably be a raajyam/ kingdom; they are synchronically bonded in such a way that it would be an exception if either of them (king and kingdom or raajavu and raajyam) existed independently. However, no such bonding occurs between muppu and Swaroopam, at least at the level of language or in any other evident social articulation. The king is unique to the kingdom because this position is defined in terms of a disposition to 'contain' an 'entire/total' territorial domain. Counterfactually, if there are 'kings' for deshams or naadus, then they would function to contain deshams or naadu but they in turn will be 'contained' by the king of that particular kingdom in which they belong. This undermines the function of kings of the former units (desham or naadu). In the case of muppu vaazhcha, several Swaroopams can coexist 'with distinction' without being mutually exclusive and without involving linear successive containment of any one by the other. Further, even when more than one Swaroopam comes within a muppu vaazcha of a person, the identity of the individual Swaroopam remains unaffected. Such a situation cannot occur in the case of the raajyam or kingdom. Two kingdoms having one king is an anachronism; but not in the case of Swaroopams. I will be elaborating on such situations later.

While the 'king' has a set of functions and authority that constitute the position, the muppu position derives its significance not from functional considerations alone, but from the place of the particular position among other positions in the Swaroopam, and also among muppu positions of its sub-units like clan, thaivazhi etc. When we take the Swaroopam as a unit, there would be only one muppu position for it, but at the same time, there would be respective muppus for its thaivazhies. However, there was no delegation of authority to these positions by the Swaroopam muppu. The Swaroopam muppu was the most conspicuous among the various positions present in different social units, and muppu vaazhcha was the most distinctive activity. But then, muppu vaazhcha does not involve 'containment' as in the case of any other muppu positions in Swaroopams, unlike in raaja bharanam. This aspect will be taken up for further elucidation contextually.

The positional aspect of muppu will now be elaborated in order to understand its positional aspect within a Swaroopam. When the word muppu was introduced in this section, it was pointed out that this word directly refers to the seniority of age among 'certain' members of the unit in question. This word 'certain' requires elaboration. It is also true that the term muppu circulates as a relative term. It is a position (*sthaanam*) that has two implications. While it is a position of distinction, the distinctiveness that was conferred upon it had been derived from the place and position within a matrix involving the swaroopikal. Therefore, it can never be absolute as in the case of raaja. The word thus means both position and place. There is a field of co-existence of several positions in which the muppu is distinctly placed. That is, there is a spectrum of individuals (swaroopikal) from which the seniormost is singled out. In the case of a Swaroopam, its muppu would necessarily belong to a swaroopam; others in the Swaroopam unit were also placed in different positions of importance but not as the muppu. This is, the first level of disaggregation to 'identify' the 'certain' members (swaroopikal). Thus, for a Swaroopam there was a single swaroopam family, this family was defined in terms of kinship relations, from which individuals would be identified and drawn to occupy the position of the muppu. The same individual would be the muppu of that family as well. Here, the specific individual who occupies this position in the family/ swaroopam is not my primary concern. The central problem here deals with where these individuals are drawn from. Rather than the particular individual and personal names, it is the serialisation of the members of a family unit, whatever may be its criteria, that is critical. A swaroopam is identified with Swaroopam in such a way that the former would be the legitimate hereditary reserve of the heirs to the positions of distinction in the organisation of the latter.

Before we proceed further, a question becomes germane: what gave legitimacy to the recognition of the eldest? Such recognition might not have been problematic during the period because the legitimacy of the eldest as muppu had already been normalised (not structurally). The fixity of this normalised recognition was a distinctive feature of the period under consideration. Alternatively, the existence of such normalised recognition enables us to mark a distinguishable period (as a period in which the Swaroopams existed)[26]. In that case the question would be concerned with what the mechanisms that perpetuated the normalisation or recognition were. This question will be addressed later, but it is raised here to allude to the recognition of muppu and others in the political field.[27]

At present, what has to be recognised as important is not so much the unit-entity of the swaroopam. But it is important to treat it as a composite unit consisting of kinship relations inclusive of affinal relations, and as a network of "genealogical relations"[28] immanent in the interlocking of several component joint families, (which can be roughly called "genealogical relations"). These genealogical relations are taken as homogeneous at this level of disaggregation. Another question is whether the swaroopam as a family is a kinship group linked to a single ancestral root or not. This question is difficult to pursue in our present state of knowledge but it is still a question that can be formulated clearly. The right of hereditary succession to the muppu positions in the Swaroopam rests on the genealogical relations among the members of the swaroopam and the relations that bind it to other unit entities of significance in the Swaroopam. It should also be kept in mind that the swaroopam and the Swaroopam can be conflated; there is no suggestion that the essence of the Swaroopam can be found in the swaroopam. One is not reducible to the other; they are mutually irreducible.

The Distribution of the Distinguished

For a Swaroopam there had to be a muppu (there were instances of absence of a muppu in Swaroopams; I shall return to this aspect later) and he had to be drawn from a definite family unit that belonged to Attingal. The broadest unit was the Attingal family and an age-based hierarchical distribution of the female members prevailed in it. It was a unit in which the female members (mothers and would-be mothers) of S(s)waroopams resided while the adult-male spouses (except children) resided at Kilimanoor till one became a muppu. The female members of the Swaroopam were also serialised on the basis of age and kinship. What is appealing is that in the palace of the Attingal family, only the female members resided more or less permanently. The sons of them (mothers) were the existing muppus and potential muppus. The male offspring of these 'mothers' were also hierarchically distributed, once again, in terms of their age and their kinship location with respect to their mother's position in the hierarchy. In hierarchically distributing the mothers and offspring, there were two terms critical in guiding the distribution; they are kuuru and mura.

The muppu would invariably be a member of the Swaroopam, but he/she need not necessarily have to be the eldest one among the population (swaroopikal) of the swaroopam. Desegregation and serialisation of the genealogical relations lead to the isolation of a set of individual members who could be the hereditary successors to the positions of distinctions. At this level of operation over the set of relations, the swaroopam is not treated as a homogeneous entity, but as a set in which the elements/constituents are differentiated in terms of both kinship order and seniority of age including gender distinctions. Only a specified set of the senior-most among those included in the kuuru-mura can be found. This set can be characterised as a diagram[29] in which the distribution and serialisation of the existing and potential muppus are vivid. This diagram primarily presents the distribution of the set of swaroopikal and specifies both inter-individual and inter-positional or subjective relations, and endows agency roles on each of them.

Let me dwell upon these two terms (kuuru and mura) before proceeding further as it helps us to decipher the discursive diagram which was functional and was also a guiding principle. This diagram was something which they cherished and wanted to perpetuate. The operation of the diagram involved a 'precisioning' of the time of birth and an ordering based on kinship and seniority in age. That is, both biological and anthropological dimensions can be deciphered from kuuru-mura diagram. As an initial move, it is possible to state that both the terms entered into the structuration of not only the succession rights but, more importantly, the inter-subjective relations of those on whom it operated from their birth to demise.

Lexically, kuuru means 'love', 'affinity', "in conformity with" and "dependence filled with love", fealty to the vaazcha mura[30]. Kuuru marks individuals with ranks such as the first (*mootha*), second (*illam*), third and so on. The term mura can mean rule, order, method, custom etc.[31] Those within the mura series (a given ordered sequence of swaroopikal) were the legitimate occupants of or successors to the position of muppu in different Swaroopams. There is a muppu-mura by which successions took place and the remaining members in the mura would occupy less important positions of distinction in the S(s)waroopams. Therefore, the mura also distributes individuals in the orders of hierarchy. The elaboration of the term mura can isolate principles that enabled one to justifiably occupy positions of distinction, especially the Swaroopam muppu because it means "what is binding", 'duty' etc, and can come in a place to refer to "having a turn of duty".[32]

The kuuru-mura diagram (hereafter, the diagram) may be conceived as a schematised representation exempting indecisiveness, which reveals certain patterns of priority that are internal to the swaroopam. It is possible to state that the diagram precessions (the precise time of birth is observed as it is critical for the distribution and ordering of individuals across positions, besides writing the *jathkam* (horoscope) the time of *jananam* or *janmam* (the terms refer respectively to birth and birth right). It consists of several persons in a serialised order of priority to become the muppu. The objects of the diagram are individual members of the Attingal family (both male and female swaroopikal). If the mura diagram is the form, then these members were the *ullatakkam* (what is contained or content). Individualisation of the membership in the unit was concomitant with the operation of the diagram which binds the distribution of members of the swaroopam with the positions of power in the Swaroopam organisation. It was indispensably those individualised members, from the moment of their birth, whom it bound. It differentiated individual members in the genealogical relations in terms of their positions, and created an 'inside' and 'outside' within the swaroopam; some members were placed within the diagram and others were placed outside it. The diagram recognised the place of the individual within kinship relationships and projected normalised distributions of kinship relations into hierarchies of power. That is, this diagram distributed individuals in the hierarchised orders of potential positions and places of the swaroopikal. It is at this level that kinship bound age distribution entered into the process of aggregation and desegregation of individuals within a swaroopam.

Here, the political dimension, as in the identification of the swaroopam with the Swaroopam, is not present. The ways in which kinship and politics operated within the swaroopam could be seen in the ordered inclusion that the diagram entails. To repeat, the nature and form of politics that were implicit in the grouping of certain individuals within the swaroopam differs from the identification of the swaroopam with the Swaroopam. This leads us to the question of lineage and succession to positions of distinction; the principles of inclusion into the diagram.

The principle of exclusion is unanimously said by historians to be founded on kinship relations. But the specific kinship basis of succession is still not very clear. There have been attempts to see whether matrilineal or patrilineal orders of succession were prevalent, but no unchallenged conclusions in this regard have appeared.[33] Nevertheless, it is believed that a matrilineal system of succession prevailed, but without any reliable substantiation.[34] There were marital relations by the swaroopikal with both matrilineal families as well as the Tamil patrilineal groups.[35] In addition, there existed knowledge about other models of kinship and successions. Further, the different orders of lineage and succession were followed by different groups of people at different points of time. These factors could have influenced historians in specifying the existed succession system and criteria of inclusion of swaroopikal into the diagram. What is important at present is to note that there is a certain amount of ambiguity. The documents, which describe the events of succession, do not state the kinship relationship of the successor to the 'predecessor'.[36] This in itself is a question that needs to be addressed.

The available documents on succession in general refer to the following: the proper names of the demised and the successor, the time, date and year of successor's birth, the proper names of the family to which the successor belonged (at times this was clubbed with the name of some ancestral family known as Kilperur which existed prior to the reference here), the temples that the successor visited and the offerings that were made, gifts and other ritualistic gestures of 'giving', oblations to various human dignitaries and extra-terrestrial deities (in general, *padiyum paditharavum*). With minor variations, these are the items that generally appear in the documents that refer to succession (*padiyet Itam*).(Correct?) What is curious is that although many things are precisely stated, the documents do not state the kinship relations of the successor to the predecessor. This has already been pointed out[37], but the answers that exist now in historiography are not credulous. The existing explanation is that the kinship relation had been obvious, therefore it was not included in the documents. Posing a counter-question could bring out the weak basis of this explanation. If the kinship relation was not included because it was quite obvious, does it mean that the other details in the documents stated were far from evident?

I would like to reiterate that the siblings of these women at Attingal were eligible members to become a muppu and no one else had this right. This implies that those at Attingal were the mothers of the present and the potential distinguished ones (muppus). These mothers were serialised in terms of their age and the eldest one was expected to be the senior-most or the most distinguished in the diagram of Attingal and her eldest son had the maximum distinctiveness to assume the muppu position. But even if any junior mother had the eldest son in the Attingal family, then he had the first priority to be or to become the muppu. This was a speciality of kuuru-mura.

Relatively, more than kinship, what was considered more significant was time of the incumbent's birth into the family; not so much about the kinship relation of the successor. Although the distinctive qualities of the successor were inscribed, the kinship relation of the successor to the predecessor, and the diagrammatic position of his mother were almost left undermined in the documents. Therefore, it is difficult to make statements about whether one can find a correspondence between the position of the mothers and their sons in the diagram; if there is correspondence then it is not only age, but the kinship order that is equally important. However, this is not the case.

The diagram operated only within the swaroopam or any other entities which had such boundary conditions; for instance in the tharavade. It orders both male and female members separately, that is, any one diagram would consist exclusively of female or male members of the swaroopam. An existing diagrammatic order gets altered in the event of death of male members but not in the case of mother's death. The demise of a male member in the diagram leads to chain effects in the sequential ordering in the diagram. In the event of birth, the order gets expanded. These alterations in the ordered sequence can be called as a change in the diagrammatic ordering. But there can also be shift in the order, if a transition had taken place from *marumakkathayam* (matriliny) to *makkathayam* (patriliny) and vice-versa, or from a multilineal to a unilinear system of succession, or as a result of the adoption of individual members into the swaroopam who happened to be elder than at least any one of the existing members in the diagrammatic order.[38] In such cases, we can state that there is a shift, rather than a change in the order. Change does not involve improbability, whereas shift involves probable consequences in the existing power relations. Shifts can bring in unanticipated, legitimate, or the illegitimate ordering. This point will be taken up while discussing about adoption.

Whatever may be the system of succession, the diagram is an ordering that moves from the existing muppu to the sons of age-based priority if makkathaayam was prevalent or to the eldest nephew in the case of marumakkathaayam. Succession to the muppu position involved precisioning of the temporal, and the founding of a hierarchical web of individual relations based on it. Precise ordering based on the time of birth and its status as the foundation for relativisation of a certain set of individuals in the diagram stabilised the system of succession and maintained inter-positional relations. Therefore, whatever may be the specific system of kinship relations involved in the hereditary succession, once a group of individual members were serialised and included in the diagram, the process of inclusion/exclusion based on kinship was terminated. What is most explicit in the documents of succession is the successor's positional relation with others in the kuuru-mura diagram.

The diagram relates different individuals and positions, and prescribes a precise set of aims and activities to those whom it isolates and sequences in the hierarchy. Its function was not to represent a world of individuals. Rather, it was a blueprint that was coextensive with the whole social field. One need not think that there was a single grand scheme of diagram that enabled the ordering of each and every member of the Swaroopam. But this diagram must be kept in mind to understand the interior of the swaroopam organisation and the way in which it created exteriority and interiority among the members of the swaroopam and how it serialised members and distributed them with positions by 'individuating' the swaroopikal.

It can be seen that age works to order different siblings of the Attingal family, and is concomitant with the kinship basis of ordering and succession. Age works in a central way in the diagram. The distribution of individuals within a particular kuuru-mura diagram does not follow the principles of kinship relations alone, but on age[39] based seniority. An important aspect that needs to be noted here is that the coverage of individuals included in the diagram is limited. This limited coverage of the order is exemplified by the high incidence of not having enough successors, and this in turn led to the adoption of both the genders. I will be describing the incidence of adoption in one of the subsequent chapters.

Determinateness

If the inter-positional relations among the members included in the diagram are based on age and kinship, then it can be perceived as a deterministic matrix which pre-empted ambiguity and indecisiveness. However, if age is the determining factor in the internal ordering of the matrix and its outer boundary is defined by the kinship principle, then this matrix may not be deterministic as the internal ordering can be altered through the adoption of both male and females. If 'mother's age' is not considered, and only age of the male members are considered, then there will be a unilateral descending serialisation of individuals (only a vector). To simplify, if the second ranked mother has an older son than that of her elder sister, then who will be the seniormost in the diagram? Obviously the elder son would be the muppu. The search for an answer to it is worthy to seek for, but at present I meet with an impasse. The diagrams for the male members and the female members were independent of one another. There was no common diagram that plotted the modalities of the inter-positional relationships between men and women (mother) in the organisational realm of the swaroopam. This interstice has given room for indeterminacy and has been prone to strategic manipulations. At present, one can propose that the muppu as the eldest is the primary determinant of the muppu mura and not so much kinship relationship, although it determines the outer boundary of the vector. In this case, the age factor undermines the exclusive determinability of kinship. Perhaps it was kinship which determined the outer bounds of the vector in which swaroopikal were distributed, but its internal distribution of the individuals across positions rests on age.

It is important to note that the diagram combines several members of the swaroopam into a universe by grouping a set of individuals from the entire swaroopam in terms of the relations to the mothers. Simultaneously, it individualizes and reallocates each of them (included in the order through age) and assigns to each a specified place within the web of inter-positional relationships.[40] The diagram becomes visible in its finalised functions from succession to the positions of distinction and at the moments when the positions came into contact with one another. This system of the succession and perpetuation of the inter-subjective relations in the swaroopam were formalised in the diagram and its application. The field of kinship was open in the sense that modifications could be accomplished, say, through adoption. An entire chapter is devoted to this aspect of adoption, therefore I am not elaborating this point. It is the centrality of the age factor in distributing people in time, space, places and positions that makes it temporarily determinate. It is temporary because the age seniority of the adopted engenders a shift in the interior of the diagram.

The diagram and the ordering therein can be analyzed further. The word *kuuru* also means part, share, alliance, attachment, etc.[41] All these qualities, which were already eulogised in the past itself, are made ordinal by reducing them to age (in distinction to efficiency) as in the diagram. The distribution of individuals over a precisioned time-scale, based on their respective time of birth is immanently unequal. Age relations are to be placed in a continuum; the time of janmam was invariably hierarchical. The time was be measured on the basis of the moment of birth of those who were to be included in the diagram. The precisioning of the time of birth (of any mortals) has always been quite meticulous as is seen in the astrological calculus prevalent from the ancient era. The moment of birth is measurable with precision and thus employable in the relations of inequality requiring a non-arbitrary criteria. The moment age-wise distribution cuts across kinship hierarchies, and this hierarchy become all the more 'precisionable'. There are two hierarchies, namely the order in the diagram and positions of distinction. For the present purpose, it can be inferred from the above decomposition of the diagram that what is made stable and fixed were the hierarchy achieved through the diagram and corresponding positions. The determinacy and un-arbitrariness in the distribution of the swaroopikal in the distinguished positions were accomplished through the determination of the time of jananam. This in turn gave stability, continuity and apparent permanence to the Swaroopam. This precisioning of time as in the diagram was permanent, exhaustive and continuous at least during the time in which there were Swaroopams.

Permanence, Continuity and Certainty in the Diagram

The kuuru-mura diagram may be elaborated further. The diagram individualizes swaroopikal or members of the Swaroopam. Thereafter it places them in a sequence of positions and constitutes inter-individual[42] relations. This was expected to be permanent during the span of the muppus and their successors who existed in this world. Thereby, the hierarchical distribution of positions in the organisation of the Swaroopam becomes normalised with the age-based diagrammatic ordering. This order is not only applicable to the swaroopam muppu but implies a general classification of positions in the organisation of that Swaroopam that specifies which individual member should occupy which position. The members in the order would be assigned positions spread across the Swaroopam. But the principles behind the designation of each and every specific position, that is, the spatial distribution of these positions, are not discernible from the existing historical documents.[43]

Further, the diagram is not only active at the instance of succession, but more than that, it has permanence in the sense that it maintains a one-to-one-correspondence between the diagram and the distinctive positions. It ensures that the individual included in the diagram is assigned a fixed place in the inter-positional relations. One need not to become a muppu, but the fact that everyone knows that so and so will be the next muppu provides a sense of permanence. But then, the schema operates most visibly at the point of succession where it becomes the basis for justifying one's claim to be the successor. It was also important when it came to the negotiations between the muppu, sabha and *ettarayogam,* (I will be elaborating on these two entities afterwards) who were extremely important and decisive elite and powerful groups in the organisation of the Swaroopam.

The diagram is more than just a guide in the sense that it provides a permanent map of the inter-positional relations within the Swaroopams. This has a profound ramification for the life and activity of individuals from birth to death; specifying not merely the functions that one is expected to perform but even determining and ordering his daily life within a ritual grid. Thus, the diagram constitutes a continuum both across space and time. That is, it cuts across the distinguished positions in the Swaroopam and the swaroopikal's entire individual's life span. It was influential in shaping the subjectivities and inter-subjective relations that they had to maintain. Nevertheless, the actual historical experience might have been different because the diagram might have been overlooked at times. But those 'deviations' become perceivable because of the active presence of such a diagram.

Above all, the diagram not only orders the present but also the future as it anticipates future incumbents. An extreme example can be given here. When an unborn child is designated 'Garbhastha Sriman' (literally, one who has succeeded the throne while still in the womb) it was not merely a honorific title but a palpable reality in experiential terms. This ordering of the future made possible the calculation and control of the size and nature of the set of people whom should be included/excluded from the kuuru-mura. Thus, when one is designated as the Garbhastha Sriman it not only 'anticipates' the successor but also anticipates the displacement of others positions and thus a shift in the diagrammatic order.

In short, the diagram was continuous and perpetual. In the diagrammatic distribution of people, one can decipher "ordering in time" and "distribution in positions".[44] The materiality of the diagram is achieved when it gets correlated with the ordered/hierarchical positions, and that is where kuuru-mura and politics converge. In other words, in the diagrammatic distribution there is a power convergence of kinship, age and positions of power. The diagram enables the enclosure of strictly individualised relations within the swaroopam and the serialisation of them in terms of relations of inequality. The application of the diagram is a non-arbitrary and stabilising mechanism for inclusion, ordering and placement, which are not only legitimising but always already legitimised.

Age as a principle of serialising individuals and diagrammatically distributing them in the positions of authority were least sensitive to differences in individual capabilities; this was another positive feature of the diagram that retained it. Once the age norm is applied, the outcomes—decision about who should be designated to which position—follow decisively and they are least prone to ambiguity and imprecision. It has to be noted that the age factor as normalised and generalised criteria for hierarchical ordering is discursively formed. The justifications for age based hierarchy among those included in the diagram are made possible within the discursive formation which is contingent and responsive to human will. But then, in the precisioning of time as noted above, one can see man's will to create principles and norms which once begin to operate, escape from the individual's will and become autonomous. The norms and principles then work as if from 'above' and shape the course of actions and the way men of distinctions becomes. Although they are formed in discourse, once formed they get affected by and effect non-discursive realm. The lure for the human artefacts is most significantly decipherable in the way time is precisioned and put to use in distributing individuals in the field of inter-subjectivities. Persons in the order from the seniormost to juniormost commonly shared the legitimacy of the diagrammatic placement.

There ought to be a senior-most when we consider several swaroopams together because the respective muppus are, of course, different in age. This is another terrain where the age factor engages in the critical power relations when there is a co-existence of more than one Swaroopam. So, in this situation also, it was not kinship that was the basis of inter-positional relations among the Swaroopams. The kinship relation was a necessary condition for one to be included in the diagram as we know well by now, but to be the muppu, criteria regarding seniority of age are to be met with. At this terminal point of application of the diagram, inter-positional relations are mediated by the technology of precisioning time. That is, if we ask the question, "what is the sanctity of age in determining inter-positional relations?", the answer has to search the discourse on 'age'. Now a general question can be raised as to whether there is any society that has devised precise modalities for mediating relations between equals. Once the equals are identified, the next question is who among the equals should succeed. This question becomes crucial because the positions are already hierarchised with fixity.

Once the hierarchy of age comes to be commonly accepted by all the members of the swaroopam, then the inter-positional relations become beyond individual will. This can be explained by differentiating the situation in question with a hypothetical alternative. If the primary factor which determined the nature of the inter-positional relationship had been 'individual efficiency' or 'personal capability', then, obviously, the conditions of succession differ. If efficiency is the parameter to determine the hierarchical positions under conditions of competition, the exercise of will for the enhancement of one's efficiency becomes a prerequisite. The efficiency norm makes it possible for any one individual in the diagram to aspire to higher positions in the hierarchy and competition becomes normalised. Acquired efficiency in turn, becomes deployable on any 'other' to become a muppu surpassing the age factor. Superior efficiency justifies such surpassing. 'Efficiency' as the norm of superiority is also inherently arbitrary, for different measuring principles order efficiency differently and this, at times, results in the inversion of age-order relations. Thus, an efficiency-based norm is more amenable to strategic manipulations conducive to the furthering of one's own interest. At the same time, the irreducibility of efficiency to any single principle of measurement makes it arbitrary and non-permanent. Efficiency as a norm is intrinsically amenable to one's will in determining the place and position of higher order within inter-positional relations. If the norm for relating one position to another is based on age, then these relationships would be determinate and predictable, and the nature of the interrelationship cannot be changed by contingent or historical factors. Unlike the efficiency-based hierarchy, the age-based norm is determinate. One cannot restructure a determinate factor like age, but efficiency is amenable to contestation and manipulation. An indeterminate efficiency norm would provide justification for preferences according to one's notion of efficiency. This would lead to contingent resolutions and indeterminacy.

So far I have been discussing about the determinateness of the diagrammatic succession to the position of muppu and other positions of importance. It was a normal practice followed by the Swaroopams. But in the organisation of the Swaroopams, there were few other organisational bodies apart from muppu such as ettarayogam and a set of *ettuveettil pillamar*. The members of these bodies were also landlords. They had significant say over the eligibility of one to be or become a muppu. In other words, they had right to intervene into the matters of succession and continuation of one in the position of muppu. These bodies have little to do with the organisation of swaroopam, but in the case of the organisation of the Swaroopam, they had an important role because swaroopam and Swaroopam were mediated through the temple of Padmanabha where the tutelary deity had been consecrated. In the matters of this temple, both these bodies and the muppu converged. Therefore, the relation between muppu and these bodies is critical to the extent that the determinacy about which I have been discussing comes to question. Therefore, the generalisability of the diagram engenders a question.

The Generalisability of the Diagram

All the members in the swaroopam would be positioned in one diagram or other. Any possible inter-swaroopy relations could be ordered by activating this kuuru-mura diagram, whatever was the level of aggregation or disaggregation of the S(s)waroopam. It could either appear momentarily, for example, at the time of deciding on the continuation of one in the position of the muppu or succession itself. Further, one swaroopy would appear simultaneously in different Swaroopams. This age-bound inter-positional and inter-subjective relations within multiple unit-entities leave none outside some or other variants of kuuru-mura diagram. It is in this wider sense that this diagram achieves its repeatable materiality during the period that falls within the purview of our analysis. It is generalisable in another sense also.

This diagram had material repeatability not only among the members included in it and others in the swaroopam but also among those who had a cardinal agency role in the organisation of the Swaroopam. For instance, there were several occasions when muppus were challenged by one of the most conspicuous bodies known as ettarayogam. This Yogam consisted of Brahmins, who had control over the matters of the main shrines, arable land, and several people and also over the main economic exchanges. It invoked the diagram to debilitate the muppu on the basis that the diagram had generalised acceptance. Those counter moves had different basis such as the argument that succession to the muppu has to be deferred due to his unconventional relations with the Padmanabha Swamy temple or that he had a lesser position in the kuuru-mura etc. Such occasions of conflicts took place at times and it showed the relative power position of the muppu in some of the important matters of the Swaroopam organisation. More importantly, for us here, they suggest that even those elite groups who were not swaroopikal had also shared the truth of the diagram and thus deployed it in the relations of power. It can be seen that the diagram was generalised and normalised to the extent that it was deployed in relations of negotiations, self-disciplining and contestations.

The generalisability of the diagram should not be taken to imply that some single continuous diagram could be activated over the whole social body of the Swaroopam, with the muppu at the pinnacle of the linear hierarchy. In fact, as the diagram individualizes and posits each of them with well-defined rights and obligations, there would be a non-generalisability of any one position over others in the order. There would be fields where an individual in a position could not exercise his authority even over its next junior position (ilamkuuru), it be a position immediately lower to it or far distanced from it in the order. Generalisability does not mean exhaustiveness with respect to the territorial spread of the Swaroopam. Nor was the individual unit with its manifold relations completely brought under any particular hierarchy. There is no one diagram encompassing the whole swaroopam or Swaroopam, although this diagram may be working everywhere but not always. Yet, there is a generalised acceptance of diagrammatic ordering.

Another question regarding the functioning of the diagram is the following: Is there any hierarchy between two orders based on gender? Once again, the ultimate determinant is the age factor, and hence the position of muppu. Once age becomes the determining factor, in the final instance, the male siblings are grouped together irrespective of the age of their mothers. If there is a mother muppu (or elder sister-muppu), then she is commonly related to all the siblings as the mother. The internal ordering of the mothers/sisters is thus independent of the order of their male or female siblings. The vertical serialisation and the ordered relation of muppu mura does not influence the female order. The specific physical parentage of the muppu both in terms of maternity and paternity is thus nullified in the diagram, but his position is linked to the other muppu namely the muppu of a matrilocal family at Attingal. The precisioning of the birth time and serialisation of age does not undermine kinship. In the diagram of inter-positional relations and the field of politics, what is more visible is the precisioning of time of birth. Usually the son of the eldest women in the kuuru-mura becomes first in the kuuru-mura of the male members. In this sense, kinship also finds a place in the diagram.

Had a hierarchised schema of positions been created in correspondence with the diagram, then the system would have become determinate, leaving no room for arbitrary individual manoeuvres. The diagram interconnects and relativises different swaroopikal, and different positions of distinction in the Swaroopam. This enables a justified distribution of them into relative positions of hierarchy including muppu without any exogenous factors to influence it. One is required to be only the first in the diagrammatic order to be the muppu of a Swaroopam.

If there is only one diagram of a swaroopam which is applicable to more than one Swaroopam then a complication is introduced. Over time, there can be changes in the specific swaroopam from which muppus are derived, but that aspect is not considered at present. Here the question is, if the source of the members included in the diagram remains the same and if there is only one order applicable to more than one Swaroopam, what would be the principle of designating members between, say, two Swaroopams? Some principle or criteria external to the diagram would be required for placing two hierarchised members on two different muppu positions of these Swaroopams or else, the Swaroopams should also be hierarchised. At least the existing works do not raise this issue.[45] This issue takes us to another dimension of muppu vaazcha.

Are there any documents which would enable us to decide whether any one muppu or any other person occupying a distinguished position exercised general control over the entire aspect of the Swaroopam? The answer to this question takes us to a different trajectory. A partial answer is that since there are other bodies such as Sabha and ettarayogam, muppu alone cannot extend his power over entire aspects of a Swaroopam. Other than poetical eulogies there is little that attributes pre-eminence to any position superior to the muppu. The title of 'Kulashekhara Perumal' is at times said to indicate such a position, which had general authority over several Swaroopams and by implications over other muppu positions.[46] But it can be argued that it was the title assumed by the *ilaya-Threppapppur-muppu* (immediate junior muppu), at least during the period under consideration.[47] The hierarchy of age had implications for inter-muppu relations about which I will be discussing in the next chapter. Perhaps, the superiority of age of one muppu over others did not give rise to formation of any other super-position, which warranted delimitation of muppus younger than the eldest muppu. It is probable that the relations of a muppu with his respective Swaroopam may be independent of his relative age among other muppu positions. Of course, the younger will have to give customary respect to the elder, but between them as two muppus there is no such binding. There seems to be a distinction between inter-personal relations and inter-positional relations.

The distinctiveness of inter-muppu relations in a Swaroopam organisation could also be examined in another way. There is hardly any historical evidence to suspect that a muppu by virtue of simply being the eldest imposed himself over another muppu who is his next junior. Additionally, there is an instance in which one of the senior-most muppu had to be persuaded to assume the position of Threppappur muppu, a position which was generally occupied by the senior-most among the contemporary counterparts in other Swaroopams.[48] Therefore, the senior-most among the contemporary muppus cannot be portrayed as the head of the hierarchical pyramid of muppus in the context of the co-existence of different Swaroopams. The right of one to become the senior-most muppu or any other position within a Swaroopam and their inter-relations are grounded on age.

Another Order Out of an Order

It was mentioned that there could be shifts in the diagram with probable consequences in the power relations. One of the main ways in which a diagram gets shifted is through adoption about which a chapter long discussion is included in this book; for the present purpose, only the link between adoption and the shift is to be highlighted. When a new adoptee is elder to someone who is the seniormost in the existing diagram, his position gets lowered in the ranking, and then there will a shift in the ordering. Obviously, this has a direct implication to the power relations among them. As age is the consideration in positioning the new adoptee, his entry orders the diagram by repositioning the already included in relation to the new entrant. A new anchorage of reference appears.

The shifting of the diagram according to will is not possible; but such adoption reconstitutes the inter-subjectivity[49] and reduces the determinateness of the diagram. It is at this the moment that agency role becomes important. During the course of time under consideration here, several such strategic adoptions of male members took place and effected destabilisation of the organisation of S(s)waroopams[50]. The point is that human agency could shift the order in the diagram but only by identifying itself with the basic grammar of the diagram. Such shifts were always intentional or could be contextual. But once the kingdom of Thiruvithamkur came into being by the middle of the eighteenth century, the way the diagram was drawn and the way it circulated became comparably different. That is, shifts became impossible; this issue can be taken up now for it will also bring out the subtle nuances of the diagram better.

This strategic adoption became a recurrent feature in successions and it sparked off several violent exercises of power[51] both in the Swaroopams and during the formation of the kingdom of Thiruvithamkur. After the co-existence of different Swaroopams ceased to exist and they were clubbed as the Thiruvithamkur kingdom, the diagram got redrawn in such a way that it pre-empted any possibility of shifting the diagram through adoption. The new procedure of adoption permitted only unmarried girl children from specific families to become an adoptee, that even, only to the Threppappur/Attingal family. They were immediately included in the mura and their male offspring were distributed in the diagram, and the eldest male was to be the eligible successor or the first prince. There is redrawing, in the sense that it is not debunking the diagram, but a re-diagramatisation of the order of succession and the positions includable in it.

This has several implications; one that the diagram was all pervasive and had several influences on the positional and inter-subjective aspects that touch even remotest aspects of life; but with the redrawing it got reduced to a thumb rule to guide succession to the throne of Thiruvithamkur alone. Another aspect is that there was shrinkage in the diagram.

The diagram included several elders and at least more than one Swaroopam at any given point in time. This was so at the time of this redrawing. But once the re-drawing was effected, the diagram included only those who would become future muppus/kings. Because other muppu positions were eradicated, only the position of king got perpetuated. As part of the centralisation and elimination of the intermediaries (especially ettara yogam) between the king and the people, several members who had been in the diagram and occupied the positions of distinction that their kuuru-mura permitted were eliminated or got reduced considerably. That is, with the redefinition of the content of the diagram, the total number of members and the positions in it got reduced to one. This implied that those positions became open to swaroopikal who could display better efficiency; 'efficiency' as a foundation of judgment was getting formed. It should be recalled here that efficiency was kept out in distributing members in the diagram.

Another aspect is that the king had much more space to play. Here the king could decide according to his discretion, unlike the former diagrammatic successions. There are differences between the agency roles with respect to succession and placement of people onto distinguished positions in the situation of the co-existence of Swaroopams. One can perceive the swelling of the agency role in this case of kingdom. The diagram of succession to the muppu was made out of bounds.

So far the discussion had, by and large, focused on the interior of the S(s)waroopam. Now the discussion should turn towards the forces and fields where several Swaroopams and muppus got interrelated. In the next chapter, the attempt will be to delineate how actually muppu positions get filled, when several Swaroopams are taken together. It also deals with how at times the force of the precisioned time involved in the diagram is altered to meet any contingencies. This opens up a field of cultural and political interaction, and a field of politics that is immanent in the relations among the Swaroopams. This would shed light not so much on whether there were separate diagrams for different Swaroopams or whether there was a single kinship network which formed the content of the diagram etc, but on other untraced patterns such as multiple muppu vaazhcha.

Notes

1. It is often stated that *Swaroopams* emerged from '*naadu*'.
2. At times the S*waroopams* that I will be discussing are combined as 'Venad *Swaroopam*' (Ganesh, K.N., 2016: viii) The *Swaroopams* that

emerged from *naadu* form of authority relations during ninth to eleventh centuries. (Ganesh K.N., 2016:97).

3. Ganesh, K.N., (2016: 240).
4. For details see, Raghava Varier, (2014, 2016): p. 127.
5. For example see Parameshwa Iyer, (1961) the M.Doc. (Mathilakam Documents or Mathilakam *Grandhyavari*). I, in T.K. Velu Pillai, Vol. II, (1940).
6. Perhaps the last document that bears these terms would be the one made in the year 1378. For details see, M.Doc:24, Parameshwara Iyer. S. (1961).
7. Chiravay *Swaroopam* appears in one of the documents referring to the year 1217. See, Shivashankaran Nair, K, (1993:57). Threppappur *Swaroopam* also got documented by the same time, see the *Kantiyur shasanam* reprinted in Shivashankaran Nair K, (1993: 61).
8. Deshinganad *Swaroopam* and its *muppu* appear from the year 1335 onwards in the documents. From 1345 onwards Kunnummel gets mentioned, Shivashankaran Nair, K, (1983:7879).
9. Ganesh, K.N. (2016:114).
10. "… an effort was made to provide a preliminary account of the transition from *natu* to *swaroopam* in the context of the history of Venad from tenth to thirteenth centuries CE." Ganesh, K.N., 2016:114; (*emphasis mine*).
11. Raghava Varier, (2016:127).
12. Raghava Varier, (2016:127).
13. At times K.N. Ganesh also conceives *Swaroopams* as family units. For instance he states that "History of Medieval Kerala has been shaped by the growth of a number of small kingdoms controlled by ruling households called *swarupams*." Ganesh, K.N., (2016:97), *emphasis mine*).
14. I am referring to these two authors not because the *swaroopam* was never mentioned before; but because they are relatively recent and sufficiently persuasive.
15. For details about Perumals of Kerala, M.G.S. Narayanan (1996, 2013),
16. Ganesh, K.N, (2016:74).
17. I use the term 'genealogy' in the Nietzschean-Foucaldian sense. For details see, Foucault M. (1977:139-165).
18. I shall explain about *Yogam* later. It was a body of landed aristocracy which had several rights on the matters of the Padmanabha Swamy temple and the organisation of the *Swaroopam*.
19. It is noteworthy to mention that "(T)he interrelations among different power centers such as the *swarupams*, Brahmans temple, village

communities and trade networks constituted the social formation of the post-perumal period." K. N. Ganesh, (2016: 84).

20. When I use the term 'formalised', it does not suggest any stationary state. It has no binding to any static model either.
21. For details, see Gundert H, (1872:1072-73); Pillai. Sreekanteswram. G. P. (1923, 2011: 1748) *Sabdatharavali* (Malayalam Dictionary).
22. I am aware that *muppu* of different *Swaroopams* are said to belong to Kilperur, but there is references such as Chiravay *Illam* and different *thayvalies*.
23. The documents that are at stake give the exclusive term *vaánaruli*, whenever they refer to the S*waroopam-muppu*.
24. This is the recurring expression in the published documents.
25. In this study this shift is not taken up for any discussion.
26. Even when I talk about the "period of Swaroopams", I am not saying that there were other forms of organisations such as *naadu* etc. The *Swaroopam* and *naadu* coexisted.
27. The term political refers to the act of generalisation of the interest of a particular individual-unit (in our case, *swaroopam*) as that of a collectivity (*Swaroopam*).
28. I borrow this phrase from Radcliffe-Brown, A.R. (1979).
29. Here 'diagram' implies the following schemata. Assume that there are four female members in Attingal palace who are named as a1, a2, a3 and a4. They have their sons. If son of a1 is the eldest among the male sons of the four female members, then the next successor to *muppu* position is he, that is a11. But if son of a4 is the eldest one (a41) among the total number of male members, then a41 will become the next successor not a11. Differently, if son of a3 is the eldest, then the next successor will be a31. That is the seniority of the male members matter in the instance of succession. That is there is a vector of male successors irrespective of the age of the female members. Since there are four *Swaroopams* and possibility of multiple-*muppu vaazcha* (about this I will be elaborating in the next chapter) the vector becomes a matrix. This matrix, I call as 'diagram'. It is from this notion of diagram derives 'diagrammatic distribution'.
30. Balakrishnan, B.C, (1994), Vol. 2: (358).
31. *Ibid.,* Vol. III: (1118).
32. Gundert, H, (1872:839).
33. Rajaraja Varma Raja, M, (1941:38) and Ganesh, K.N., (1990:17) etc.
34. This general belief that matrilineal system of succession was followed is evidenced in Ganesh, K.N, (1990: 21) Surprisingly enough, in the

same text the contrary belief that there is indecisiveness about it is also offered, for details, see, Ganesh, K.N, (1990:17). This reveals the intensity of the indecisiveness regarding the question.

35. Raajaraaja Varma Raja, M, (1941:38-40).
36. Raajaraaja Varma Raja, M., (1941:38).
37. Rajaraja Varma Raja, M., (1941).
38. It will be shown that this situation is not merely hypothetical but something for which there is documental evidence.
39. Trautman, T.R., (198:418).
40. This interpretation is based on the decomposition of the kuuru-mura schema that is presented in the previous section.
41. Gundert, H, (1872:286-87).
42. I am not using individual in the modern sense. Here individual is someone separated from other swaroopikal to occupy positions of distinction of various grades.
43. There are documents like those appeared under the title "Some Travancore Dynastic Records" published by Rajaraja Varma Raja, M, (1928-33) especially the Document No.VII, see, Rajaraja Varma Raja, M, (1931) which provides an example for the way positions are assigned to members of swaroopam. In this document each one is specified to specific locality, but the nature of the rights they have over the locality and people are not specified. Another aspect worthy of note in the document is that there is no mention of the basis for specifying each one to respective localities.
44. These categories of analysis have similarity to usage of Foucault, M.'s (1979:163) analysis of power.
45. Nevertheless, for the time being it can be said that at least the kuuru-mura of Threppappur swaroopam was applicable to Chiravay and Deshinganad swaroopams also. This issue is elaborated in the next chapter.
46. For example, some hold the view that "The senior-most among the Venad Swaroopam were made Kulashekhara Perumal by the ceremony performed by the Brahmans", Ganesh, K.N., (1996:104).
47. For a self-evident document exemplifying this point, See Document No. XV, Varma Raja, M., (1928).
48. Document, No. XV, Rajaraja Varma Raja (1928).
49. The term inter-subjectivity refers to the kind of relationship that one maintains with others (including corporeal, non-corporeal, and epi-phenomenal worlds) and with oneself. It also refers to the subjectivity

of an individual in terms of one's relation to oneself that is mediated through the imagined/real gaze of the 'other'.

50. Sivasankaran Nair, K, (1983).
51. Ibrahim Kunju, AP., (1990).

Chapter - 4

The Diagrammatic Distribution of the Distinguished

In this chapter, the central question is about how the swaroopikal included in the kuuru-mura diagram were distributed across different Swaroopams as muppu. The Swaroopams considered are Threppappur, Chiravay, Deshinganad and Kunnummel Ilayetam. Was there any tendency to localise power either with the most distinguished position or with the swaroopikal/individual placed there? These questions are important because there were four Swaroopams and a diagram. These questions will have to be tackled obliquely so that some interesting forms and patterns immanent in the muppu vaazhcha can be brought out. Moreover, the tone of this chapter is primarily empirical in nature and no attention is paid to explain the specific patterns traced. How the relative autonomy, primacy and non-erasure of the co-existence of different Swaroopams through what could be phrased as 'multiple muppu vaazhcha', is the main question that is being addressed. It is also proposed to inquire as to how the Swaroopams co-existed without infringing upon the internal coherence of one another, even when a single person occupied the position of muppu of more than one Swaroopam.

Towards the end of this chapter, the way multiple muppu vaazhcha got functionalised as a part of the strategy to alter the primacy of the co-existence of Swaroopams and to amalgamate them to form a kingdom will be sketched. This is taken up mainly because it was the multiple muppu vaazhcha which enabled the said co-existence of different Swaroopams. The question is how through the legitimised practices of multiple muppu vaazhcha, which the diagram permitted, and the position of muppu and the Swaroopam were erased, and a king and kingdom were posited. Three different Swaroopams namely, Threppappur, Deshinganad and Chiravay, about which we have reliable and continuous data have been chosen to trace the nature of the successions that have taken place in them. The other Swaroopam, which had been portrayed as the fourth constituent part of medieval Travancore by historians, namely Kunnummel Ilayetam[1] has not left adequate information to pursue the questions posed here. The required information has been compiled from different sources which are mentioned whenever found essential. The lack of clarity in them or the inference made out of them would not affect the propositions and general arguments that follow. This is so especially because tracing out the chronological order of successions is not our objective.

I have shown in the previous chapter that the distribution of individuals on the basis of age essentially rank or prioritize them in the diagram and mutually relate them in terms of 'activities' that each position entails. The diagram not only defines the individual positions but also objectifies and subjectifies the swaroopikal. In the previous chapter, we found one generalisable aspect which is the precisioned distribution of swaroopikal in terms of age. Generally, diagrammatic distribution appears determinate but it will be shown that it is not always so. Distributional problems are integral if there are two or more identical positions occurring in different Swaroopams and there is only one in the diagram from where individuals would be chosen to fill those positions. But then, it is known that Swaroopams were also serialised and there were correspondences between them and the order in the diagram which is primarily hierarchising. The hierarchy among these three Swaroopams might have changed over time.[2] For instance, at times Chiravay was at the top end and Threppappur appeared next to it. The reverse of it has also happened. Such changes are sensitive to time and context. The context includes the specific nature of the issues at stake. For instance, in the matters of the Padmanabha Swamy temple, Threppappur has had a relatively higher role. How such a serialised hierarchy of Swaroopams were formulated and their co-existence had been perpetuated are questions to be taken up separately.

Since the Swaroopams were also hierarchised, three differently positioned members in the diagram could not become muppus of three different Swaroopams without positions and hierarchy among them. This is so because the principles of mutual differentiation among them preempted any relation of equivalence. Given this, if there was an asymmetry between 'similar' positions (say, the muppu positions of two Swaroopams), then the diagram required the help of no external elements in distributing individuals between positions. The diagram necessitated a serialisation of inter-positional relations wherever it operates, and the hierarchy of the Swaroopams brings about distribution of muppu determinate. One of the underlying theoretical postulates is that there is no functional and correspondence relations between this hierarchy referred here and the hierarchy that was viewed as a changing pyramidical power structure. The hierarchy among the Swaroopams was flexible and fluid at a point in time, at different occasions/events (ritualistic or otherwise) and over time.

Multiplicity in Muppu Vaazhcha

When information on the patterns in the distribution of swaroopikal in the most distinguished positions in the Swaroopams are gleaned and conflated, we find that they had a common heredity and a common diagram. Even when one or more persons were adopted from different lineages, they were placed within the heredity. A characteristic of the muppu vaazhcha is that one is not fixed to any one Swaroopam; one might be the muppu of a particular Swaroopam but at the same time or with a time lag, he may occupy a muppu position in others as well. One may become the muppu of a Swaroopam or more at the same time, but without dissolving or amalgamating the Swaroopams. That is, even when one becomes the muppu of more than one Swaroopam, the intrinsic features of the Swaroopams are maintained. Such a feature can be characterised as multiple muppu vaazhcha. The Table (Table No.1) of successions presents a list of those who occupied the position of muppu in more than one Swaroopam, either sequentially or simultaneously or with overlaps. Such instances are referred to in this analysis as multiple muppu vaazhcha[3]. If a swaroopy occupies only one Swaroopam in his life span, then it is referred as a simple muppu vaazhcha. Therefore, in the muppu vaazhcha one can trace two broad patterns: (1) simple muppu vaazhcha and (2) multiple muppu vaazhcha. Multiplicity arises because one can occupy more than one muppu in different Swaroopams without merging the positions and also by retaining the identity/intrinsic-features of Swaroopams. Multiplicity arises also because there were de-successions about which we have much to write about later.

Here the importance is not given so much to succession (simple muppu vaazcha) to the muppu within a Swaroopam, but to those instances in which a swaroopy occupies the muppu position in more than one Swaroopam, and also to the way in which certain Swaroopams—without losing its primary identity/intrinsic features as a Swaroopam—got combined and not merged through the multiple muppu vaazhcha.

Certain unique patterns in multiple muppu vaazhcha are discernible:

(1) At times a person becomes the muppu of a Swaroopam after renouncing the position there and succeeds to another Swaroopam. Ravi Varma becomes muppu of Chiravay in 1485 and terminates in 1488 and he succeeds to Threppappur in1488 and terminates in 1512.

(2) There were also instances of an individual succeeding and terminating to the positions of more than one Swaroopam at the same time. Unni Kerala Varma succeeds to muppu of Threppappur and Deshinganad in the year 1547 and terminates in the year 1568. Rama Varma succeeds to Threppappur and Deshinganad in 1595 and terminates in 1606. Rama Marthanda Varma succeeds to Threppappur and Deshinganad in 1609 and terminates in 1607.

(3) One muppu occupying muppu of all the three Swaroopams. Sequential succession is discernable here in this instance as well. Udaya Marthanda Varma succeeds was muppu of

Chiravay from 1516 to 1532; he was muppu of Deshinganadu from 1520 and 1535 and he becomes muppu of Threppappur in1527 and terminates in1535. Likewise, another Udaya Marthanda Varma was muppu of Chiravay from 1544 to 151554 and he becomes muppu of Threppappur and Deshinganad in 1547 and continues till 1568. Another instance is, Ravi Varma becomes muppu of Chiravay in 1677 and terminates in 1685, in 1784 he becomes muppu of Deshinganad and terminates in 1718; same Ravi Varma was muppu of Threppappur between 1685 and 1718. In this case but succussions and terminations are at different time points.

At the general level, it can be observed from this table that for all the three Swaroopams taken together, there were at least thirteen instances where a swaroopy had occupied more than one muppu position during the 225 years covered in it. No continuous data for the previous period could be elicited. To be clearer, it is important to compare the above thirteen instances with the total number of successions that had taken place in each Swaroopam as there were instances of simple muppu vaazhcha as well. The numerical values that are provided are only indicators, and their referential field is what has to be reckoned with. Although only 225 years are covered, it does provide us with a pattern. Such a pattern probably might have occurred before and after the period covered here.

The multiplicity occurs in two ways in terms of the number of Swaroopams that are combined by multiple muppu vaazcha. They are (1) dual muppu vaazhcha (instances of one becoming muppu of two Swaroopams) and (2) triple muppu vaazhcha (here, instead of two it is three Swaroopams).[5] The dual muppu vaazcha suggests a swaroopy occupying muppu of two Swaroopams and triple muppu vaazcha suggests a swaroopy occupying muppu of three Swaroopams. It should be mentioned here that multiplicity need not take place simultaneously. Of the thirteen instances listed, only little less than one-fourth (23.3%) of them were triple muppu vaazcha pattern and the rest were instances of dual muppu vaazcha (76.9%). Out of the total of thirteen successions that took place in Threppappur, eleven of them (85%) involved twin/dual multiplicity and the rest triple multiplicity. These proportions for others are 85% for Deshinganad and 46% for Chiravay (six out of sixteen). Together they show a higher incidence of multiplicity when compared to Chiravay[6]. Chiravay had a simple muppu vaazhcha as well as multiple muppu vaazhcha in roughly equal proportions, whereas Deshinganad and Threppappur had a high incidence of multiple muppu vaazcha. On the whole, contrary to the commonly held notion that simple muppu vaazhcha was the rule and multiplicity an exception, it is evident from the Table that multiplicity was the characteristic of the muppu vaazhcha.

As mentioned earlier, simple muppu vaazhcha means that once an individual succeeds to the muppu in a Swaroopam, from then on he never succeeds to any other such a position elsewhere till his terminal point in time. But then, it had been a rare occurrence when muppu vaazhchas of all the three Swaroopams are considered. Further, the duration of the multiple muppu vaazhcha as a percentage of its total (inclusive of both simple and multiple types) in each of the Swaroopams are the following: 81% (186 years out of the total 230 years) for Threppappur, 91% (207 years out of the total 228 years) for Deshinganad and 47.5% (107 out of total 225 years) for Chiravay. It can thus be inferred that multiplicity was prevalent during a substantial part of the total duration considered here, especially in Deshinganad and Threppappur. Even in the case of Chiravay, it could be said that it prevailed for a significant period of time. Although multiplicity was phenomenal, it still remained undiscerned in its own right in the historical accounts.[7]

Multiplicity Discerned

How did the Swaroopams get combined through the multiple muppu vaazhcha? An observable pattern is that it links Threppappur and Deshinganad most frequently. Nine out of thirteen times, they were combined through it (about 69%), whereas only five out of thirteen times Threppappur and Chiravay, and Chiravay and Deshinganad got combined (39%). Another feature is that a single swaroopy combined Chiravay and Deshinganad twice. One thing that needs to be highlighted is that whenever Chiravay got combined either with Deshinganad or Threppappur (each of the couplings took place five times), three out of five times they got combined in multiplicity of a special kind, where the same person became the muppu of all these three Swaroopams.

As the Table shows, among other things, the instance of a swaroopy becoming the muppu of two Swaroopams was more frequent than one person becoming the muppu of all the three. This leads to the conclusion that multiplicity can be disaggregated. The usage of 'multiple muppu vaazhcha' can be retained to denote the general condition of a swaroopy taking up muppu vaazhcha in two or more Swaroopams. The triple muppu vaazhcha (hereafter, tripling) did not take place successively but with significant numbers of successions in between and with time gaps (Table 1). Numerically, the main feature in terms of the frequency of occurrence of multiplicity is dualising (85%). Tripling had been rare; it had a ramification when it came to the exercise of authority. It should be noted here that there was no tendency to perpetuate such tripling because in certain cases there were de-succession. This implied that one desucceeds before taking up the muppu position in another Swaroopam.

Multiplicity combines either Threppappur and Chiravay, or Threppappur and Deshinganad, or Deshinganad and Chiravay. It should be mentioned here that multiplicity combined the other Swaroopam, namely Kunnummel Ilayetam too, although we do not bring it for analysis due to the unavailability of data. As mentioned earlier, of the total multiplicities, there were ten instances of dualising. Now the question is, does one become the muppu of more than one Swaroopam simultaneously or at different points in time? This opens up the question of the different ways multiplicity takes place.

Both tripling and dualising needs to be further disaggregated in terms of the nature of successions. The disaggregation has to first take into account the specific time of each succession to the muppu positions in different Swaroopams. For this is the variable factor that influences the nature of multiplicity. One will have to analyze the time span of the muppu vaazhcha of each swaroopy in each column of the Table. What is to be taken into account is the time of succession, 'discontinuation' and 'desuccession' (act of relinquishing muppu vaazhcha) of each of the names entered in the Table across

Swaroopams. This gives rise to patterns that can be termed as a "sequential succession" when it involves multiplicity. At the outset itself, it should be stated that this 'discontinuation' and 'desuccession' are not to be regarded as acts of secession, as no separation of a 'part' from the 'whole' is involved, nor any withdrawal from the alliance. One has to emphatically specify that these three specifically or the four Swaroopams together did not constitute a whole. The patterns of succession and de-succession involved in the multiplicity mirror what the diagram enabled and disabled.

Sequential and Simultaneous Successions: Overlapping and Desuccession

Sequential succession in dualising and tripling can be discussed separately. In the dual muppu vaazhcha there are four discernible patterns of sequential succession; they are overlapping, desuccession, simultaneity and discontinuation. Overlapping would occur when one succeeded to a second muppu position after remaining as a single muppu for some time. Please note that the single muppu vaazhcha is different from simple muppu vaazhcha as already mentioned.[8] It can also occur during dual situations in which one has simultaneously succeeds to the muppu of two Swaroopams and lets some time to elapse before desucceeding from one of them. Desuccession is the termination of a muppu position by one while he is a dual muppu. Thus, there is the possibility of a single muppu turning into a dual muppu or a dual muppu turning into a single muppu. Overlapping takes place only when the muppu vaazhcha of two Swaroopams get combined or intersect with a 'pre' or 'post' single muppu vaazhcha. Of the ten dualizing 60% were with overlapping. Among these six, three i.e. 50% took place between Deshinganad and Threppappur; about 33% (two out of six) of the total overlapping took place between Chiravay and Deshinganad. There is only one instance (17%) of dualising with overlapping between the Chiravay and Threppappur Swaroopams.

Simultaneous multiplicity (to be distinguished from simultaneous succession) would mean that the initial and terminal years of one's dualising would be the same. That is, it is a situation where the time of succession and the termination of one's dual condition in both the Swaroopams are identical (here after referred to as 'simultaneity'). Out of the ten instances of dualising, three were simultaneous types. Among the 30% of the simultaneous types, all the three instances took place combining Deshinganad and Threppappur. Simultaneity was a pattern exclusive to these two. In the other two possible combinations, simultaneity could not be found. This is suggestive to the background of the war fought between Deshinganad on the one side and the Threppappur - Chiravay combine on the other during the formation of the kingdom of Travancore in the second quarter of the eighteenth century.

Discontinuance occurs when one terminates[9] the singlemuppu vaazhcha of a Swaroopam before succeeding to the singlemuppu vaazhcha (singularity) in another Swaroopam. That is, although one becomes the muppu of two Swaroopams there is no overlapping (S.No. 2 in the Table). In this case, first there is a succession to the Chiravay and then a termination of this position before succeeding to Threppappur.

The overlapping nature of the dualising warrants further disaggregation and the nature of the 'pre' and 'post' periods of overlap needs to be detailed. Within the pattern of overlapping, two possible types of sequentiality can be schematised: (1) from singularity there is a movement to dualising, and (2) from a deualised condition, there is a movement to singularity. To detail, in all the six cases of overlapping, type (1) could be identified; in this case once overlapping begins then it is continuous till the end. There was one instance of a sequential movement of type (2). If we introduce the nature of the sequentiality also into the above schema, then another pattern emerges. The number of sequential movements could be one or two. Of the six overlaps, all except one instance had only one sequential movement. In one case (S.No. 3) there are two sequences, that is, first there is a movement from single to dualising, followed by a movement back to it. In this instance the features of types 1 and 2 are combined. That is, the period of overlap during dualising is preceded and succeeded by singularity. The overlapping period in this case combined Deshinganad and Threppappur.

It has been noted that there were three instances of tripling. There was a time gap of 33 years between the occurrence of first and second tripling, while the third one took place after 90 years. Nothing can be stated about the regularity of such occurrences. In terms of the nature of sequentiality involved, each of the three instances show a certain distinctiveness. What is common is only that there is desuccession or discontinuance at some point of time (with or without overlapping) and sequential movement ends with dualising. The first instance of tripling (S.N. 4) shows a sequential movement from the single muppu of Chiravay becoming a dual muppu by succeeding to Deshinganad in 1520. From then onwards, there was an overlap of 12 years combining Chiravay and Deshinganad. After seven years, the second sequential movement from a dual situation to tripling occurred in 1527 without either desuccession or discontinuance. Therefore, from this time onwards till the desuccession of the muppu from Chiravay in 1532 - that is for five years - there was an overlap involving all the three Swaroopams.

Multiplicity thus presents a spectrum of possibilities. At one end, a Swaroopam may remain independent of the other Swaroopams with its own uniqueness, and at the other end all of them may relate to each another with a common muppu. During the entire period under consideration, it was only during the five years between 1527 and 1532 that tripling took place with simultaneity. In the other two cases of tripling, it combined at most two Swaroopams with simultaneity. Throughout the history of muppu vaazhcha and Swaroopam, this five-year period, however short the duration may be, remains unique.

Moving on to the other two cases of tripling (S.Nos. 7 & 13), desuccession from the dual situation took place before succeeding to the third one. In both cases de-succession took place in Chiravay. When overlapping is considered, tripling combines at most two Swaroopams simultaneously except during the five years mentioned above. Therefore, though these instances could be termed as tripling, it is to be noted that overlapping involving all the three Swaroopams is a unique event. That is, a significant portion of the tripling consists of simultaneous dualising. But then, this dual situation needs to be distinguished from the simple form of dualising that has been discussed earlier. Once one desucceeds, (in this particular case twice from Chiravay) then under his auspices an Ilamkuuru from the diagram succeeds in the Swaroopam.[10] At this level, we can again see the operation of the age-factor. But one should keep in mind that the age factor works only in the relations between these two muppus[11] as elder and younger. However, it need not influence their relations with the affairs of the respective Swaroopams. The muppu who de-succeeds before tripling, will have a relation with his successor muppu as the "earlier muppu".

The desuccession observed in the context of tripling is not to be taken as a prerequisite. Given our present state of knowledge, we can only state that such events could also happen and nothing more. The only another instance where all the three Swaroopams were combined was during the formation of the kingdom or the 'centralisation' that marked a departure from the co-existence of different Swaroopams and the muppu vaazhcha. It is important to differentiate this from the tripling or multiplicity involving desuccession.

In the first place, for the first time all the four Swaroopams referred to above and many more have not merely got connected but amalgamated, and not through multiplicity but through kingship. Further, when all three Swaroopams got merged through the kingship of Marthanda Varma, it did not involve any de-succession either before or after the event. Moreover, in the case of tripling before the mid-eighteenth century, the connection ceased with the demise of the individual who occupied the positions. That is, once the individual muppu passed away, the multiplicity also ended. Hence, such instances never undermined the boundary between the Swaroopams nor was there any deprivileging of the muppu positions. The multiplicity was bounded on the individual life and in turn on its transitory nature. It was not necessary that a successor had to inherit the multiple muppu vaazhcha of his predecessor, and in that way multiplicity had no rule of temporal continuity. The combined existence of all the three Swaroopams in tripling was never given any permanence as it was purely contingent upon the life of the mortal individual muppu. Its impermanence is further exemplified by the instances of de-succession. These are the main differences between the tripling of Swaroopams which took place prior to the mid-eighteenth century, and the successions that took place since the kingship, beginning with the so called Marthanda Varma epoch by the first quarter of the eighteenth century.

Yet another aspect of tripling needs to be highlighted. In the second instance (S.No.7), the sequential succession is marked by an interval period between the termination of the first single muppu vaazhcha of Chiravay and the subsequent simultaneous succession leading to dualising in Threppappur and Deshinganad. This discontinuance is peculiar because once the discontinuity occurred, there was a rather long interval lasting for 14 years before the next succession. The discontinuance that was present in this dualising is different from this one for there was no interval involved in it. Udaya Marthanda Varma (S.No.7) after discontinuing the muppu of Chiravay moved to Kalakkad[12], the region that was under the Chiravay Swaroopam, and took the charge of it, till tripled eventually succeeding to Threppappur and Deshinganad. As he abstained from taking up any of the three muppu positions during the period when he was at Kalakkad, there were other muppus for the three Swaroopams. Only after a lapse of fourteen years did Udaya Marthanda Varma assume the muppu position (in the year 1568). Discontinuance, therefore, can be of two types: one is discontinuance with immediate succession, and the other discontinuance after lapse of time before next succession. The presence of the interval has significant implications on the diagram, especially when it comes to the exercise of authority. In the case of the movement from a single muppu to either dualising or tripling without an interval, there was no point of time at which one was without any of the muppu positions. The interval is to be contrasted with other instances of discontinuity and desuccession, because here one relinquished the position without entering into another position of equal status, if not higher. Such an interval has a bearing on both the concept of authority employable to describe and analyze the muppu position, as well as on the diagram.

As the muppu abstained from assuming any of the muppu positions, a shift occurred in the diagram, for in his absence, the muppu position was occupied by others belonging to the diagram. For instance, Udaya Marthanda Varma (S.No.7) terminated his Chiravay muppu vaazhcha and remained without assuming any position, yet continued to be the seniormost in the diagram.

Other than demise, there are various reasons that enter into the distribution of the individuals over positions. Discontinuance or desuccession that were noted in all forms of multiplicity are types in which one could terminate the position in a Swaroopam and immediately succeed to another one or two without altering the hierarchical sequence. Such successions took place only at the instance of a 'change' in the diagram. While when one discontinues a muppu position without succeeding to another, and after an interval again assumes muppu position(s), there would be corresponding 'shifts' in the relative positions of muppus. The shift could therefore occur twice. These shifts occurred because there was no change in the distribution in the diagram corresponding to the shifts in the redistribution of swaroopikal across positions. No principle internal to the diagram is at work in this kind of discontinuance and resuccession. The critical determinant, namely the age-factor, is not at work in such realignment of the members. The diagrammatic order can be said to be sensitive to historical specificity and the alterations that the contingent forces warrant. Nevertheless, it should be emphasised that whatever may be the factors or principles that effectively work to realign the order during such a situation, they are neither 'external' nor 'exceptional' to the organisation of the Swaroopam. After the long interval when a dualising took place in Threppappur and Deshinganad simultaneously, no legitimacy problems arose. The historical conditions under which this peculiar discontinuance and resuccession took place are important, but an elaboration of them is outside the scope of the present analysis.

In the third instance of tripling (S.No.13), there was no discontinuance with interval as in the above instance, nor any overlap involving the three Swaroopams as in the first instance. Concomitant with the succession to the third one in 1685, the first position was relinquished and the dualised vaazhcha was perpetuated. Therefore, in the previous and this instance of tripling, there was either a single or dual muppu vaazhcha at a given point in time. Once again, we see a nonamalgamation feature in tripling.

Now it can be hypothesized that the fact of being the eldest among the muppus of different Swaroopams is no guarantee for superior authority or permanence in one's position. A simple muppu of a Swaroopam, although the senior-most among others, does not exercise authority over other muppus. I shall illustrate this; while Unnikerala Varma was in Deshinganad (S.No.10), he was the eldest among the contemporary muppus. However, he had hardly any influence in Threppappur or Chiravay. At the same time, his younger brother Ravi Varma (S.No.11) was quite influential as the Chiravay muppu. It should also be said that though he had influence in Threppappur, he was not its muppu.[13] It is one thing to be a simple muppu in the presence of other simple-muppus; it is another thing to be a simple muppu in the presence of a dual-muppu. These differences would get reflected in the inter Swaroopam and intermuppu relations. One hypothesis that can be forwarded now is that there is considerable difference in the effects of muppu vaazhcha under the situations of multiplicity.

Questions like 'Which muppu has preponderance over the others?' and "Which Swaroopam can wield general authority over the others?" are untenable because the relative authority of a muppu is dependent upon the nature of his muppu vaazhcha and also that of others. If the hierarchy among the muppus or Swaroopams is to be described and analyzed, then the types of muppu vaazhchas that coexist at a particular point in time need to be focused on. This is especially so because particular constellations of them are far from stable. The analysis therefore should concentrate on the diverse complexities in the specific constellations and the nature of sequentiality and overlap. Rather than trying to search for an authority that is bestowed with a fixed position or with permanence, the constellations due to multiplicity need to be considered as the term of reference for discussing the exercise of authority or power structure. These shifting constellations thus preempt and undermine, to a great extent, the tendencies towards localisation of power either in a particular Swaroopam or in any muppu position.

To recapitulate, the specific types and nature of the muppu vaazhchas that coexisted at different points in time and the Swaroopams connected through multiplicity were different. These changing constellations show that the types of muppu vaazhcha that co-exist at a certain point of time change due to the demise of the individuals occupying the positions or because of discontinuance, or de-succession or re-succession. The exercisable authority cannot be assumed as localised or embodied in one or the other muppu or in any Swaroopam. The exercisable authority of any muppu was related more to particular types of the muppu vaazhcha that one assumed and the relation to others in other Swaroopams. Therefore, any search for a single position or set of positions wielding authority over all the Swaroopams or search for any permanent hierarchical structure of positions and Swaroopams should begin by considering the multiplicity and specificity of the muppu vaazhcha at each point in time. The belief usually found in existing accounts of the so called "medieval Travancore" is that one or the other Swaroopam or muppu wielded general authority or something similar to it. But the fact seems to be that changes in the extent of authority across Swaroopams have to be sought for the spectrum stretching from single to triple muppu vaazhcha. The complication is not merely due to the existence of several types of muppu vaazhchas with corresponding implications on authority, but due to the fluidity and irreducibility of the constellations. These complications persuade a historian to search for an alternative characterisation of authority by tracing the patterns and diagrams of all the variable forms in muppu vaazhcha, without assuming that there is any permanent locale for authority. Changes in the location and the extent and nature of authority when all the three Swaroopams are considered in their mutual relations were closely associated with the changes in the types and nature of multiplicity, de-successions and the nature of sequential succession.

Directions of Sequential Succession

This section begins by briefly probing into the direction of sequential succession of muppus across Swaroopams. The results of this would be conflated with some of the trends observed in the previous section to problematise multiplicity—especially in the contexts of desuccession and discontinuance—and its implications upon the exercise of authority.

There instances of sequential movements of the muppus from one Swaroopam to another, retaining the position of muppus or with desuccession. The sequential movement does not show any fixed origin. Nevertheless, in all the cases of tripling, the Swaroopam of origin had been Chiravay and the final destination Threppappur (S.Nos. 4, 7 and13). The sequential movement of muppu vaazhcha (successiveness) begins with a succession to Chiravay as a singlemuppu and then desuccession (S.Nos. 4, 7) or discontinuance (with an interval, S.No.7) from it before succeeding to an overlapped dualising in Deshinganad and Threppappur. In tripling, no sequential movement could be observed that begins either from Deshinganad or from Threppappur. Chiravay muppu vaazhcha was either desucceeded or discontinued before tripling. Chiravay never figures as the terminal Swaroopam in sequential succession. When there was a time lag between the second and third successions (S.No.4 and 13), the movement had always been from Deshinganad to Threppappur and never from Chiravay to Threppappur. In these instances, the movement had been in three stages: first, a succession to Chiravay, then to Deshinganad, and finally to Threppappur. This three-stage successiveness can be of two types.

In the first type, at the time of succession to third Swaroopam, that is Threppappur, there takes place a de-succession from Chiravay (S. No. 13). In the second type, desuccession occurs only after a period of overlap combining all the three Swaroopams (S.No.4). Invariably, the terminal Swaroopam in all the sequential successions involving tripling had been Threppappur. Threppappur was the terminal point in the sense that once muppu vaazhcha of Threppappur is assumed by any one, no more sequential successions or discontinuance or desuccession appears to have occurred.

Under dualising involving Chiravay and Deshinganad, the sequential movements never originated from Deshinganad. The movement had always been from Chiravay to Deshinganad (S.Nos.1 & 12). Another important pattern observed is that there were three instances of the dualising involving movement from Deshinganad to

Threppappur (S.Nos. 3, 5 & 10). Except S.No. 3, in both the instances of dualising, there had been a time lag since one had become the muppu of Deshinganad before the second succession to Threppappur. In the case of S.No. 3, the pattern is different; after being dualmuppu of Deshinganad and Threppappur for some time, there was a desuccession from Deshinganad and retention of the position in Threppappur. Therefore, one can state that, once one reached Threppappur, then there is no discontinuance or desuccession from it even in the dual muppu vaazhcha as it is in tripling.

Whenever dualising takes place simultaneously in Deshinganad and Threppappur then also neither discontinuation nor desuccession (S.Nos. 6, 8 and 9) from them took place. Out of the two dualising, which combined Threppappur and Chiravay, there was a discontinuation from the latter (S.No. 2). The other succession to Threppappur gave rise to overlapping without any desuccession or discontinuity from Chiravay (S.No.11). In the movements from Chiravay to Threppappur also, once the terminal Swaroopam, namely Threppappur is reached, then there is no instance of discontinuance or desuccession.

One of the general trends noticed with regard to sequential movements is that Threppappur was invariably the terminal Swaroopam in any type of multiplicity, be it dual or triple. The distinctiveness of this Swaroopam among others is apparent from this trend. Another aspect is that Threppappur never figured as a Swaroopam of origin or as a transit point in sequential successions. Therefore, it is also important to examine whether the Swaroopam of origin falls into any pattern. Of the ten, dualisings, Threppappur and Deshinganad got combined seven times. Chiravay and Threppappur came together thrice, and only once do we find Chiravay combining with Deshinganad. When we look at the particular Swaroopams that got combined through dualising, a shift in trend could be observed. Up to the mid-seventeenth century, apart from one instance, the sequential movements to Threppappur always originated from Deshinganad. After that no clear trend could be found for the next 75 years. During this period, the movement took place from Chiravay to

Threppappur, so perhaps this could be treated as the indistinct beginnings of a trend.

It is well known that since then Threppappur and Chiravay became close allies, and Deshinganad got distanced from both of them. What is important at present is to state that in spite of the shifts in the inter-Swaroopam alliances, there was continuity in the co-existence of the Swaroopams and in multiplicity. Although there was a directional change in the origin of the sequential movement, the Swaroopams retained their distinctiveness.

The above complexities in the patterns of succession could perhaps provide some suggestions to the distinctiveness of each of the Swaroopams and the intricate mechanisms that their interrelationships entailed. The distinctiveness of both the Threppappur Swaroopam and its muppu vaazhcha within the referential field of multiplicity and the sequential successions involved in it are clear. However, the distinctiveness of it as the most visible Swaroopam should not be viewed in the light of the afore-mentioned trend in the sequencings alone.

There is still another complication; it was not necessary that only a singlemuppu of a Swaroopam could succeed to the muppu vaazhcha of Threppappur. And a gradual progression from the Chiravay or Deshinganad Swaroopam to Threppappur was not a precondition. It should be recalled that there were three instances wherein Threppappur had simplemuppu vaazhcha. That is, in these cases, the successors were never the muppus of any other Swaroopam; so there is no question of multiplicity and sequential succession. The distinctiveness of Threppappur, in terms of the terminal status and features of nondiscontinuation and nondesuccession, is significant only within the referential field of multiplicity. When there is simplemuppu vaazhcha, there is no question of such centrality or distinctiveness for Threppappur and its muppu. The features born out of the multiplicity should be situated in the possibility that Threppappur could have had simple muppu vaazhchas also. Unlike in multiplicity, there is no concomitant bonding of the Swaroopams in the case of simplesuccession. The uniqueness and centrality of Threppappur as the terminal point of sequential successions, and nontermination of the muppu position appears to be irrelevant in the simplemuppu vaazhcha. The occurrence of it cannot be treated either as an exception or as a superior, ideal situation. The inter-Swaroopam relations should not be described solely on the basis of multiplicity either.

Discontinuity and Authority

The specific nature of multiplicity was influenced by simultaneity, discontinuity, de-succession and overlap. The discontinuance with and without interval between successions and desuccessions (in general, discontinuity) could be analyzed further to bring forth other dimensions and implications that they had on the co-existence of Swaroopams. Whatever be the historical specificity of discontinuity, either demise, conflict or disorder etc, such instances were inextricably linked to the diagram. At least the option for succession were preferred or resorted; and it was the way that muppu vaazhcha took place. Stretching further, it could be mentioned that during those days, these discontinuities had never caused any non-particular problem, rather this was the way co-existence prevailed. Moreover, continuity/ discontinuity, duality, tripling etc, might not have entered into the reasoning of the muppu vaazhcha as something strange or as a complication.

The kind of discontinuity in multiplicity can be recapitulated by schematizing it into five types:

(a) One becomes triplemuppu from singlemuppu after an interval.

(b) Discontinuation of singlemuppu to succeed to another singlemuppu of a different Swaroopam without an interval.

(c) Desuccession from a muppu while being triplemuppu to remain as a dualmuppu.

(d) Desuccession from a singlemuppu to become dualmuppu simultaneously without lapse of time between discontinuation and successions.

(e) Desuccession from a muppu while being dualmuppu to remain as a singlemuppu.

So does discontinuity influence the duration of the muppu vaazhcha of each individual? We know that such duration is inextricably linked to the power of the muppu. This consequence of discontinuity could be gleaned from the average length[14] of the vaazhcha in each Swaroopam. The calculated average lengths are 18.4, 16.5 and 14.1 years respectively for Deshinganad, Threppappur and Chiravay. The frequent discontinuity from Chiravay could have brought down its average when compared to Deshinganad and Threppappur. Discontinuity increases the frequency of successions, which brings down the average period of the vaazhcha of a swaroopy. The same reasoning cannot be applied in the case of Threppappur; another factor has to be taken into consideration to give an account of the numerical figures. This Swaroopam being the terminal point of sequential succession, only at a relatively older age did one succeed to Threppappur. This brings down the possible duration of the vaazhcha. What makes the average of Deshinganad relatively high is simultaneity and a lower percentage of discontinuity. Further, this high average is also due to the absence of the factors that pulled down the averages in the other two Swaroopams.

It can be said that the average length was sensitive to the differences in the nature of multiplicity. This aspect of the average duration is significant as it had a direct bearing on the political desires and a possibility for political maintenance and alterations in the inter-Swaroopam relations. This is especially so because age-factor is integral to the hierarchy of members within the swaroopam. Further, it is also well known that hereditary transfer of positions employs kinship to political purposes; it has been shown that this is true with respect to South India in general.[15] However, the usual hypothesis or explanation that the low "average length of reign" is due to one or other kinship based lineage system, and 'matrilaterality' especially, is questionable.[16] The average figures under consideration have closer correlation with the multiplicity and especially discontinuity.

To move beyond these general propositions, the complexities are to be brought into deep focus. The following situations can be simulated and counter-posed to each other. There can either be discontinuance/de-succession, or there can be simultaneity/

overlapping. There can be an extreme case of overlapping of all the three Swaroopams at a point in time and then a discontinuity. When these situations are compared, problems of explanation come to the surface. As the tripling or overlap of two or more Swaroopams was a legitimate possibility, the question arises as to what condition engenders discontinuity. Alternatively, under what conditions does an overlap or simultaneity occur? For example, there have been instances of discontinuity in sequential succession while at the same time simultaneity was also normal. Now, what made these two extreme instances possible?

Can 'kinship' help to answer these questions? To suggest the subtler implications of this question, an example can be taken up. In S.No.3, it can be seen that Kerala Varma became a muppu in the year 1485 as a singlemuppu and by 1513, took place dualising through him, but after fourteen years, in 1527, he relinquished one of the positions and reverted to singlemuppu vaazhcha of Threppappur till his demise. This is one of the instances in the history of muppu vaazhcha that cannot be explained simply in terms of the diagram. There is hardly any correlation between the natures of multiplicity and kinship or age distribution in this case.

It is quite possible to think that simultaneity and overlapping were necessitated by the insufficiency of members in the diagram. This problem gets resolved, may be through adoption, but discontinuity would occur. It will be shown soon that this could be an adequate answer, because multiplicity happened even when there was sufficient number of successors. What were the historical conditions that influenced simple to multiplemuppu vaazhcha with its different patterns of sequential succession? What could have been the principles of selection employed to place people to simple, single, dual and triplemuppu vaazhchas respectively? These questions are important especially because both the forms (simple and multiple) were possible. If the criteria of selection were external to the diagram, how did it come to be qualified under those conditions? In other words, how did the distribution of members included in the diagram get reordered at the instance of the occurrence of multiplicity? At present, there is hardly any reliable data to answer these questions.

Nevertheless, it is possible to examine whether the principles of selection or discriminant factor for differentiating Swaroopams in terms of 'family' existed or not.

There were three family names that recurred in the documents along with the names of the muppus; and they are Threppappur, Deshinganad and Kilperur. Members having these family names occupied both simple and multiple muppu vaazhcha. Bearers of these family names also resorted to discontinuity. Therefore, family-wise differentiation is not a discriminant factor.

Another possible trajectory of inquiry is along the lines of differentiation between the adopted successor and the nonadopted successors. Here also the differentiation between simple and multiple muppu vaazhcha could not be made in terms of the above criteria; the adopted also engendered dualising, even with overlap. The status in terms of adoption can neither be a discriminant factor in the explanation for the differentiation between multiple and simple forms, nor can it be the basis for differential options from the possible types of successiveness and multiplicity. What can be asserted is only that it was not because of the shortage of individual members in the diagram that multiplicity took place or was resorted to. Even when there were Ilamkuuru (junior) members, the multiplicity occurred[17]. Further, even if there was a shortage of members, it is well known that this could have been solved by adoption (the next chapter is exclusively devoted to the patterns of adoption). To answer the question of when discontinuity was opted for as against overlapping and simultaneity in a clearer manner, perhaps the unearthing of new source materials would be a prerequisite.

Discontinuity and Play of Power

Although a causal explanation need not (or should not) be given to the phenomenon of discontinuity, it could not be meaningfully viewed against the power relations immanent in subordination/ unification, and in invasion/containment. These models are referred to demonstrate the play of power in the muppu vaazhcha from them. Further, these specific models are chosen because they are fairly familiar and recur frequently in historiography.[18]

For the sake of brevity, let us phrase the propositions using notations. If there are three Swaroopams named S1, S2, S3 and respective muppus for each of them, namely M1, M2 and M3, then in the instance of any overlapping between S1 and S2, M1 can act in S2 as its muppu only after succeeding[19] to the position of M2. As the muppu of 'Threppappur' or as the eldest among the muppus, one cannot exercise authority of the muppu over others unless he assumes the muppu vaazhcha of them also, otherwise the legitimacy of the muppu becomes questionable[20]. When M1 sequentially succeeds to S2 and engenders duality, then he would be recognised and addressed only as M2 in S2 and not as M1, although he would continue to be referred to as M1 in S1. M1 cannot act the role of M2 in S2 unless he succeeds to it and vice versa. For example, when a Deshinganad muppu becomes, say, the Threppappur muppu also (with overlap), then while exercising the acts as the Threppappur muppu, he would be referred to as Threppappur muppu, and while exercising the acts of a muppu in Deshinganad, he would be referred as Deshinganad muppu. If a muppu discontinues one of his muppu positions, from then onwards he would be referred to only as the muppu of that Swaroopam in which he retained his position. When a position is discontinued, from then onwards he would not be referred as the muppu of that Swaroopam. Therefore, even if M1 becomes the muppu of S2, neither the identity of S2 nor the continuity of the M2 position is displaced. There is no erasure or alteration of S1, S2 and M1 or M2. The boundaries between the Swaroopams, as well as between the respective positions, remain the same irrespective of simple or multiple muppu vaazhcha. This implies that these patterns in the rule do not have properties of cumulative power or tendencies of amalgamation.

Overlap and duality do not necessarily mean any notion of subordination or unification of Swaroopams and the erasure of positions. This is one of the peculiarities of the co-existence of Swaroopams as engendered by the multiplicity and de-succession, as against the expansionist and universalising tendencies of kingdoms. In the Swaroopams, a tripling or dueling may be immediately followed by a single muppu vaazhcha. There is no fixity to the nature of multiplicity and discontinuance.

The very descriptive term 'kingdom' exists with reference to a king. The 'kingdom' may be derived from the concept of king, but in the case of a Swaroopam, there is no such derivation because it is a 'selfform'. The king and kingdom have the same etymological root, but this is not the case for a Swaroopam and muppu. Further, the muppu position can be there for the units such as Swaroopam or a family, whether it is a joint family or not. A family cannot have a king. The king of a kingdom K becomes a king of another domain (K2) only when that domain becomes a part of his kingdom (then the difference between K1 and K2 ceases to exist). Otherwise, K2 becomes under the hegemony of K1 and its king metamorphoses into a tributary. There cannot be any discontinuity or desuccessions in this case without the territoriality of the kingdom or the nature of kingship getting altered. Within any sovereignty model, the moment an individual becomes the king of another kingdom or domain, there after the order of several positions and inter-positional relations undergo a drastic transformation. The legitimacy of any existing muppu or the justification for localising the muppu positions in terms of the Swaroopams was never questioned under multiplicity and discontinuance. Further, they never altered the integrity of the Swaroopams nor is there any tendency to perpetuate the coming together of them as a consequence of multiplication. Thus, 'dualkingship' or 'multiplekingship' are conceivable only as exceptions, while in the organisation of Swaroopams such duality and multiplicity are treated as normal. The power relations, however, were incomparably different. Perhaps the kingdoms did not recognize any duality at all. The discontinuity and multiplicity in the unificatory idiom of sovereignty would imply that this was some sort of an 'abnormality', but they were not treated as such in the co-existence of Swaroopams.

In multiplication, what is apparent is not so much the tendencies of subordination and amalgamation or unification, but something different. Even if unificatory tendencies were present, de-succession preempted them. That could be the reason why the nature of multiplicity and sequential succession was never fixed. De-succession was imminent in the muppu vaazhcha; it did not necessarily take place either under exigency or due to the lack of successors alone. It did not amount to cessation. However one should not assume that the tendencies in the organisational form were friction free, and therefore no such eulogy should be foisted on these patterns and types of discontinuity and de-succession which have been singled out.

In the light of the above discussion, it is possible to propose that the muppu vaazhcha in any one Swaroopam did not entail any authority that could be generalised into others as well. Let us now recall a trend in the sequential succession across them – that the terminal position was always in Threppappur. There could be something that is exclusive to it when compared to the other two Swaroopams in this respect, but this distinctiveness cannot be interpreted in terms of either the presence of a "general or overall authority" over others. If the Threppappur muppu (let it be any other one) had been the "center of power or sovereignty" or "king/chieftain having overall authority", as is usually believed, why should over-lapping and simultaneity take place in it followed by a situation of the singling in Threppappur. If this position had overall authority, then why under some conditions should there be duality combining it with another one, and why under some other condition, does the same individual de-succeed from one of the Swaroopams? This implies that there is no sign of localisation of power due to multiplicity; it does not have any signs of anti-localisation either. The diagram is seen as having operated outside both these forms and tendencies. The reference here is to inter-muppu relations. There was a hierarchy among the muppus of different Swaroopams, but this was not in terms of sovereign power but through superiority in terms of age.

It is true that there is a clear-cut difference between the single or simplemuppu of Threppappur and a multiple one combining it with any other one. These two situations are significantly different and reflect the specificity of authority relations that have implications on both inter and intra-Swaroopam relations. It could be hypothesised that the conception of a general authority need not be valid here. What is more significant is the varying varieties from the simple to the triple muppu vaazcha with different implications on exercised authority. The specific nature of the muppu vaazhcha influenced particular authority relations among Swaroopams, be it Threppappur or any others.

Another implication of de-succession is that it is against one of the prevalent notions that the muppu was 'merely symbolic' and that the kind of activity that he had to perform were 'mere rituals'. The de-succession with time lag before subsequent succession shows that the muppu position had significant functional implications on the organisation of the Swaroopam. Otherwise there would be no need for de-succession and resuccession. Multiplicity is definitely important for authority relations and is quite different from the king's relation to the kingdom.

Therefore multiplicity not only constitutes the internal relations of the Swaroopams and the respective muppus but also the inter-Swaroopam relations. Moreover, even if the position was 'symbolic' and the activities performed by this position "merely ritualistic", it can be safely suggested that the organisation of the Swaroopam found more materiality within the symbolic and ritualistic orders. It is perhaps within this symbolic realm that the political rationale was meaningful, effective and significant. Besides, the political truth might have been constituted through the symbolic and ritualistic practices. Here, there is no distinction between the symbolic, ritualistic, materialistic, political etc, as they are all folded together into the age factor (biological factor). Discontinuity was not to be treated as the cessation of one's relation with the position or Swaroopam that one leaves; rather it redefined his relations with the immediate successor to that position.

It is important to ask whether dualising in any way meant superiority over simple or single situations. This question is important especially because the common factor in all the dualising, except in two (S.Nos.1 and 12), one of which had been Threppappur, the terminal Swaroopam in the sequential succession. Muppu vaazhcha of Threppappur along with that of the other Swaroopams was the most distinguished position that any one individual could have within the possible trajectory of multiplicity. At the same time, a simple muppu vaazhcha of it and a dualising that combined it with Chiravay was substantially different. Therefore, once again one is compelled to distance one–self from the fallacy of a "Threppappur muppu possessing the greatest authority".

Further, the dualising that combined Threppappur with any other one did not mean that this gave rise to exercisable roles in the remaining third one also. In what way was a dualising related to a single muppu and vice versa, is another question to be taken up. The third instance (S.No. 3) in the Table gives an example that counters the obvious answer that dualising was superior to the single muppu. Although Kerala Varma was the senior-most member of the entire family by 1520s and actually had great prestige and respectability, he was only a single muppu. This implies that simply because one is a single muppu, he cannot be considered as inferior. Therefore, when one searches for relations (hierarchical or otherwise) among different Swaroopams, the question of how multiplying combines them would be the most crucial one. The specific combinations need not have any fixity over time, because it is sensitive to the specific historical contexts and situations.

Methodologically, the description of relations should be distanced from any format using (implicitly or explicitly) concepts which assume fixity and continuity. The fluidity of relations due to the variety of unique constellations that are possible in the muppu vaazhcha (simple and single, simple and dual, simple and multiple, single and multiple and so on) seems to have withstood any determining principle or structure from within. This fluidity can be hypothesized as having mitigated both the frictions of power in multiplicity and intersubjective relations among the different kinds of muppus.

The multiplicity and de-succession that are roughly sketched above helps one to analyze muppu vaazhcha and successions without reference to one or other forms of localised authority and fixed principles. The principles that directed de-succession, dualing, tripling etc, are not known. In the analysis that has been carried out so far, the diagram or kuuru-mura order is found to be all the more complex and this order forms only the foreground in determining the specific nature of multiplicity which was a persistent feature of the Swaroopam organisation. The diagram however provides a serialised ranking which is fixed and stable because of the age factor. The multiplicity and the varied patterns of sequential succession that complicated it were normal and immanent in the co-existence of Swaroopams.

No localised authority having power over all the four Swaroopams could be identified. Even when different Swaroopams were combined, say, in tripling, it was neither fixed nor overarching. That is, just after tripling, a singling could follow, where by the Swaroopams which were combined returned to their prior state of single/simple muppu vaazhcha. Within the multiplicity, such a generalised and permanent local authority was not an overwhelming presence at all.

It is also quite clear that when multiplicity and de-succession are phenomenal, the established argument or conclusion that the rule of each Swaroopam was delegated to the 'branches' or 'fragments' of the Vanchi dynasty or to the Venad (at times referred to as Kilperur family) royal family/dynasty cannot stand empirical scrutiny. The argument would not be able to withstand any test for internal coherence either. Although two or more Swaroopams are combined (quite frequently) in various types of multiplicity, it does not mean that the unity thus formed is either fixed or continuous. Under multiplicity, there is no alteration/transformation of the identity of the Swaroopam nor is there any destabilisation/erasure of distinctive positions such as muppu.

The specific nature of the muppu vaazhcha has been open to a wide spectrum of possibilities. These in turn may take place with sequential succession involving discontinuity, desuccession, overlap and simultaneity. It is the specific constellation of the muppu vaazhcha in which each muppu is placed in different Swaroopams and this determines the intermuppu relations. There is no linear law or principle that influences the succession of a person to different kinds of multiplicity; therefore there is no determinacy/predictability either. The question as to which individual would be able to assume one or other multiple positions and under what conditions was not reducible to any pregiven criteria. At the same time, this did not result in chaos or anarchy which are presumed to be imminent in such 'indeterminacy'. I use the term 'indeterminacy' because we do not know the criteria that was decisive in determining a particular form of multiplicity.

The Erasure of Multiplicity

During the early 1730s, an army was sent to Deshinganad by Marthanda Varma, the Chiravay muppu, mainly to compel its muppu to abandon the adoption that had been conducted, and to lay claim to a portion of land in it which was supposed to belong to Threppappur[21]. What is critical here is the demand to abandon the adoption that Deshinganad had conducted some time before 1727[22] fearing a dearth of successors in it. Without difficulty[23] it can be said that the strategic reason that persuaded Marthanda Varma to make such a demand was that he intended to become the dual muppu and combine Deshinganad and Chiravay. As a male member was adopted, his claim to become the Deshinganad muppu was preempted. Had the adoption been abandoned, then after the death of the existed Deshinganad muppu, Marthanda Varma could legitimately succeed there as well by employing the legitimate possibility of multiplication.

By demanding the land of Threppappur, Marthanda Varma was also playing the role of Threppappur muppu, which was at that moment lying vacant, although he could formally become the muppu of Threppappur only decades later. In fact, it was also a time of erasure of the distinction between Threppappur and Chiravay as two different Swaroopams[24].

Here, one can see that multiplicity had become instrumental in a project for the erasure of differentiation of Swaroopams and their co-existence. As multiplicity and sequential succession were legitimate and there was dearth of successors in the diagram of Deshinganad at that juncture, the only thing that could be done was to prevent any one from entering the diagram through preempting adoptions into it. That is, when there was lack of members in the diagram, and if one was able to prevent adoption, then multiplicity would be the necessary consequence. As multiple muppu vaazhcha was legitimate and possible, it became an instrument in the hands of Marthanda Varma for undermining the differential coexistence of Swaroopams. He was already the muppu of Chiravay and was attempting to become the muppu of Threppappur, Deshinganad and Kunnummel Ilayetam. The multiple muppu vaazhcha was getting altered in such deployments of multiplicity through erasure during the second quarter of the eighteenth century and by the 1850s, the differential co-existence ceased and the Thiruvithamkur Mahaarajyam got formed.

The possibility of multiplicity (tripling) that combined the three Swaroopams generated friction among the Swaroopams as it challenged the primacy of differential co-existence. When the possibility of multiplicity became instrumental in the strategy for abolishing Swaroopam boundaries, it created a re-alliance between the Deshinganad and Kunnummel Ilayetathu Swaroopams in order to resist the other alliance consisting of Chiravay and Threppappur. Both the actions of Marthanda Varma in the year 1730 and the reactions of the other alliance resulted in war and violence. The Chiravay muppu, Marthanda Varma, was denied the succession to Deshinganad and in Threppappur succession was getting deferred. The ploy of Marthanda Varma became well articulated by the second quarter of the eighteenth century itself, and by the mid-eighteenth century, he held the muppu vaazhcha of all the four Swaroopams and many more regions north of Deshinganad. The nature of the multiple muppu vaazhcha was transformed to the raja bharanam of the kingdom of Thiruvithamkur.

The nature of sequential succession had undergone fundamental changes, and no more was there desuccession or discontinuance or multiplicity etc. Marthanda Varma combined all the four Swaroopams not as the muppu of each of them in isolation as he would have done under multiple muppu vaazhcha. The Swaroopams that came under the Threppappur muppu were declared to be the kingdom of Thiruvithamkur belonging to Lord/god Padmanabha at Padmanabha Swamy temple through a ritual known as *threppadidaanam*. The *threppadidaanam* is a ritualistic bestowing of entire territory of a muppu/king to a god. And the muppu of the Threppappur Swaroopam was the muppu of the Padmanabha Swamy Temple as well (he was known as Sri Pandarakaryam Chaivaarkalaya Threppappur muppu).

The primacy of the Swaroopam differential was undermined by unifying all of them within a regime centralised through Lord (God) Padmanabha. Their independent existence as Swaroopams had become secondary to their existence re-defined in relation to a unified territory of the Padmanabha Swamy temple. The re-defined relation between the Threppappur Swaroopam and the Padmanabha Swamy temple now got projected onto the other Swaroopams also. After the threppadidaanam, a ritual that had tremendous power effects among the clites, the Threppappur muppu could wield all exercisable authority that the muppu had over Threppappur in other Swaroopams also, without formally becoming the muppu of them. That is, the muppu position of Threppappur was prioritised as the most superior one and the muppu got redesignated as Sri Padmanabha daasa. Thus, an immortal 'Sri Padmanabha' and a mortal "Padmanabha daasa" formed a center around which the totality of a kingdom consisting of what had previously been Swaroopams came to be conceived and constructed. From then onwards there was no Threppappur muppu or for that matter the position of muppu itself, as the former had been identified as the king of Thiruvithamkur. There were no Swaroopams or muppu but only a king and kingdom containing/compulsively amalgamating all the Swaroopams.

This centre consisting of the Temple and the king was given fixity by the erasure of the muppu positions. Further, the succession to the Sri Padmanabha Dasa (king) was streamlined and it was decided that only the eldest male children of the Attingal Ranis (Threppappur) would succeed to the throne of Travancore. This has lead to a redefinition of the diagram and one is left with only the single mura of the male children of the Attingal Ranies. The diagram becomes a vector. The diagrammatic order of the female members of Attingal fell into disuse as the Attingal matrilocal family was annexed to the kingdom. There was never any problem of the distribution of members of different kuuru-muras across different Swaroopams. In short, the phenomenon of multiplicity began to have another status in Marthanda Varma's strategy for erasing the differentiation between the Swaroopams. Once again, the multiplicity in which the position of each of the muppu was left unaltered irrespective of the nature of multiplicity and sequential succession transfigured into the "Threppappur muppu" as the "raaja of Travancore".

I am not suggesting that the diagram became totally unfunctional; for instance, while there was the conspicuous presence of the British Resident, the issue of succession became critical with respect to the power equations. The Resident revisited the diagram and made the final verdict on the basis of the documents on previous successions. While Resident wanted a female to succeed, the male members in the diagram opposed it. Since then the function of the diagram has become a part of the past. The Constitution of Thiruvithamkur (Travancore) kingdom through amalgamation of all the four Swaroopams took place by the first quarter of the eighteenth century. The king became at the apex and a pyramidal power relation got constituted. An enquiry into the historical conditions that constituted such power relations is a matter concerned with social history and it is not attempted here. While the diagram is primarily hierarchizing, it follows another cosmology of power relations which is not pyramidal or accumulating due to multiplicity, de-succession etc. They can be thought of, yet it is also left un-attempted here. What is attempted in this chapter is to open up trajectories of enquiry that would have been impossible if one gets besieged by 'over reading' and "interpretational skidding" about which I discussed in detail in the first chapter.

There was no centrifugal force pushing one to the apex of the pyramid, rather the forces seems to have been independent of and non-comparable to such a movement. This in turn, is related to the fact that adoption was also subjected to such contexts. Otherwise, multiplicity due to the non-existence of successors should not have occurred; the adoption that took place while there were enough members in the diagram should also not have occurred. Adoption and its relation to the diagram will be the central theme of the next chapter.

Notes

1. Here after, Kunnummel Ilayetam would be referred only as Kunnummel.
2. Shivashankaran Nair, K. (1993).
3. The specific ways in which subjectivity of the muppu is posited in roles that are proper to the muppu vaazhcha of Swaroopams.
4.

Table: Types of Multiplicity

S. No	*Threppappur*	*Deshinganad*	*Chiravay*
1.	N.A	Adithya Varma	———
		1480-1485	1460-1485
2.	———	N.A	Ravi Varma
	1488-1512		1485-1488
3.	———	Kerala Varma	N.A
	1513-1527	1485-1520	
4.	———	———	Udaya Marthanda Varma
	1527-1535	1520-1535	1516-1532
5.	———	Rama Varma	N.A
	1542-1547	1535-1547	
6.	———	Unni Kerala Varma	N.A
	1547-1568	1547-1568	
7.	———	———	Udaya Marthanda Varma
	1568-1595	1568-1595	1544-1554
8.	———	Rama Varma	N.A
	1595-1606	1595-1606	
9.	———	Rama Marthanda	N.A
	1606-1607	Varma-1606-1607	
10.	———	Unnikerala Varma	N.A
	1620-1650	1607-1650	
11.	———	N.A	Ravi Varma
	1650-1662		1610-1662
12.	N.A	———	Rama Varma
	1668-1671		1662-1671
13.	———	———	Ravi Varma
	1685-1718	1684-1718	1677-1685

Source: Compiled from Shivashankaran Nair, K, (1993).

Not applicable (N. A) Indicates that the individual entered in that row has not been the muppu in the column of Swaroopam. The lines show that the name entered in the row is applicable to the specific Swaroopam head also. For instance, in the case of No. 13, Ravi Varma was the muppu of all the three Swaroopams and the period is given just below.

4. Here onwards, both dual and triple muppu vaazcha are referred to as multiplicity.
5. An important argument to be made here is that if Venad was divided into different Swaroopams and assigned their rule to each kinship

segments of blood relatives (the so called 'branches'), then how can a multiple muppu situation can take place? That is, when a multiple muppu situation is possible then one cannot link the way it is usually done without dispute.

6. Generally this type of succession or muppu vaazhcha is considered as the deviations from the simplemuppu vaazhcha. But what is found out here is that this need not be formatted in the framework of normalx abnormal, or usual x exceptional, or convention or in practice (For a recent example for such an argument, see Ganesh, K.N., (1990:18).
7. For analytical purposes, the single muppu vaazhcha should be differentiated from the simple muppu vaazhcha. Single muppu condition occurs only within the system of multiple muppu vaazhcha, it takes place only when there is a time lag in one muppu to become the dualmuppu. The pre-dual-muppu vaazhcha of a muppu is the single-muppu vaazhcha. The simple-muppu vaazhcha is independent of the system of multiplicity. In terms of the exercised authority of the muppu and the inter-Swaroopam relations, this difference in the system of vaazhcha is important.
8. This discontinuance should be distinguished from the one that is observable in the case of overlapping, which is referred as de-succession.
9. For details see Document No. XII, Rajaraja Varma Raja. (S.1,1928:20). This document refers to the year (1587).
10. How this age factor works in the intricate interrelations among muppus alone and not in the rights and authority that each muppu exercised over his Swaroopam will be shown later.
11. Shivashankaran Nair, K, (1993:95).
12. Document XV, Series I, Rajaraja Varma Raja. (S.1,1928:21).
13. I am aware of the fact that any measure of average would conceal variance in the duration of each one's muppu vaazhcha, which this is the drawback of any such summery measure. Moreover, the absolute value of the figure is not very significant in our study as we use it only for comparative purpose, even if high variance is present, it would be equally applicable to all the Swaroopams.
14. Trautmann, T. R., (1981).
15. For an example of a kinship based explanation for the shorter average length of the reign in 'Travancore', see Trautmann, T.R, (1981:419).
16. There are several instances of this kind, for example, see Document No.XV, Series I, Rajaraja Varma Raja. (S.1, 1928:21).
17. Counterfactually, one may think why I am not taking something like the Greek city states as the model to make a contrast.

18. Here succession includes performance of several ritual ceremonies called padiyettam.
19. For an exemplary event of this kind, see Document. No. XV, Rajaraja Varma, M, (S.1,1928: 21-25).
20. Shivashankaran Nair, K, (1993:223).
21. Shivashankaran Nair, K, (1993:139).
22. The history from the early eighteenth century had been fairly well explored and documented.
23. Rajaraja Varma Raja, Documents I&2 (S.8, 1931: 100-106).

Chapter - 5

Redrawing of the Diagram

The word 'adoption' is quite familiar and requires no elaboration. The Malayalam word *dathetukkal* has been translated to English as adoption[1]. But then, dathetukkal in the context of Swaroopams cannot be translated as adoption. Dathetukkal of a different kind had been quite frequent in these Swaroopams. Dathetukkal from other families with which none of the swaroopams under consideration had a kinship relation had been significant. Once dathetukkal takes place, whether the adoptee is a boy or girl or adult, the diagram expands and sometimes the hierarchy in it gets reordered. Reordering took place especially when men were the adoptees. Such adoptions not only expanded the kuuru-mura diagram but also reordered the diagram, especially when men were adopted. Since the adoption process reordered the diagram, it is pertinent to delve into it.

Dathedukkal into a Swaroopam involved the positioning of the adoptee in the diagram and thus getting drawn into power relations in terms of age. The specific procedure that went into arriving into a consensus on where and who should be adopted is not known. In any case, such adoptions were outside the realm of the biological reproduction taking place within the Kilperur or Attingal family. This implies that a willful alteration in the diagram was possible. That is, the possibility of alterations of the diagram was brought in without challenging the truth of the determining diagram. We will focus on this event of adoption (hereafter called 'event') not only to get to know the way it functioned and how it was employed in strategic moves, but also to bring out the moments of marking the exterior and interior of the Swaroopam interactions. This had effects in the Swaroopams when conceived as interacting units. The manner in which the Swaroopam as an identity defined its interior and exterior, vis-à-vis other Swaroopams as well as within itself through sub-divisions is shown to be an evasive one, particularly when Swaroopams were engaged in the act of dathetukkal.

The evasiveness mentioned above is such that in this act, the unity and coherence of the concept of the Swaroopam, and the continuum between the swaroopams in terms of kinship are found to be perpetually problematic. The patterns of the exterior and the interior of the Swaroopams, as traced from the interactions and co-actions of the Swaroopams in the act of dathetukkal are different from those found in the normalised biological/natural kinship relations in the multiple-muppu vaazhcha.

Although the Malayalam word dathetukkal can be meaningfully translated as adoption, in our context it is not tenable because such a translation becomes tenable only by the middle of the eighteenth century. The reason for this is that it had more ramifications and it involved different power relations. Therefore, at times we will use the term 'conjugate' for the word dathedukkal instead of 'adoption' and show the ways in which it becomes translatable as adoption towards the end of this chapter. However, I will be employing dathetukkal and conjugation interchangeably depending on the context of the discussion.

Dathedukkal need not be Translated as Adoption

Let us begin with some quantitative dimensions of this particular form of conjugation; i.e. the effect of this situation of conjugating. An aspect that made dathetukkal a unique phenomenon in Swaroopams was that a majority of the muppus and ilayathus/ilamkuru (junior to the existing muppu in terms of age) who succeeded as muppus in the Swaroopams were conjugants; this had been so till the first quarter of the eighteenth century. The known continuous evidences on dathetukkal that took place between 1620[2] and 1729 show that of the six Threppappur muppus, four (67%) were conjugants either from Vellarappalli (a family situated in present day Cochin) or Kolathenadu (situated in the present day Kolathenadu in north Kerala).[3] Similarly, of the twelve Chiravay muppus, seven (58%) were conjugant from Vellarappalli, Kolathenadu and Puka thaivazhi (situated somewhere in present day Travancore).[4] Then in the case of Deshinganad, between 1607 and 1730's, all the muppus except one were conjugant.[5] These figures are self-evident as far as the frequency and preeminence of conjugality is concerned; but the dependence on them need not take us beyond that.

In the forthcoming part of this section, the act of conjugation will be analyzed in greater detail to bring out its complexity, by differentiating this act from adoptive practices. Such a differentiation is made because it has been a normal practice to translate dathetukkal as 'adoption', and this translation has led to a metaphorical reduction of the complexities involved in it into some monolithic kinship framework, in which the term adoption has a definite place and significance. In other words, adoption has been conceived in history books as something rare that takes place only when the lack of successors occurs. A few lexical meanings of the word to 'adopt' can be selectively invoked here: "to take up from someone else and use as one's own, as a phrase, practice, or creed, or to take into one's family or as one's child by legal means… the legal act whereby an adult person takes a minor into the relation of a child or the acceptance of a word unchanged in form from a foreign language, or the receiving into a clan or tribe of one from outside, and treating him as one of the same blood" etc.[6]

The following observations can be made on the basis of the lexical definitions of the word adoption. There is a transposition of someone or something, be it a person or a word, from a given unit to another. These units are conceived through the difference between an outside and an inside - foreign/someone-else and ones-own/of the same-blood, etc. Further, their differential relations are well-bounded, especially when transposition takes place. The difference between the one and the other, or the same and the foreign is the necessary precondition for the conjugative act. Therefore, only under such a condition does the need emerge to situate one as a conjugant and the other as a 'conjugater'. They converge in the act of transposition while retaining their separate positional identities as conjugant and conjugater. Such a separation is what makes the conjugant different from the conjugater. But in dathetukkal as used here, once the adoption takes place, be it a child or matured person, he/she becomes a swaroopi.

First, if the precondition is not satisfied as in the case of transpositions that took place between swaroopam and its thaivazhi, then dathetukkal cannot be treated as a conjugative act in any analysis. That means, there is no way in which a swaroopam and its thaivazhi can be separated as two distinct unities having a separate interiority; together, they constitute a whole and its part. In spite of such unity, if the distinguished members of them act as conjugater and conjugant, (it has taken place, and we will take it up in detail elsewhere) then either they should be considered as independent of any unifying relationship, especially kinship. It can also be said that there takes place a repositioning within "one's own" unit and no transposition from one to the other as it occurs in the case of adoption.

Secondly, if different Swaroopams were primarily linked in terms of kinship relations that defined a 'total inside' consisting of the four Swaroopams, then such a conjugation between the Swaroopams would be an anachronism. This is so mainly because conjugation takes place when there is no kinship relation between the conjugater and the conjugant, and the act of adoption establishes the kinship relation between the conjugant and the receiving entity. But if conjugation takes place in spite of the existing kinship linkages, then one can say that the 'one' and 'the other' are not defined in terms of kinship, which will be an anomaly. Alternatively, it can be said that there was no such kinship tie among Swaroopams that can be comprehended as a fixed-total unit as in the existing historical accounts, so that dathu-form of conjugality between the Swaroopams could take place. It can also be said that Swaroopam entities were primarily defined in terms of self-reference rather than in terms of any other criterion such as kinship.

The presence of a 'lack' or the 'absence' of a swaroopy is the necessary condition for the above-mentioned transposition. It should be remembered that this 'lack' becomes perceptible only when there is a clear-cut separation between an inside and an outside or only when a clear exteriority and interiority are conceived. But the historical fact is that there were several instances of conjugational acts that took place even when there was no such 'lack' or 'absence'.[7]

Thirdly, if the conjugant did not have much of a role or function in the space into which he/she had been transposed, but had roles only within the space of origin, as in the case of Swaroopams, then also the appropriateness of the term adoption would become questionable. This is so especially because, in this instance, there is a lack or an absence to be overcome. That is, there was no condition of lack or absence in the swaroopam that demanded adoption; rather the trans-positioning took place not because of them, but because of something else. This complicates the term adoption and compels one to see the complexity of the term dathetukkal which involved all the above mentioned hypothetical situations. The act of dathetukkal does not seem to satisfy the preconditions for adoption, nor is its context and consequence similar to that of adoption.

Although the person who is transposed is the critical factor in the attempt to overcome the perceived 'lack', he/she is conceived of as passive, often a child, therefore the conjugant as a member includes not merely the person who was brought in but also those who participate in the event of conjugating as persons related to that member. The conjugater is active, but once the transposing has taken place, even after a time lag, the conjugant becomes active as he fills the absence or lack in the diagram. But when two Swaroopams come together in conjugating without any passive body, then also the situation is different from that of adoption. There were situations in which elderly persons or bearers of important positions in muppu vaazhcha got exchanged between two Swaroopams as conjugants. In these events, both the conjugant and conjugater were active and there was no transposition of the conjugant without separating him/her from the positions that he or she had been holding. But in this case also the conventional term 'adoption' would be inappropriate; because there is no separation between conjugater and the conjugant. Both are at the same time the conjugater and conjugant.

Once the convergence of one and the other occurs or once the transposition takes place, as in the case of the adoption, then it is followed by a separation of the conjugant from his/her unit of origin and, from then onwards, the conjugant becomes active to the extent that he can be the conjugater of the Swaroopam into which he was received. Once the transposition takes place, the individual is cut off from the unit of origin, 'renamed' and placed in the diagrammatic order of the receiving unit.

Fourthly, if dathetukkal takes place without erasing the respective identity of the conjugater and conjugant, but with an intention and expectation of becoming more integral than they were, then also the event cannot be considered as adoption. For example, when a Swaroopam adopts a person from another one to ease any dispute between them and to realign their mutual relations, a mutual transposition without having any repositioning of conjugant in the diagram of the receiving Swaroopam occurs.

Finally, when someone is transposed to a Swaroopam where there is sufficient number of members in the diagram of successions, then the phenomena of dathetukkal becomes overtly political as it reorders the existing inter-subjective relations among the members. Such an act seems to be a part of a history, but dissimilar from the generally known history of adoption and thus it demands a re-problematisation wherein the translation of the word 'adoption' becomes objectionable.[8] These are the conditions that compel us to study this phenomenon with all its complexity and why the word conjugating or conjugate is employed to refer to dathetukkal as a better means of communication.

Even though dathetukkal can be differentially schematized, for the present purpose it can be broadly distinguished into different types in terms of the unit entities that converge in the act:

(1) The mutual dathetukkal of muppus of two different Swaroopams without placing in the respective diagrams. That implies that after the event of dathetukkal, the muppus return to their previous muppu positions (I will be discussing this type later in this chapter).

(2) Where more than two Swaroopams converge in the roles of either conjugater or conjugant.

(3) A kind of mutual dathetukkal of the muppu of two or more Swaroopams wherein both the Swaroopams assume the roles of conjugater and conjugant (I will be discussing this type later in this chapter).

(4) Within a Swaroopam, dathetukkal took place between the Swaroopam and its thaivazhi, which implies that there is a pattern of intra-Swaroopam mutual-conjugality. Sometimes there will be more than one conjugate, although dathetukkal is to one Swaroopam.

(5) Conjugation from families which were geographically and genetically distinct.

(6) The adoption of boy and girl children from families not having blood relations with the adopter.

(7) Dathetukkal of adults from outside the four Swaroopams under consideration.

It can now be recalled that the difference between the conjugant and conjugater are clearly differentiated and defined. The place of origin of the conjugant and the terminal Swaroopam are clearly specified in the documents. As already mentioned, the place of origin of the adoptee is more or less definite. The above schema brings out the nature of the units that pose themselves as conjugater and conjugant and also the complexity involved in the nature of dathetukkal.

Exterior and Interior in the Case of Dathetukkal

Let us examine the historical details of the different types of conjugality. The focus of the analysis is not the meaning of the term 'conjugality' or the historical conditions that led to its occurrence. The attempt is primarily to view once again the phenomenon itself as a new object of study, to trace the patterns in this practice of dathetukkal, and to situate it in the inter-Swaroopam relations. Generally, when two Swaroopams or a family get related through the conjugater and conjugant, they are necessarily two entities independent of each other in terms of territoriality, family unity or kinship. The conjugant cannot be within the diagram order of the conjugater's Swaroopam prior to the event of conjugating (the event);

if it were so, then the event itself would not have taken place. However, in the Swaroopam organisation, the two of them engage in the event by positing themselves as either conjugater or conjugant. There was an instance of a male and a female member of Threppappur conjugating with Chiravay in 1574-75 and the conjugants were renamed and assigned positions in the diagram of the latter.[9] The conjugants were given koikkals (residences) in Chiravay and they were made Chirava Swaroopathine utayathaaka or persons having rights in Chiravay. That is, even though Threppappur and Chiravay were inter-netted within the kinship unity, in this instance, the kinship-unity was left unrecognised, if not undermined. This suggests that in defining the boundary between the Swaroopams, kinship had only a limited role and it refers to the varying nature of its boundaries in specific instances.

The Politics of Kinship Makes It What It Was Not

The initial differential positioning and its momentary erasure at the event was embedded in relations other than kinship. In other words, they remained united in the kinship ties, but yet relations of difference was maintained which is why dathetukkal took place. Dathetukkal itself was a part of a kinship-based relational activity of a different kind. It was a relation of difference in which the respective exterior and interior of the Swaroopams were taken as well defined. Such conjugation reaffirms the differenced existence of the Swaroopams. Their separateness got reaffirmed at the moment of their convergence in the event of dathetukkal (event), and this reaffirmation not only a precondition for it to take place but also a condition that was to be maintained even after its occurrence in the future as well. Such events were critical in the inter-Swaroopam relations over and above its function in both the receiving ones and the Swaroopam of origin. These two Swaroopams were apparently independent and thus there was the need for such a transposition from one to the other. Irrespective of the possibility of multiplicity that could combine them, such conjugating events seems to be a modality for a person to be the member of the 'other' Swaroopam. This brings out the differentiation among the Swaroopams and at the same time illustrates the mutually accepted norms that governed their interactions.

Four years after the event mentioned above, there was yet another act of conjugation in the year 1579 wherein two male members from Threppappur were transposed to Chiravay.[10] This conjugating act once again transposed members from Threppappur to Chiravay, and it shows that inter-Swaroopam dathetukkal was not a unique instance in the co-existence of Swaroopams. Such events also show that even though boundaries of swaroopams were blurred within the kinship bondage, as conjugater and conjugant, the Swaroopams could define their separateness in the roles of the conjugant and the conjugater[11]. Although dathetukkal was employed as a legitimizing means for a member in the diagram of a Swaroopam to be considered as a member in another one, this was not always so. For example, there were instances of the Chiravay muppu becoming a multiple-muppu without sparking off the issue of dathetukkal.[12]

Independent of the alliance between the swaroopams that were constructed through kinship, there was another stratum wherein differential and integral relations among them were possible, which could be delineated without reference to it. That is, another stratum of a personal tie was formalised in such events of conjugation, and the conjugant's position in the Swaroopam got marked in the diagram. This means such act an event could not be reduced to the kinship idiom although the kinship terminology was employed to refer to the relation between the conjugater and conjugant.[13] To reiterate, in the event, the elements of kinship terminology may be referred to place the conjugant in the receiving Swaroopam,[14] but it was primarily into the inter-personal tie that the conjugant was transposed.

If the S(s)waroopams were branches of a 'kinship tree', then there would not have emerged any need for such a conjugation between them. The kinship ties between the Swaroopams did not pre-empt it to happen, and these observations show that the kinship ties were not emblematic of the inter-Swaroopam relations. The primacy of the identity of each of the Swaroopams was getting reaffirmed as they were differentiated into independent unities in the event. The inter-Swaroopam relations that got affirmed in the event did not exactly correspond with the kinship relations that existed historically.

The specific combinations of the Swaroopams that came to be related as the conjugater and the conjugant[15] varied with respect to the context in which it took place. The nature of the event itself varied without there being any corresponding changes in either the kinship ties or the nature of the muppu vaazhcha. One can identify different strata of inter-Swaroopam relations in each of these events and each stratum differed from others, although not necessarily in terms of the specific combination of the Swaroopams that were involved in each of them. The strata enjoyed mutual independence, thereby engendering a situation in which the active subjects, who were involved in muppu vaazhcha, had a space to alter situations in a stratum without influencing others. Thus, the practice of dathetukkal had the potential to be implicated in strategies and exercise of power without undermining or being in conflict with inter-Swaroopam relations in other strata.

Even when different Swaroopams got combined through multiplicity, there were occasions of re-conjugation; members belonging to the diagram of one Swaroopam were transposed into another one as it is in the event of 1574-75 mentioned above. Even though Chiravay and Threppappur were combined in the multiple-muppu vaazhcha of Udaya Marthanda Varma, a conjugating act had to be conducted. This event also shows that the combinations of Swaroopams that converged in the multiple muppu vaazhcha were not necessarily the same ones that came together in the dathetukkal. At the time of the event in question, Threppappur and Deshinganad were combined through a dual-muppu, and the muppu had already de-succeeded from Chiravay. Under such conditions, it is possible to assume that he has superiority, due to the age factor, compared to the then muppu of Chiravay. Further, the kinship-unity was stronger between Threppappur and Chiravay at that time.[16] In spite of all these, the conjugating event had to be conducted to include members from Threppappur into the diagram of Chiravay.

Once again, the unity of Swaroopams in multiplicity did not imply that the composition of Swaroopams in such unity was same in every instance of inter-swaroopam interactions and co-actions. Unity in multiple muppu vazcha did not preempt acts of re-conjugation between them for their relatively independent co-existence.

From the above discussion it can also be seen that even when multiplicity and kinship simultaneously combined several Swaroopams, the mobility of individual members from the diagram of one Swaroopam to another one had to be accompanied by performance of political rituals that acknowledge the differentiation between the Swaroopams and their boundaries. The specific exterior and interior of each of them were differentially defined in each of the strata made up of kinship, dathetukkal, and multiple-muppu vaazhcha. As shifts in the order of the diagram could be affected by conjugation, its performance had to be a conscious and intentional event. Therefore, the transposition had to primarily recognize the boundaries between the Swaroopams and not so much the unity of the swaroopams and the coalitions that take place in multiplicity.

The anachronism here is that if these Swaroopams had been primarily unified in terms of a "ruling family" or the 'branches' of a 'dynasty' as it is commonly believed, then why did conjugational acts took place at all between Threppappur and Chiravay or from Kunnummel Ilayetam to Threppappur and vice versa?[17] The exterior and interior of the Swaroopams were defined not only in terms of kinship or family network and in terms of the form of multiplicity, but in terms of other factors such as those involved in the dathetukkal.[18] In the event, the Swaroopams had to define their mutual differentiation by positioning, as either the conjugater or the conjugant, and in this they primarily identify themselves in terms of the Swaroopam.

For a better understanding, another event of inter-Swaroopam transposing that took place in 1623 can also be looked into. The new conjugation reached by Kunnummel Swaroopam on the one hand and Threppappur and Chiravay on the other in the year 1623[19] reveal another dimension of the political borderlines between them. This event involved the muppu of Kunnummel as the conjugant and the muppu of Chiravay as the conjugater. But in the transposition of members from Threppappur to Kunnummel, the conjugater was the muppu of the latter Swaroopam and the conjugants were the muppu of Chiravay and two junior male members along with the three senior-most members of the female kuuru-mura of Threppappur. All the members who were conjugant in this 'mutual' dathetukkal were active, as against the "passive-conjugant" in the previous examples or in the adoptive practice in general. Besides, all of them had a higher place and position in the diagram order and they were active in the organisation of their own Swaroopams.

The transposition of the elderly members has another implication on inter-Swaroopam relations. The former events, which were mentioned above, were instances of a person getting transposed from one Swaroopam into another one, implying that there was a unidirectional movement of members from one Swaroopam into another. But unlike this, this event of 1623 shows a simultaneous transposition from one Swaroopam to the other and vice versa. There is bi-directional transposition of the swaroopikal, that is, there is a mutual conjugality between two Swaroopams.

In the earlier examples, members included in the diagram of Threppappur were transposed into Chiravay, which meant that there were only two Swaroopams involved in it. But in this one, there were three Swaroopams. Two of them —Threppappur and Chiravay — were coupled in their roles of both conjugater and conjugant while Kunnummel was all alone in these roles.

Another interesting peculiarity of this mutual transposition is that the conjugants were not placed in the diagrams of the Swaroopams into which they were received, nor were they offered any positions in the muppu vaazhcha in the Swaroopam into which each swaroopy got conjugated. In other words, this event did not shift the order in the diagram or referred kinship terminology to relate between them. The new relations of the conjugant with the conjugaters were not defined; rather they were referred to in terms of their position in the Swaroopam of origin alone. They were posited into some kind of protective fold of the Swaroopams of the conjugaters as they were specified only as *swaroopathine utayathaaka*. Moreover, there was no allotment of any koikkals (palace) to the conjugants. In the earlier instances of dathetukkal, cited above, the conjugant were physically transposed into the conjugater's Swaroopam, they were given koikkals, implicated into the diagram whereby they became part of the Swaroopam and they could also become the muppu. There was no such transposition, as we have defined, of the conjugant from one

Swaroopam to the other; it was only a symbolic transposition which had 'meaning' and functionality without the conjugants physical presence or roles in vaazhcha. This event may be seen as a practice that illustrated the reciprocity between the Swaroopams in question, perhaps as a symbolic exchange of assurance for their co-existence.

The Boundaries and Their Non-Consideration

Referring back to the conjugating act of 1623, although members of Chiravay were also involved in the dathetukkal, the muppu of Kunnummel was conjugant only into Threppappur. The senior-most conjugater was the muppu of Chiravay; nevertheless the conjugants from Kunnummel were not received into this Swaroopam. No male member of Threppappur (especially the muppu, ilayathu etc.) was involved in the event; there were only the female members of the matrilocal and mother centric family at Attingal and the male members of Chiravay. This shows that the involvement of the Chiravay muppu in the event was not primarily on behalf of the Chiravay Swaroopam, but on behalf of some other unity. There was no amalgamation of Threppappur and Chiravay because Chiravay did not figure as a receiving Swaroopam. These factors clearly bring out the complexities involved in the maintenance of inter-Swaroopam differentiation and co-existence.

Even when the Chiravay muppu was the initiator of the event, this Swaroopam did not enter into the picture directly. Transposition was between Threppappur and Kunnummel and not between Chiravay and Kunnummel, although the main conjugater and its initiator was the Chiravay muppu; this is another question that stems when we analyze this particular mutual dathetukkal. Yet another question that crops up in this context is how the Chiravay muppu could be the initiator in the act of transposition between Threppappur and Kunnummel, especially when there was another muppu for Threppappur.

While the Chiravay muppu took such a position in Threppappur, Unnikerala Varma was the Threppappur muppu. Given the importance of the event in the inter-Swaroopam relations, how could the Chiravay muppu instead of the Threppappur muppu, act the roles proper to the latter? A continuum between the muppu position of the Chiravay Swaroopam and his place in the Threppappur Swaroopam can be seen. The Threppappur muppu (Unnikerala Varma) was not even referred to in the document that depicted the event. In one stratum of relations the inter-Swaroopam differentiation is maintained, and at the same time one begins to see the existence of continuity between the Swaroopams forming a different stratum. This unity is achieved neither on the basis of the Swaroopam as an identity nor in terms of multiplicity, but in terms of conjugality.

It should be recalled that Threppappur and Chiravay were not combined in any form of multiplicity at that time; moreover, Threppappur and Deshinganad were combined by dathetukkal through Unnikerala Varma. That is, by virtue of being the muppu of Threppappur alone, one could not position oneself as the conjugater of the Swaroopam (it is not known whether there was any such fixed role obligation). Even though Threppappur and Deshinganad were combined following the diagram at that time, there could be situations in which such continuity between them did not appear. The combination of positions/agents involved in this event was defined by principles other than those that legitimized one as the muppu or as the senior-most in the diagram. That could be the reason why Unnikerala Varma did not appear as representing Threppappur although he was its muppu.

What privileged the Chiravay muppu to act as the conjugater of Threppappur is not clearly decipherable. Yet it can be mentioned that the relation between the Chiravay muppu and the female members of Attingal gave shape to the composition of members in the event of a dathetukkal.

Whatever be the historical condition of this specificity, one implication is that even when multiplicity combined two or more Swaroopams, there were roles—the kind of roles found in the event of dathetukkal—which are distinguishable from the roles that were strictly and solely attached to particular muppu positions.[20] There were certain matters of a Swaroopam for which its own muppu was a prerequisite; at the same time there could be other situations in which this was not required. This suggests that there was a differentiation between Threppappur and Chiravay although they were together as conjugants, that is, they were not the joint receivers of conjugants from Kunnummel. As conjugants they were combined but as the dathu-receiving-Swaroopam, they were differentiated. The distinction between them as two Swaroopams was maintained even within this stratum; moreover the differentiation between the swaroopam and Swaroopam could also be identified in this event.

To complicate the matter, in 1630 there was another event of conjugating between Vellarappalli family in Cochin and Threppappur, in which Unnikerala Varma, who was absent in the former event, took a very active role.[21] In the case of the transposition from Kunnummel to Threppappur, only one conjugater was there, namely the muppu of Chiravay, but when Threppappur became the conjugant, there were several members as conjugants belonging to Chiravay and Threppappur. These complexities are reflexive of the minute distinctions that are active and the characteristics of inter-Swaroopam relations.

When certain results of the above analysis are conflated, it can be observed that in the previous chapter multiplicity combined Threppappur and Deshinganad more frequently, whereas in the acts of conjugating Chiravay and Threppappur happens to be a more frequent combination. Further, there is no correspondence between the combination of Swaroopams that appear in the kinship network and those who appear in the conjugation. Even when the three swaroopams, Deshinganad, Chiravay and Threppappur, are combined through a common muppu as a totality within the kinship network, in the practice of dathetukkal there is no recognition of it as primary.

Now the question is that if there was variation in the specific composition of the Swaroopams across each stratum and if several such strata were active, then did such variations in the composition of them result in instability and imbalances in their inter-relations? Different intersecting boundaries can be deciphered at the level of the specific combinations of them that appeared in each of the strata and within each of the combinations. This is so as each of them retained their respective boundaries differentially within each of the strata. Therefore, the criterion involved in the determination of boundaries might have been quite sensitive to time space and complex; but yet specific. How did this differential structuration which took place in each of the stratum perpetuate the primacy of the Swaroopam in the interactions, counter-actions and co-actions between/among them?

Though the questions raised above cannot be taken up here, still one thing could be stated: there was no permanent meta-unity that made the variable combinations of Swaroopam stationary. No tendency could be deciphered which made any one combination common to all the strata that are discussed so far. They were combined variously on different grounds; this made it possible for the formation of several strata consisting of unities and differences. The 'initial' decision to be outside any combination was endogenous to them, whatever may be the consequences that it may effect. However, once a Swaroopam decided to be part of a combination then it became active in the inter-Swaroopam co-existence. The heterogeneity in the possible combinations of them that constitute different stratum could be one of the factors that made the relatively autonomous co-existence of them possible without any meta-unity among them.[22] Both the relations of difference and integrity were conceived and articulated as normal and norm-bound.

The intricate ways in which the manifold forms of power operated in the inter and intra-Swaroopam organisations can be elaborated by examining another instance of conjugational event. When the appearance of a specific combination of Swaroopams was disapproved by any one or more of the four Swaroopams, then that specific combination gets problematised and structural equivalence gets destabilised[23]. The conjugal event could be reconstitutive of the inter-Swaroopam relations and it also could maintain the structural equivalence among them. These moves are born out of the willful intentions of agents who acted within the given possibility that continued from the past, and are perpetuated by some actors of the present. Theoretically speaking, strategic moves and problematisation did not emerge not so much from the opposition between the agents and the structures but something that surfaces in the inter-subjectivity of the agents who at the same accept 'what is given' and invent 'what has to become as something given'.

Differentiation From Within

In the year 1622, there was another dathetukkal between Threppappur and Chiravay on the one hand and Pokam/Poka *thaivazhi* of the Threppappur Swaroopam, on the other.[24] A thaivazhi by definition is a 'sub-set' or 'branch' of a swaroopam such that they ought to have close kinship relation, as they are already a consanguine descent group. Thus thaivazhi is said to be 'in' the swaroopam and in principle, the S(s)waroopam includes thaivazhi. However, at the instance of a conjugal event combining a Swaroopam and its thaivazhi, and particularly a mutual-conjugal act, they are bound to be separated as the conjugater and the conjugant. Such a differentiation can be grounded only in a stratum outside the unity achieved by consanguinity or kinship relationship, or when it is dormant/sidelined. This event also problematised the definition of thaivazhi in terms of swaroopam and its condition of "being contained" by the S(s)waroopam. The very fact that there occurred a political need for a mutual-conjugal act itself is an attestation that there was a realm in which the existence of kinship unity and the position of thaivazh as a part of the Swaroopam did not matter. A branch can be as good as its stem!

Even if a kinship-based unity existed, it was not sufficient to prove the notion that a Swaroopam was the total and the thaivazhi its part. Alternatively, conjugal acts had to be performed in spite of the existent kinship unity; this also indicates that there was relative autonomy to the thaivazhi in its relation within the Swaroopam. Kinship unity did not necessarily ensure the political unity of a Swaroopam, and even if it were so, the need for intra-Swaroopam conjugative events would not have surfaced. These observations suggest the need for an alternative conceptualisation of thaivazhi, as they contradict the existing conceptualisation of it as contained by the Swaroopam and its relation to the swaroopam and Swaroopam. The kinship based description of the relation between the Swaroopam and thaivazhi or definition of these two as the *moola-kutumbam* or 'original family' and 'descent group' or the 'centre' and 'satellites' or 'total' and 'part' is not possible. This intra-conjugative event achieved the unity that kinship ties could not effect.

Another event in the history of conjugality is the one that took place between the Swaroopam and thaivazhi in 1679, when members were transposed from Poka-thaivazhi to the Threppappur/Chiravay and later the conjugant became muppu of Chiravay in 1684.[25] This substantiates the above argument further and highlights its intensity. Now, it can be said that even for a member of a thaivazhi to become the muppu of a Swaroopam, dathetukkal was essential. Without this, such a member was treated as a kin as well as a member of Chiravay/Threppappur. But he was not considered as a legitimate successor to the muppu position. In other words, only conjugal binding introduced even the seniormost of a thaivazhi into the diagram of its Swaroopam.

To repeat, the existing kinship based characterisation of the relation between the Swaroopam and thaivazhi cannot explain this dathetukkal, and within such an ethnographic analytic-framework such an event may be treated as an 'exception', if not as an anachronism. Such characterisation and the fact that they could relate each other as two self-similar identities assume away the possibility of a different power relation between thaivazhi and Swaroopam in the political field. An analysis of this event also help us to formulate a hypothesis that the thaivazhi might have had the possibility to grow as a Swaroopam. The relation between kinship and politics and the very notion of kinship itself need to be re-problematised by the anthropologists/ethnographers/historians in the light of the observed complexity in the non-relation between Swaroopams and also between the Swaroopam and its thaivazhi. Given the complexity involved in the relation between a Swaroopam and its thaivazhi and the political implication of conjugal bindings, let us return to the political aspects by returning to the event of 1622.

Equality Between Center and Part of the Total

This event brings out how a kinship connection between the Swaroopam and its thaivazhi remains exogenous to activities which have both inter-personal, inter-Swaroopam and inter-family relations. This conjugal act is at the same time intra-Swaroopam and also an intra-family one. Earlier we had seen an intra-family and inter-Swaroopam dathetukkal but here it is an intra-family and intra-Swaroopam tranpositioning at the same time.

In the document[26] the unit entity, Poka thaivazhi appeared in the roles of both the conjugater and conjugant and it was treated as different from the Swaroopam and it was referred to only as thaivazhi; thus there was continuity in their mutual relation in general as both Swaroopam and thaivazhi. Nevertheless, in the event of dathetukkal, they mutually treat the other as an equal entity. The Swaroopam was not treated as a whole but was differentiated. One of the Swaroopam's assumed part was disassociated and thus the achieved units were placed as the Swaroopam (Swaroopam minus a part of it) and the thaivazhi. We see that the swaroopam and its thaivazhi come into mutual relation as two equivalent counter-partners of a transposition or as two teams at the beginning of a game. The thaivazhi was treated more or less as another Swaroopam. They reciprocated each other by exchanging their most distinguished positions as conjugants.

It is clear by now that the thaivazhi was not merely contained within the unity of either the Swaroopam or in any overarching kinship binding of the swaroopam; the idea of 'total' and 'parts' cannot be applied here. Even if it is treated so, the lines that mark the exterior and interior of both the total and part remain severely complex and it resists any straightforward application of monolithic concepts. Not only did the practice of strategic, optional, and conditional conjugative events unify different Swaroopams, but it also integrated units within a S(s)waroopam, maybe due to the fact that other factors that unified them were inactive. The kinship relations that posit the thaivazhi's status as part of the domain of the Swaroopam did integrate them, but it did not unify the part into the whole exhaustively, and there were spaces in which they were no more total and part, but two independent entities. The muppu or any other such distinguished positions did not entail an all-pervasive influence on the thaivazhi or any other such parts; it did not invade the autonomous space in which the thaivazhi could act as a unit in itself. That is why Poka-thaivazhi reciprocated as an 'equivalent-other party' vis-à-vis the united Threppappur/Chiravay. In other words, there was hierarchy between them at certain situations, but in the act of a conjugative event or when the need for such an event emerged, such asymmetries in their power relation had no influence on the relative positioning of them, however momentary it may have been.

Political Script

The event that we have been focusing on constituted a mutual relation between the conjugants or conjugater which was to last during both the 'desired' and 'undesired' times, and they had rights over the dead bodies as well in performing death rituals. The content of the 'mutual agreement' between them elucidates the political underpinnings involved in it.[27] In the mutual agreement between Kerala Varma, the muppu of the Poka-thaivazhi and Ravi Varma the Chiravay muppu, there was a mutual exchange of the document of treaty. Kerala Varma agreed not to see or enter into alliance with the Kunnummel Swaroopam without the knowledge of Ravi Varma, his elder brother; he also agreed not to align with those who do so. In return, Ravi Varma agreed not to make peace with the Ilayidattu family without Veera Kerala Varma, nor side with the latter's nephews (junior princes) and those of his own family and molest him. Both mutually agreed not to dishonour the ardhapranadhishthana.

The kind of guarantee that they exchanged with each other is a clear expression of the bond that had been absent, at least until the event. The significance of this treaty can be seen in the mutual agreement between them, with its documentation in written form, and in the mutual exchange of the documents and the transposition of the distinguished. Although several members were involved as conjugater and conjugant, this agreement was strictly between the muppus of the Swaroopam and the thaivazhi. This overtly articulated treaty shows the kind of power relation between the Swaroopam and thaivazhi, a kind of power relation in which they could exercise authority mutually in a more or less equivalent manner. One broad observation that can be made is that while dathetukkal that had a bearing on politics involved a group activity, the overtly political matters like the one mentioned above that involved both inter-Swaroopam relations and intra-Swaroopam relations could take place under the leadership and auspices of the muppu alone.

In the event as noted earlier, both Threppappur and Chiravay present themselves as a combine in distinction to their thaivazhi. When it came to the exchange of a written agreement about the relations that they should maintain with Kunnummel as well as between them,

Threppappur was not referred to at all. In spite of this, it can be safely assumed that the Threppappur/Chiravay combine was represented by the Chiravay muppu as the ameliorator of the discord between the Kunnummel and the combine took place within another year, which culminated in the event of 1623. The integrity of the combine continued to exist throughout the period under consideration. It should be remembered that along with these events, the rift between Deshinganad and Threppappur was also continuing, and there was also a tendency in Threppappur and Chiravay to come under multiplicity more frequently. It should be said that there was also a tendency in the Poka-thaivazhi to disassociate itself from the Chiravay/ Threppappur combine. This dissociation should not be viewed as a complete cessation of the thaivazhi from the combine or the muulakutumbam (genealogically the 'original' family).

Both Threppappur and Chiravay were facing their own unique contingency; the combine had problems with the Kunnummel Swaroopam, similarly Poka-thaivazhi was having difficulties from within. What exactly was the internal dissent that the muppu of Poka-thaivazhi faced is not a matter of concern here. What was common was that both of them had a similar relation of discord with the Kunnummel Swaroopam at that time, and the discord was intensely affecting the relation between the combine and Kunnummel. The historical situation was that a structural equivalence had to be fabricated through the aid of this 'mutual agreement' between the Threppappur/Chiravay combine and Pokathaivazhi, in which the transposition of the members or the initiation of a new conjugality was extremely significant politically.

It had been stated above that the relationship that existed between the combine and the thaivazhi in the dathetukkal had been as two equal counter-parts involved in a contract. But this proposition cannot be left unqualified in the case of the treaty. There had been an overt statement that the Chiravay muppu had superiority over the Threppappur. Their relationship was also well specified in terms of age. The technology of hierarchically ordering individuals, and their positing in the hierarchy of positions (including muppu) that were involved in Swaroopam organisation in terms of age had been observed while discussing the diagram. In terms of age, the muppu of Chiravay was superior to that of the thayvazhi. This aspect of their mutual relation is invoked into the treaty, therefore there takes place a hierarchy between them. This implies that Chiravay Swaroopam appears to be at a higher level of authority and speech due to the inter-personal relation between the two muppus, through the projection of the Chiravay muppu as the 'elder' to the muppu of the thaivazhi. The age factor gets a space in which the hierarchy could be retained within 'some' relations, although outside it is not the case.

What was the need for an overt agreement/treaty between the Swaroopam and its thaivazhi? This question is pertinent because there already existed an age-based hierarchy between the two muppus. Further, the mutual obligations had to be written (mozhi-olay was written) and they were exchanged so that both the parties could possess the copies/olay. The question here deals with why there was such a complicated and systematic practice, if the relation between the two muppus were structured in terms of an age based hierarchy within the same diagram. Was it not a custom, as commonly believed, that a thaivazhi muppu had to obey what the Swaroopam muppu demands? If this is so, why did Ravi Varma have to get consent from Kerala Varma, who was junior to him, before negotiating with Kunnummel for reconciliation; and reciprocally, why did the attempts of reconciliation between the thaivazhi and Kunnummel have to be conducted only with the knowledge of the former? It also points to a possibility that they belonged to two different kuuru- muras. If this is so, once again, the received view of the relation between the Swaroopam and thaivazhi needs to be rephrased; and broadly speaking, the relation between the thaivazhi and muulakutumbam will need to be re-conceptualised in the light of such complexities (not complications). Another question is regarding whether the thaivazhi was one of the parts of the Swaroopams, and why there was a need for measures like treaty and dathetukkal at all, as if without these acts and the subsequent treaty, the structural equivalence might not have been realised. Was the unity between the Swaroopam and its thaivazhi a matter of negotiation between the respective muppus; and alternatively, was it something that had been decided solely by the Swaroopam muppu? Was the relation between Kunnummel

Swaroopam and Poka-thaivazhi independent of a combined opinion of Threppappur/Chiravay? These questions are formulated to indicate the intricate ways in which power relations worked between them. It also alludes to the non-linear, non-fixed and non-localised ways in which the technologies of power operated, which made possible the co-existence of different Swaroopams.

One of the possible principles that operated in the Swaroopam organisation was that there were several things that a thaivazhi could conduct, irrespective of what it's Swaroopam thought about it. The Swaroopam was not to intervene into these fields of activities of the thaivazhi and any intervention had to be preceded by mutual consent. That is, there were spaces created in the relation between the Swaroopam and thaivazhi in which the latter could act autonomously, provided that it did not alter or contradict the persistent practices and systems of the Swaroopam organisation. While the Swaroopam had relative advantages due to the hierarchy, there were occasions when its engagements with the thaivazhi were conditional and bound by negotiation. This should not be read as a limitation of the Swaroopam, but rather as a shared principle between them. The authority relation between the Swaroopam and thaivazhi shows a non-generalised exchange of forces and an irreducibility of power to the Swaroopam muppu or any other single location in the Swaroopam. There were discontinuities within the flow of authority between the Swaroopam and thaivazhi as can be seen in the above instance of a conjugative act and mutual agreement.

There took place a generalisation of particular interests of the Swaroopam combine which made possible the co-action of the Swaroopams and thaivazhi in the strategy against their common opponent, namely Kunnummel. In this, the thaivazhi also gained as it could ameliorate its internal dissents. The terrain of politics is quite evident. The treaty that followed the dathetukkal and the dathetukkal itself can be viewed as strategic operations embedded in both the inter/intra-Swaroopam relations. The strategic moves were conducted primarily to prevent any structural realignment between the Swaroopam-combine and the thaivazhi that could be anticipated in favour of Kunnummel.

Action and Shift in the Diagram

Even when there were sufficient successors and members in the diagram, a conjugality of a different type, which had been not mentioned so far had taken place as young members from Vellarappalli (in the present day Cochin) were transposed to Threppappur in 1630.[28] The conjugants were given specific positions in the Threppappur family by placing them in relationships with each of the conjugaters using kinship terminology. There were two conjugants and eight conjugaters including the Chiravay muppu, his ilayathus and the female members of Attingal. The length of the list of conjugater itself shows that there were enough members in the diagram. In spite of their existence, these two conjugants were introduced into the diagram of Threppappur.

After one year, in 1631, another such an event was repeated between them[29], in which yet another member was transposed from the same family. That is, in addition to the two conjugants, there was a new one who got transposed and in turn placed as the 'elder' to the two conjugants of the previous event.[30] The new entrant was placed as 'uncle' to the already existed non-muppu members in the diagram;[31] thereby a shift in the diagram took place. Interestingly enough, not only that there was sufficient number of successors but also that this newly introduced member was to succeed to higher positions faster than the other two conjugants. Such a shift, due to the super-positioning of the new conjugant over the existent members undeniably altered the relations among the members in the diagram as they were further distanced from their anticipated positions. It might have created a new relationship between the conjugants and those who were already there. The age-based determination got sidelined and concomitantly such determinability got functionalised thereby allowing the precise-determinacy/restrains of the diagram to be overcome.

Therefore, one can say that the diagram was primary even when there were attempts to shift it. The determinacy was by-passed not by ignoring its truth value but by re-functionalising its sanctity. The truth of it was functionalised with a view to overcome the prevalent system of succession that this ordering effected. The foundation of the determinability and fixity of the diagram was the biological factor of age and birth-time. When through dathetukkal and placement of the conjugants, the order of hierarchy of positions in the diagram was accomplished, the determinate character of the schemata would be altered. Given such an instance of purposive shifting through dathetukkal, it can no more be considered as a schema that determined the distribution of individual swaroopikal across various positions solely in terms of the 'place'/family of birth, although age factor is retained. But it was only instrumental in legitimizing the purposive choice of the swaroopikal and their redistribution across positions of consequence according to the intention and will of the existing muppu and the conjugaters.

Another aspect worth noting here is that Unnikerala Varma, who was the muppu of Threppappur, entered into the picture of the consecutive-dathetukkal about which we have already referred to. But at the same time, although the dathetukkal took place in Threppappur, he was not mentioned as the conjugater. Rather, his role was confined to the decision making process in which other female members of the Vellarappalli family were also present. In that way he was identifying with Vellarappalli and displaying his closer affinity with this family rather than with Threppappur. It should be noted that he was also a conjugant from the Vellarappalli family who became the multiple-muppu of both Threppappur and Deshinganad. Here we begin to see the differentiation of a muppu in terms of whether he was a conjugant or not.

On the other hand, in the subsequent dathetukkal, even though he was not the conjugater, he played an important role by mediating between the conjugater and the family or the place of origin of the conjugants. He played this role in it because the conjugaters were from the Vellarappalli family to which he himself belonged before he was transposed into Deshinganad. In the document that refers to the consecutive dathetukkal,[32] the conjugant was specified in relation to Unnikerala Varma and the conjugants of the 1630 adoption.[33] Generally, the conjugants were referred in terms of the kinship relation that they were to have with the Swaroopam into which they were transposed. Therefore, even if one had been transposed through dathetukkal from one family to another Swaroopam/family and he became the muppu of that Swaroopam or Swaroopams—as in this case—his pre-dathu family history was never de-linked as generally believed.

One of the questions that can be raised now is the following: which Swaroopam was to be concerned about the disagreement of others that had bearing upon the equivalence and whose disagreements were to be warded off? There might have been conclusive answers to this question at specific instances, but they were not static across time and space. Hence, this peculiarity opened up space for tension between the Swaroopams. Whether the instability in the structural equivalence was the reason for a particular way of dathetukkal or vice versa cannot be specified. This instability was closely related to the deviations from the usual practice of a collectively negotiated dathetukkal,[34] that is, by taking care of the disagreements of other Swaroopams. There were several instances of structural instabilities between Swaroopams on account of un-negotiated dathetukkal and its strategic fictionalisation, especially during the turn of the seventeenth and the beginning of the eighteenth century.

There was another dathetukkal in 1672 which led to a disagreement between the muppu of the Attingal family and Chiravay on the one hand, and the Poka-thaivazhi on the other.[35] The Threppappur muppu, Adithya Varma, along with the Attingal family members wanted to transpose a member from Vellarappalli. This muppu of Chiravay was the one who was a conjugant from the same family in 1630[36] and he suggested his nephew Rama Koil Pandala as the successor, while the muppu of Poka-thaivazhi proposed that Rama Varma of his family should be the conjugant. This disagreement however, was affably solved, but conjugative events continued to create instabilities in the structural equivalence among Swaroopams.

There were several differing sets of combinations of Swaroopams during the period under consideration, and the specific combinations of the Swaroopams interacted and co-acted differently over time. The specific patterns and the combination of the Swaroopams/thaivazhies involved in the event not only differed over time, but also did not correspond with those observed in both the kinship-based differentiation/union and the multiplicity combine (multiple muppu vaazcha). The interaction between the Swaroopams or between a Swaroopam and any other kinship-unit shows the way the Swaroopam identities got perpetuated without recourse to any essential referential relation to any model involving an 'exterior' and 'interior' defined in terms of kinship or swaroopam. Just as in the multiplicity, what gets affirmed as real and primary is the concept of the Swaroopam. But then, an instance of problematising the coherence of the interior of the Swaroopam itself could be found in the event of dathetukkal.

The conjugality, when analyzed, reveals the interface between the swaroopam and Swaroopam, the manner in which they become one at times, and the modalities by which they were separated. Moreover, this event had wider implications as it also redefined and reordered the inter-subjective/individual relations among those included in the diagram as it could result in a shift in the existing order in it. This shift directly affected the specificity of the existing or the potential multiplicity; in other words, it implies that this strategic rational conjugality affected the political relations among the Swaroopams and between those in the diagram. Although the subjectivity of the actors involved in the event had been grounded more firmly on Swaroopam than in swaroopam, there were instances when this coherence between Swaroopam and swaroopam were overlooked. Such instances also exemplify the exteriorisation of a part of the interior of the Swaroopam.

The occurrence of frequent dathetukkal in the Swaroopams also testifies to the fact of the small coverage within the greater kinship network, and the possibility of altering the kinship hierarchy and the diagram. Despite the increasing instances of the event, the coverage of the diagram was restricted to a small fraction of the kinship network. It is not only that the coverage remained at the same level but also the frequency of dathetukkal remained high despite the possibility of multiple muppu vaazcha. If the lack of successors to muppu had been severe, then either the coverage could have been extended to include other members into it, or instead of dathetukkal, multiplicity could have been opted for. Instead, we find that the former had been an opted during the period under consideration. It implies that over and above the task of overcoming the lack of successors, dathetukkal had more to do with inter-subjectivity and inter-Swaroopam relations. When such a dathetukkal takes place, human agents get a chance to intervene and alter/shift the hierarchical order in the diagram or kuuru-mura and the way it functioned in the successions to muppu positions. That is, instead of the pre-given scheme determining the serialisation of individuals, the human agency becomes decisive in determining it or altering it. The interface between the 'structure' and the 'active agent' can be deciphered in such events of dathetukkal. All these added to the significance of dathetukkal in Swaroopams, and it compels the analyst to accept the complexity that was imminent in the perpetuation of the Swaroopam.

When two Swaroopams, say, S1 and S2 have relations with exactly the same set of other actors (for example, the family/ Swaroopam of the conjugant), even if S1 and S2 have no mutual relations, it can be said that there exists a structural equivalence between them. Therefore, there could be a structural equivalence between two Swaroopams or swaroopams when they have a common Swaroopam/swaroopams or any other unit from where they adopt. When they together change the unit of the conjugant from one to another, it can be stated that the structural equivalence between them is maintained.

Although there were realignments among the Swaroopams due to dathetukkal and a shift in the diagram, the primacy of the Swaroopam identity was retained. Even when the muppu and ilayathu or a given set of members of the Swaroopams were transposed to another one, as observed earlier, they were not introduced into the diagram of the receiving Swaroopam. They were not directly implicated into the kinship network, although the conjugater-conjugant relation was phrased using kinship terminology. To be precise, such conjugants were never placed in the kuuru-mura schemata. If they had any such position, for instance, when the Chiravay muppu was transposed into Kunnummel, he would have become the muppu of Kunnummel Swaroopam but it did not take place although the former was elder to the Kunnummel muppu. Whenever dathetukkal took place with the intention to fill or shift the diagram, then their relation with each of the conjugaters in the order was well defined.[37] But in the mutual dathetukkal (both inter-Swaroopam and between Swaroopam and thaivazhi) of the distinguished positions, realignment took place in terms of Swaroopam itself and the interaction was between the units having their own exterior and interior, be it the Swaroopam or thaivazhi. Thus, such events did not cause any shift in the diagrammatic order. The unity of the Swaroopam is highlighted not to establish that kinship relations were absent, but to emphasize the primacy of the co-existence of Swaroopams and to demonstrate the limited role that hereditary kinship relation had in determining the inter-Swaroopam unity or intra-Swaroopam coherence despite frequent dathedukkal.

Conjugational events took place when there was a lack of successors as well,[38] or a shortage of members in the diagram.[39] The lack of successors need not mean that there was a shortage of swaroopikal to succeed to the muppu position, but it could also take place due to several other ritualistic needs; for example, the conjugant might be required to perform one year long death rituals which a muppu cannot afford (a one year long deeksha) etc.[40] In this type of conjugality, the kinship factor was pertinent. Another pattern that could be observed is that when it took place to fill the diagram, then the conjugants were never from any of the Swaroopams that we have mentioned so far. Why this is so is a question that is important but left unaddressed here. They were generally from faraway places like the Vellarappalli family in Cochin and also from Kolathunaadu in northern part of present day Kerala. There had never been any mutual dathetukkal between any of the Swaroopams and these families of Cochin and Kolathunaadu. These are historical issues to be discerned, but we turn our attention to something else here.

Adoption Becomes Translatable as Adoption

A conjugative event took place when there was no successor in Deshinganad and therefore a male member was transposed from Kayamkulam (a region north of Deshinganad) during the first quarter of the eighteenth century under the auspices of the muppu of the Swaroopam. This was not agreeable to Marthanda Varma, the muppu of Chiravay. Had this event not taken place, the Chiravay muppu would have combined Chiravay and Deshinganad through dualing. Perhaps this can be the reason for the squabble between them. Their disagreement engendered violent reactions from the Chiravay side against both Kayamkulam and Deshinganad.[41] The latter combine also retaliated in the same manner. The structural equivalence between Deshinganad and Threppappur/Chiravay got destabilised as and when the new unit namely, Kayamkulam was introduced into their relationship. Here the inter-Swaroopam differential relation got problematised before and after the conjugational event. What we can understand from this is that Deshinganad should have consulted the Chiravay muppu and received his consent before the dathetukkal from Kayamkulam; in fact this was the argument. As a result of this, there was a breach in the followed norm of negotiated dathetukkal. This was one of the arguments based on the diagram and the custom of conjugality. The fact that Deshinganad did not consider the potential disagreement of the Chiravay muppu itself shows that there had been an attempt to de-link Deshinganad from the system of multiplicity.

Thus, the precondition of this dathetukkal itself shows that there had been political interstice between Deshinganad and Chiravay/Threppappur. This non-negotiated event furthered the already existed crevice. On account of this event, another un-experimented reactive practice of recurring violent encounters between Chiravay and Deshinganad had begun. That is, the process was not to correct the failures involved in that particular dathetukkal, but to functionalise the failure with a view to achieve certain definite ends. Here, it was no more the result of a structural disequilibrium, as in the above mentioned moment, but a legitimating reason for the use of violent actions. The reason given to fight against Kayamkulam was that they allied with Deshinganad. This shows that any instability in structural equivalence due to dathetukkal had far-reaching the consequences. The lost possibility of the existing Chiravay muppu to succeed to the Deshinganad muppu position due to dathetukkal itself become instrumental in the strategy that resulted in violence on the members of another Swaroopam and destabilised the idea of the co-existence of the Swaroopam itself. That is, dathetukkal was a site of strategic operations as well as the cause for the resulting violence at the same time.

Such a strategic rational practice of dathetukkal shifted the hierarchy in the diagram and this in turn determined, however partially, the possibility of a person to succeed to the multiplicity. The inter-Swaroopam relations not only influenced the dathetukkal, but the latter also influenced the former. This circular relation determined which individual from the diagram could assume multiple positions and it also created a link between dathetukkal and multiplicity. The determination of the successor was made sensitive to several factors exogenous to the diagram.

The nature and consequences of dathetukkal was sensitive to factors such as where the conjugants were chosen, when it was chosen, who all the conjugaters were, contingency that necessitated it, the expectations about multiplicity, and so on. The manner in which these factors influenced it varied significantly from one instance to another. It was quite 'amorphous' in the sense that it functioned as a cause and means for unification/differentiation, as a result of alterations in the structural equivalence between Swaroopams, as a site for maneuvering inter-Swaroopam relationships, etc. [42]

Several factors intensified the potential of dathedukkal to be implicated in political and symbolic practices and custom-bound maneuvers in manifold ways. They ranged between the need for a substitute for performing death rituals,[43] the succession or perpetuation of political alliance, the reconciliation of rivalry between Swaroopams and so on. When it becomes a cause or the 'explained reason' for acts resulting in violence, then one can say that failures in observing the norm of the negotiated dathetukkal legitimated the acts that caused violence and altered the possibility of co-existence of the Swaroopams. It should be noted that not only the norms related to and practice of it had political functions, but failure to follow the norms also had political functions. Failures in following the norms were functionalised to legitimize the acts of *duraachaaram* (literally this word means violation of customary rules) and waging war against another Swaroopam. To put it briefly, the 'truth' involved in the practice of dathetukkal and the notion of transposing individuals had become an ideology in inter-Swaroopam disputes.

The repeatable materiality of them in the wide spectrum of sites, strategies and contexts finally got reduced to a monolithic form by transforming it into adoption. I shall elaborate this point. No more could the swaroopams[44] engage in dathetukkal since 1748[45]. If any swaroopam faced the problem of lack of successors, then it was to be resolved through dathetukkal into the Attingal family. It should be remembered that the Attingal family was a matrilocal/matrifocal one and the Attingal palace was the residence of the female members of the swaroopams and children. This gave added fixity to this localisation of dathetukkal/adoption. During the second quarter of the eighteenth century, the autonomy of this family was dislodged and it was made part of the Thiruvithamkur raajyam (by amalgamating the Swaroopams and occupying/containing nearby regions). Along with such changes, the practice of dathetukkal also got redefined. The alteration of dathetukkal and the perpetuation of the new rules of adoption were mutually agreed preconditions between the Attingal family and Marthanda Varma, the first Travancore raja, before the alteration of the matrilocality/matrifocality of the Attingal family. The transformation of dathetukkal was part of the containment strategy applied on the Attingal family by Marthanda Varma. The new condition of dathetukkal was that whenever it took place, the conjugant was not to be transposed into any of the Swaroopams or any of the diagrams but only to the Attingal family. This localised the right to conduct adoption to the Attingal family under the auspices of the raja.

Further, only female members were to be the conjugants. No more male dathetukkal could be practiced. This made the purposive shifting of the order in the diagram impossible. In addition to this, the family of origin of the potential conjugants was specified and reduced to Kolathunaadu alone. The range of families and places from where the conjugant could be chosen got reduced to one single family or naadu and no more inter-Swaroopam or intra-Swaroopam dathetukkal was possible. Thus, dathetukkal had become localised between the fixed family of the conjugant and a single family into which they were to be adopted. There emerged a located center and a specification of a gender route.

The condition of adoption also got defined in terms of purpose; it could be conducted solely when a lack of successor was anticipated. No more it could function as a means of a treaty between the Swaroopams and a means to ameliorate conflicting relations within a Swaroopam. If at all, only the sons of the conjugant female members (conjugant or not) of the Attingal family were to become the muppu of the Swaroopam. By the time of such changes, the Chiravay muppu was said to function as the muppu of the Padmanabha Temple and did what had been called rajya paripaalanam as against muppu vaazhcha.[46]

Concomitant with the above redefinition of dathetukkal as adoption, the number of diagrams also got reduced to one, which became common to all the four amalgamated Swaroopams under consideration—and other regions too. The successors to the Travancore kingdom could only be from the Attingal family.[47] As the Swaroopam entity ceased to exist, only one diagram was sufficient as the eldest would succeed as the Sri Padmanabha Daasa and the king of Travancore, and other members would occupy junior positions. Once there was only one general diagram for the single unit of Travancore, as against several Swaroopams, there was no question of dueling and multiplication as we had been discussing so far. No more was the Swaroopam the primary unit conceived for succession, but the Raajyam.

The Travancore raajyam contained within it the Swaroopams, and inter-Swaroopam boundaries were hardly recognised in the raajavaazhcha (vaazhcha by the raaja). Since mid-eighteenth century onwards, the four[48] Swaroopams together with many other regions south of Cochin was categorised as Venad/Thiruvithamkur raajyam till the formation of Kerala in 1956 with changes in its outer boundary.

With the disappearance of the co-existence of Swaroopams and the primacy of Swaroopam itself by mid-eighteenth century, dathetukkal had also metamorphosed as an act that became perfectly translatable as adoption. In the beginning of this chapter, we had stated that dathetukkal cannot be translated as adoption, but this is true only for a period prior to the mid-eighteenth century. Since the redefinition of dathetukkal in 1748, it became perfectly translatable as adoption and matter of kinship alone.

Notes

1. The Malayalam word for 'adoption' is dathetukkal or dathevakka, Gundert, H, (1872).
2. Documents showing dathetukkal prior to 1620 are also available, but the available information is not sufficient to create continuous series.
3. This has been compiled with the help of the genealogical tree of the Travancore royal family as in Nagam Aiya, V, Vol. I, (1906: 332) and information contained in Shivashankaran Nair, K, (1993).
4. Shivashankaran Nair, K, (1993).
5 Shivashankaran Nair, K, (1993).
6. Webster Comprehensive Dictionary, International Edition, Chicago: J.G. Ferguson Publishing Company, Vol. 1, (1986:276).
7. Document No. G, Rajaraja Varma Raja. M, (S. 3,1930:130-133).
8. Although in the following pages the Malayalam word dathetukkal is used, words like conjugater and conjugant are retained for easier communication.
9. See Document No. VIII, Rajaraja Varma Raja, M, (S.1, 1928:18).
10. Document No. A, Rajaraja Varma Raja, M, (S. 3, 1930:123-124) and also see p.114 of the same Series.
11. Here a *Swaroopam* is treated as conjugant in the sense that when someone is conjugant from one *Swaroopam* transposed to the other then, what is given importance is not only the conjugant person but the *Swaroopam* to which he/she belongs. Thus we conceive of the conjugant as a swaroopi.
12. Both Unnikerala Varma of Deshinganad and Ravi Varma of Chiravay are the best examples for this.
13. The conjugant would be renamed and he would be placed in kinship relation with members of the kuuru mura.
14. For a detailed description of the nature of placement of the conjugant in the new kinship relations, see Document No. E, Rajaraja Varma Raja, M, (S.3, 1930:127-129).
15. It should be remembered that here conjugant does not mean the person/ conjugant alone, but includes all those who were involved in the transposing.

16. See Document IV, Rajaraja Varma Raja. (S.1, 1928:17).
17. See Document No. D, Rajaraja Varma Raja, M, (1930).
18. If kinship is more primary and all encompassing including the Swaroopam identity and still adoption takes place in the intra-kinship structure by partitioning it into two, then the kinship structure itself should be redefined for the context.
19. Document No. D, Rajaraja Varma Raja, (S.3, 1930:126-129).
20. In the next chapter, the muppu-specific roles will be taken up for detailed discussion and therefore it is not taken up for discussion in this chapter.
21. See Document No. F, Rajaraja Varma Raja, (S.3, 1930:129).
22. Another premise for this statement is the differential relation that Unnikerala Varma, the multiple-*muppu* of Threppappur and Deshinganad, maintained with Threppappur during the early seventeenth century.
23. For an example of such destabilisation, see Document No. H, Rajaraja Varma Raja, (S.3, 1930:133).
24. Document No. B, Rajaraja Varma Raja, (S. 3, 1930).
25. Shivashankaran Nair, K, (1993:122).
26. Document B, Rajaraja Varma Raja (S.3, 1930:119).
27. Document B, Rajaraja Varma. Raja (1930:119).
28. Document E, Rajaraja Varma Raja (S.3, 1930:127-129).
29. Document E, Rajaraja Varma Raja (S.3, 1930:127-129).
30. Document E, Rajaraja Varma Raja (S.3, 1930:127-129).
31. This shows beyond doubt that a new conjugant need not be placed at the tail end of the kuuru-mura sequence, and also that the conjugant can be placed in a superior position than some of the conjugaters. One of the conjugaters involved in this dathetukkal was Ittunni, the new conjugant was placed as the uncle to him.
32. Document No. E, Rajaraja Varma (S.3, 1930:127-129).
33. Document E, Rajaraja Varma (S.3, 1930:127-129).
34. As in the dathetukkal that took place in the year (1630-31).
35. Document G, Rajaraja Varma Raja (S. 3, 1930:130-133).
36. Rajaraja Varma Raja (S.3, 1930:122).
37. Document E, Rajaraja Varma Raja (S.3,1930:127-129).
38. For example, Unnikerala Varma was conjugant from the Vellarappalli family and he became the *muppu* of both Deshinganad and Threppapur. For details, see Rajaraja Varma Raja, (S.3, 1930:120).
39. Document No. G, Rajaraja Varma Raja, M, (S.3, 1930:130-133).

40. Document G, Rajaraja Varma Raja (S.3, 1930:130-133).
41. For details, see Shivanshankaran Nair, (1993:123-25).
42. For details, see M.Doc. CC and M.Doc CCI, Velu Pillai, T.K, (1940: Appendix). There was a conjugant from Kolathunadu named Kerala Varma, who was the *ilamkuur* to the ruling king of Travancore in the year 1799. With his demise in the year 1799, there was nobody other than this Kerala Varma to succeed him, but his succession was challenged and he was sent back to Kolathunadu. In fact, the problem of indecisiveness about the legitimate successors had begun to surface by the early eighteenth century itself. The legitimacy or unique determinability of the kuuru-mura or this schemata itself was getting questioned over and again. For example, see Document No. F and Document No. E in Rajaraja Varma Raja. (S.3, 1930).
43. See Document G, Rajaraja Varma. Raja (S. 3, 1930:130-133).
44. By this time the Swaroopam organisation had been metamorphosing into a kingdom and the muppu vaazhcha was giving way for vaazhcha of the raja or king. But it should be pointed out that there was a difference between raaja bharanam and raaja vaazhcha. In this context, recall the distinction that we have made in the second chapter, between bharanam and vaazhcha.
45. M.Doc. CXXXIV, Velu Pillai, T.K, Vol. II, (1940: Appendix).
46. M.Doc. CXXXIV, Velu Pillai, T.K, Vol. II, (1940: Appendix).
47. M.Doc. CXXXIV, Velu Pillai, T.K, Vol. II, (1940: Appendix).
48. Then onwards the territory of Travancore was south of Cochin.

Chapter - 6

Truth in Custom and Customary Power Play

A trajectory gets opened up with the question: When and how does a legitimate successor take up the muppu vaazhcha of a Swaroopam? It explores the principles and procedures that are not intrinsic to either the swaroopam or the age/kinship diagram. Did the successors require the fulfillment of any requirement other than sanction of the kuuru mura diagram? Therefore, we will move on to the exterior of the diagram. Unlike the previous chapters, the analysis is not confined to the principles that determine 'which particular individual is the legitimate successor'. Here, another stratum of ruling of the self can be gleaned from the manner in which different formalised groups and individuals relate to each other within a shared aachaarakramam (the order of custom).[1] An analysis of aachaaram has significance in terms of legal history as well as in political and cultural analysis.

Let me introduce another agency, namely the brahminical sabha or ettarayogam[2] of the Padmanabha Swamy temple situated at Thiruvananthapuram devoted to the tutelary deity (Padmanabha-swamy). It was at the same time the deity of the swaroopams as well as the favourite deity (*Ishta Devan)* of Threppappur. Compared to the swaroopam, the *ettarayogam* as a unit of analysis has more or less similar importance (however this is not to say that they are professedly same in any ontological sense) as it engaged in power relations with the ruling elites; but then, their activities and interactive spaces were quite distinct. The Yogam had a role in the conduct of everyday affairs to those which had longstanding implications in the governance of the temple. This temple has gained a high reputation among the vaishnavaites well-known through Bhakti poetry and the people who maintained belief in the pantheon. Its reputation was not confined to the Swaroopam alone but it was the one which gained glory and power outside it as well[3]. The elite groups made both material and non-material investments on it and its rights over arable land was immense thus it was a site and effect of power relations.

The Yogam/sabha (I may interchangeably use Yogam and sabha. It is not clear as to when onwards ettarayogam began to be called as sabha) was primarily a Brahminical body to look after the temple affairs. It was a body consisting of seven Potti Brahmins, one Nayar noble and muppu.[4] The administration included everything from the executions of daily rituals to long term decision making. In the decision making process, the muppu of Threppappur was also part of the assembly of the sabha. In the co-existence of the Swaroopams, those in the diagram including the muppu and the body of the sabha shared a negotiated realm playing different roles and positions. It was the commonly shared aachaaram (I will be elaborating this term aachaaram soon) that combined and distinguished them and ordered their respective roles. There was another body of Pillamar/Nairs known as *Ettuveettil Pillamar*[5] which had a direct role in the affairs of the temple, especially in collection of taxes from the tenants of the temple land and the lands of the nobles within Threppappur. It is often said that if one can conceive the sabha as the brain, then the Ettuveettil Pillamar are the hands. It is the aachaarakramam or aachaaram which was commonly shared by the muppu, sabha/ ettarayogam and Ettuveettil Pillamar. At times, it is said that the muppu had little influence over the temple.[6] But elsewhere, another authority tells us that "It was the king (read as muppu) who appointed the highest dignitary of the temple, the swamiyar."[7] The presence of this swamiyar was indispensible for the sabha to conduct the assembly.[8] And therefore, the muppu had highhandedness over the sabha. Both these arguments are born out of the application of the sovereignty models and we will show that such statements cannot hold good, because the relation between the muppu and the sabha varied over time and across events. The relation was sensitive to how the aachaaram can be interpreted and invoked. It is proposed in this chapter that we see instances where the muppu was obliging the decisions of the sabha and occasions where the muppu was sidelining them. The discussions that are included in this chapter will touch upon such instances and occasions. Even when the muppu obliged the sabha, it was not because of the sabha's power over the muppu but because the muppu was obligated to the aachaaram as much as to the sabha, and this is one of the arguments of this chapter.

Therefore, let us look at the aachaaram more closely because it is the aachaaram that binds the muppu, sabha/ettarayogam and Ettuveettil Pillamar. In other words, there was a shared domain within which the selfhood of each of them have their specific place and function. Power relations could sprout when any one of them deflected from the perpetuated domain of the aachaaram in which their mutual interests intersected.

The lexicon translates aachaaram as 'usage', "established custom", 'reverence', "to observe good manner" etc[9]. In another dictionary, it is translated as 'custom', "traditional practice", "customary rites" etc[10]. But then, it is too cursory and thus we may move over to the classifications of it. The term's plural form 'aachaarams', are classified in varied ways, one classification differentiates it into shaastraachaaram (written aachaaram) and lokaachaaram (prevalent aachaaram) and recognizes several other differentiations of aachaaram in terms of caste, time, locality etc[11]. For instance, there are about 45 associated entries in a recent exegetic dictionary when it refers to this word, aachaaram.[12] I will be using aachaaram as "a practice so long established that it has the force of a law".[13] In verbal expressions, the term aachaaram was often suffixed by another term *maryaada* which means 'limit', 'boundary', 'custom', 'propriety', 'civility'[14] etc. Thus, aachaara-maryaada was a phrase that had the function of comprehending and judging activities within a normative anchor. The difference between the term and activity can be seen in the way they were treated in those days. In contra-distinction with the *aachaarakanakke* (written account of aachaaram) there was separate account for *chaithe* (activity), known as *chaithikanakke*.[15] Although acts of the rulers are to be fine-tuned to aachaaram and even if they differed with respect to the positions of them the aachaaram prevailed.

The chaithikanakke records the prevalent practices, events and incidents, be they ritualistic, political, social or not, which may be evaluated on the basis of the aachaarakanakke. The aachaarakanakke distinguishes three types of aachaaram, namely aachaaram, anaachaaram and duraachaaram. Aachaaram involves the observance of generally expected actions on particular occasions. Anaachaaram refers to deviations from the aachaaram without attaching any derogatory suggestions to it. Duraachaaram involved the breach of aachaaram or activities against it.

If chaithi, as in the chaithikanakke, is a concrete act, the aachaaram can be visualised as an abstract diagram that validates or invalidates or permits or denies an act (aachaaraprakaram). While the diagram of kuuru-mura, which we have been discussing is primarily distributive and hierarchizing; both are connected to the subjectification of individuals in general and swaroopikal in particular in different ways.

Further, the aachaaram is not embodied by any individual or collectivity as in the logo-centric conception of law and power that foist these things on the Lord or the state. It is something that is flexible circumstantially and temporally; nevertheless it is also something that is never to be willfully flouted and it is something to be willfully perpetuated. Thus, the aachaaram is something that does not vary across time and space in the case of the organisation of Swaroopams. In general, specific aachaarams differ from place to place, religion to religion and caste to caste etc.

It is something that cannot be changed by anyone, and if at all it changes, it changes by itself, through processes immanent in it. Such processes are self-justificatory. It is something that gives value and content to charanam (movement). The particular constituent elements of the aachaaram may change (aachaaraparishkriti)[16] but it as such does not disappear. It does not vary with time although its specifics may, and its operation is always context-specific and particular. It can be tested whether an activity is in conformity with it or not. The functionality of it could be seen most clearly in its transcendental existence and its independence from conjectures. It gives meaning and value to the movement in general and to one's process of becoming. It is omnipresent in the ebb and flow of social interactions, but even when it is 'universally'[17] applied, it is differentiated from within.

It is heterogeneous in the sense that groups can be differentiated in terms of the aachaarams that they follow. Each unit entity identifies itself with a diagram of the aachaaram and their relation with itself and others and with the world out there that is conditioned by it. This differentiation of 'one' from the 'others' on the basis of the aachaaram is not absolute or fixed, so there is a possibility that there existed other aachaarams which made their union possible, and wherein the 'you' and 'I' become merged into a collective 'we'. So both the integration and differentiation of the unit entities could be carried out on the basis of the aachaaram that one follows. The Aachaaram at the same time individualises unit entities with respect to the janmam (birth), role, position, space - Swaroopam, kuuru, graamam, deesham, naadu, kara, pradeesham, itam, etc. Though impelled by different aachaarams, disparate groups converge upon sites of collective activity as in the assembly of the sabha and create a common frame of the aachaaram. Therefore, the interaction and intersection among different aachaarams can be deciphered in the relations between identifiable groups or sets of people. It differentiates groups in terms of their respective aachaarams and maryaada[18] (custom, propriety, rule of society etc). While each one holds on to his/her own aachaaram, certain elements of an aachaaram may be commonly shared, and a relationship of mutuality gets constituted.

Aachaaram should not be understood in terms of whether it is written or not; aachaarakanakke existed in written form right from the medieval days. Rather, it should be seen as a segregated, rational, and normative diagram. It is something that lives alike in the soul of the ruler and the ruled (or any such differentiated and hierarchised social unit-entities). They are expected to uphold the aachaaram that they are supposed to adhere to and never to abandon it. It is, in turn, formalised as aachaarakramam, implying the existence of a regularised, proceduralised and ordered aachaaram which insists on regularity and recurrence.

Now let us turn our attention to the question to how the interactions between the muppu positions, the sabha and their mutual relations took place within a field of aachaarakramam. The interactions between the Temple sabha and the swaroopam involved and revolved round the aachaaram that was specific and more or less defined. There was an all-pervasive will—whether conscious or not—to perpetuate aachaarams, especially those which influenced the interactions between the sabha, the Temple and the swaroopam. In other words, aachaaram was ingrained within the muppu vaazhcha. Deviations from the aachaarams was thought to burn the soul of the deviant and the victim of the deviant action and anyone who become aware of such breaches; it was the deviations that made aachaarams to work most conspicuously, as they were instantaneously written down.

It can be safely assumed that no one would consider themselves as having the intention to breach or question the aachaarams as an end in itself.[19] The recognition of one's own being in this world was intimately related to one's activity-status evaluated by one self or by others in terms of the aachaaram; one was to observe one's aachaaram and one could not compel or influence others to deviate from it without committing anaachaaram/duraachaaram. Whatever were the differences in the specificity of the aachaarams that each one observed, in general, the existence of every person was embedded in the grid of the differentiated and differentiating aachaarakramam. The observance and perpetuation of one's aachaaram involved the recognition that others had their respective aachaarams to follow. The aachaarams were formalised in the sense that the manifold, specific aachaarams of the diverse unit-entities were never expected to contradict one another. There were formalised principles that made it possible to distinguish both anaachaaram and duraachaaram from aachaaram. I am not stating that aachaaram was in a state of stasis, but changes in it had to follow some or other aachaarakramam. The prevalence of a field of stable inter-relations among various individual social units was assumed in the aachaarakramam, which influenced or conditioned one's being and becoming in the world. The interrelationships between the Yogam and swaroopam, especially that which was related to the aachaaram of padiyettam (ritualistic succession) and daanam (donations to the temple and its dignitaries), needs to be viewed in the light of this.

With the discussion of the sabha, the inquiry once again turns to the intrinsic relations involved in the muppu vaazhcha. The multiple muppu vaazhcha persisted within an aachaarakramam that displayed its potential in perpetuating the co-existence of the Swaroopams as a 'constellation'.[20] The way in which knowledge about things, others and one's own self is closely implicated in one's relation with others and with one's self is well known. The manner in which the aachaarakramam functions is analyzed indirectly by explicating the relations among the swaroopams, the muppus of the Swaroopams, the sabha and Ettuveettil Pillamar.

After a brief account of select facets of the aachaaram and the interface between the sabha and muppu, this discussion moves on to a detailed analysis of the event known as padiyettam (literally, 'entering the gate', or 'ascending the steps of a temple'; in general, the initial customs followed at the temple as one succeeds to muppu). This exemplary event, when analyzed, sheds light upon the intricate and complex ways in which the aachaaram worked on individuals and joint actions. Padiyettam is an event that can be viewed as an instance when the aachaaram comes to the centre court in such a way that the judgment made on the basis of it had both symbolic and material implications.

The Diagram of Proceduralised Custom

One common factor that can be identified in the relationships between the muppu/Swaroopam and the Temple is the sabha, although there are others as well such as Ettuveettil Pillamaar. It is in the assembly of the sabha that the muppu and the members of the sabha converge as one, sharing a common aachaaram on behalf of the Temple. It is the shared belief in it and a devotion to the deity that combined them within it. In the sabha, the fields of relations that each of them (the members of the sabha and the muppu) maintain with the Temple intersect and bring into being a plane of sanctioned actions and reactions.

When we look into the documents on the affairs of the Temple, it can be seen that most decisions are formalised in the presence of the muppu and the members of the sabha[21]. It should, however, be remembered that this was not mandatory, for there have also been instances wherein decisions were taken independently[22]. Moreover, in certain cases, other representatives of various social groupings were also found to be involved in the decision-making process; the composition of this set is highly variable depending upon the purpose of the assembly. At all times, there would be a scribe (who wielded some power because he could be one of the swaroopikal). The question 'In what context did the specific composition of the decision-makers/ formalisers change?' is beyond the scope of this analysis, although the question is important.

In the present analysis, it is important to note that there were sets of activities which indispensably necessitated the copresence of the muppu and members of the sabha, and that in turn led to the constitution of a norm-bound interactive field among them. The copresence resulted in functions that ranged from minor ones like the settling of disputes between temple servants,[23] the removal and appointment of sweepers[24], the decision to regularly light a lamp in the Temple,[25] and the conduct of repairs in the temple[26] to major ones like large-scale architectural renovations[27], the appointment and removal of priests (especially pushpanjali swamiyar who presided over the meetings of sabha)[28], the issue of land grants (revenue from the land) and the conduct of extraordinary festivals.[29] The interaction between the sabha and the muppu became quite vivid when they converged to discuss 'the temple matters' and the succession to the muppu within the shared aaachaarakramam. (customary ritual procedures).

Customary-Ritual Procedures for Authentication

In the third chapter, it was seen that the situations that engendered sequential succession had no uniqueness. Now a possible trajectory of analysis is to inquire whether the muppu of a swaroopam was identical with the muppu of the Swaroopam. When multiplicity is a possibility, for reasons other than a lack of adequate members in the diagram, the relative seniority in age cannot alone be sufficient as the condition for sequential succession. If the specific place of a person in the diagram is what enabled him to become the muppu of the swaroopam, then does the assumption of the muppu vaazhcha in the Swaroopam involve the fulfillment of any other requirement? To put the question in different manner, when the muppu of a Swaroopam was to be the muppu in another one also, was there any requirement, like the conduct of the *padiyettam* rite (hereafter, 'the rite'; literally it suggest ceremonious climbing of the steps of the temple and it involves the giving of gifts to various individuals related to the temple) for succession. This rite had a multiple functionality as the conduct of it necessitated the consent of the sabha and several other elders.

Generally, it is argued that conduct of the padiyettam was 'an essential prerequisite' for initiating one's muppu vaazhcha and a way of legitimising one's authority in the affairs of the Temple[30], which was already political. Historiographically, this argument has undisputed prevalence for more than half a century in the so-called "palace histories", 'Manuals' and modern nomothetic or document-based scientific histories. It is also worth mentioning that at present, one comes to know about the successions under consideration through the 'written' paditharam[31] accounts ("scales of customary expenditure"). These accounts were made at the time of padiyettam of the Temple complex[32]. These accounts of the customary procedures, especially padiyettam, conducted at the Padmanabha Swamy Temple of Threppappur[33] and/or the Sucheendram Temple of Chiravay contain evidence regarding succession and years of reign[34]. This ritual procedure involves roles prescribed by the scriptures, customary offerings to the gods and the various functionaries of the Temple, and the observance of different rituals in the Temple.[35]

The existing interpretation is that it is a practice wherein one gets the necessary sanction to the muppu vaazhcha from the sabha and other elites belonging to the caste categories such as Pilla, Nair, Thampi, etc (*maatampies)*. This procedure was considered to be an indispensable gesture of allegiance towards the sabha and the Temple[36] that the muppu had to show at the time of succession. According to this interpretation, it was yet another inevitable authorisation that is required in addition to the sanction of the diagram which functions within the swaroopam. This means that legitimacy has to be accorded to the muppu by a body external to the swaroopam and kinship that is the conglomeration of sabha and maatampies[37]. It could also oversee whether the diagram was observed or not and if not it could have a contestation.

Nevertheless, it is demonstrated in this chapter that conduct of the rites was not an indispensable prerequisite under every condition or for every performance. It will be shown below that several activities of the muppu were performed and functions realised without it. Even if it was assumed to be a prerequisite, it acquired this status only when it was functionalised to achieve particular ends by the Temple sabha. Whatever may be the nature of the relationship (hierarchical, equivalent, circular or of dominant) existing among the sabha, swaroopam and muppu, the way they themselves got constituted and reconstituted within their mutual relations needs to be discerned. The mutual relations are magnified in the observance and conduct of the padiyettam, as various force-relations converge by referring to the aachaaram before it is conducted.

There is a field of aachaarams in which the activity-relations between the muppu and the Temple are perpetuated in a decipherable form. There is another field of aachaarams that encoded the conduct of the sabha with respect to the Temple. There is yet another field of aachaaram that gives shape to the mutual activity-relations between the two entities. These three fields should not be treated as exclusive or completely independent of each other and there are others not mentioned here; they are in fact mutually reflective. These fields define the possible and permissible interactions between the individual entities of the Swaroopam; still better, what ought to be the relation between them. As the padiyettam was a well-documented aachaaram, it provides us with an observable site where the three fields converge. However, it should be pointed out that performance of the rite should not be regarded as the sole site wherein these unit-entities converged.

The aachaaram-bound performance of this rite is of particular importance in the case of Threppappur as it was an integral part of one's simultaneous assumption as the muppu of the Swaroopam and of the Temple. The first visit to the Padmanabha Swamy Temple by the new 'seniormost', as part of the assumption of the muppu vaazhcha was an important event. This first visit to the Padmanabha Swamy temple, and also to other temples, involved ritual gift-giving to the temple servants and to the other dignitaries. Once it was accomplished, the possibility of any activity of the muppu getting questioned on the grounds of legitimacy of succession got foreclosed. The right to conduct it however rests on seniority in the diagram and the sanction from the sabha. Yet, by itself it was not sufficient for the realisation of all the potential functions of the muppu affecting the Temple[38]. The muppu vaazhcha of a Swaroopam involved a combination of the diagrammatic order that was formalised within the swaroopam and the other order, that is, the aachaarakramam of the Temple in which both the swaroopam and the sabha were implicated, or their identities were formed.

Rule Bound Game of Customary Procedure

The generally accepted proposition that padiyettam is an "essential prerequisite" for the muppu vaazhcha[39] can now be re-examined to decide whether this assertion can be retained in historiography or not. This is critical, because in the existing histories, the conceptualisation of the authority relations that existed between the sabha and the 'king'/ 'rulers' rests to a great extent on the conduct of this rite/procedure. If it was an inevitable prerequisite, the nonperformance of it should have disqualified any–one from performing the roles that were proper to the muppu position of Threppappur even if he was the senior-most in the diagram. If any instances are found wherein one had performed the muppu vaazhcha before fulfilling this 'prerequisite', then the assumption gets invalidated as per the methodology that enabled such arguments. The invalidation would be all the more drastic if a muppu vaazhcha under such conditions was found to be in conformity with the aachaaram.

Let me detail these propositions; Unnikerala Varma became the muppu of the Threppappur (S)swaroopam as per the diagram in the year 1607, but he conducted a padiyettam only in 1620. During these thirteen years, there were several instances in which he had performed roles unique to the Threppappur Swaroopam muppu[40]. These performances included appointments to distinguished positions in the Temple and the sabha. The required neettus (orders) were issued by him in his capacity as the Threppappur muppu. He acted as the Threppappur muppu both independently and in the assembly of the sabha. The fact that he was the senior-most was the sole justification for his activities. The non-performance of the padiyettam does not appear to have posed any problems, especially to the sabha. His activities in Threppappur/Temple were apparently not questioned in terms of the aachaaram of the non-conduct of the rite; that is, the nonconduct did not problematise his muppu vaazhcha. He had been recognised as the muppu not only by the Threppappur Swaroopam but also by the sabha, and they collaborated with him in materialising important functions of the Temple and the swaroopam. Therefore, although the padiyettam and muppu vaazhcha of Threppappur were related, the former cannot be generalised as a 'prerequisite' nor can it be viewed as an act conferring "freedom to the Sovereign".

Although this rite is not inevitable, it was an aachaaram that could be implicated in the interactive relations of power that connected the sabha, the Swaroopam and swaroopams. That is, the nonconduct of it could well be treated as an anaachaaram-bound performance, and, occasionally, it could turn out to be a duraachaaram in the muppu-Temple relations. Experientially, it could have been a compulsive obligation of being the senior-most in the order of the diagram. Before taking up these issues, it is necessary to schematise the main fields of the aachaaram within the Swaroopam organisation, wherein they are in an interactive relationship.

Deconstructing a particular instance of padiyettam can highlight the complex manner in which the interactive relations were interlocked within an aachaarakramam.[41] In the year 1607, Unnikerala Varma was to simultaneously become the muppu of Threppappur and Deshinganadu. From 1605 onwards, reconstruction work at the Padmanabha Swamy Temple had been going on[42]. These activities were initiated and executed mainly by the Chiravay Swaroopam. Quite often, the muppus and other elders of the different Swaroopams were physically present at Threppappur for this purpose. It suggests the importance that they had attached to the activity. By 1620, the reconstruction was completed and an auspicious date for the conduct of other rites—namely, kalasham (purification ceremony) and *mulayidu* (seed-sprouting ceremony in the Temple)—had to be astrologically found. It was at this juncture that the right of Unnikerala Varma to act as the Threppappur Swaroopam muppu got conditionally questioned. The peculiarity of the challenge was that per se his legitimacy or right was not in question; the objection was that he was not supposed to issue an *anugnja* (order) for mulayidu, a prerogative of the Threppappur muppu, before accomplishing the padiyettam in the Temple. This objection was raised in the assembly of the sabha. The tenor of the argument was that he should conduct it at least at this late stage; and one can glean from the moment and mode of raising the objection, the location of his subjectivity in the interactive relationship.

It is remarkable that Unnikerala Varma had been performing the roles of the Threppappur muppu without conducting it until this challenge was raised, but obviously he could do this by virtue of being the senior-most in the diagrammatic order. If he could not be recognised as the Threppappur muppu for the period between 1607 and 1620, as in the above objection, then it would imply that for thirteen years there was no Threppappur muppu. This, in turn, would mean that as per the aachaaram-, there would emerge situations in which no muppu existed even for a significant period of time. A kingdom without a king is an anachronism and outside the reason of the kingdom, but the Swaroopam can exist normally without any one assuming the position of a muppu as in the case of Threppappur between 1607 and 1620.

The situation during these thirteen years appears anomalous or anachronistic only when padiyettam is considered as a necessary prerequisite for the muppu vaazhcha of Threppappur. Further, one need not assume that the absence of any muppu invariably resulted in chaos or instability in the Swaroopam. Far from that, it is mainly during this period that large-scale mobilisation of wealth through the collaborative operation of various social groupings spread across different swaroopams culminated in the large-scale reconstruction of the Temple.[43] This collective operation of the reconstruction of the Temple has been described as the golden period of 'Travancore' or as an indication of the movement towards an aachaaram-bound unification of the "fragmented territories as the kingdom of Venad", a period which experienced exuberant diplomacy of the Chiravay muppu who gave the lead to the reconstruction activities.[44]

Whatever is the truth-value of such a characterisation of the 'period', what is apparent from the histories is that the value of the aachaaram had been celebrated by taking for granted and the 'observance and perpetuation of it' was an overwhelming preoccupation of the collective and individual consciousness. Just as the existence of a muppu had been crucial to the perpetuation of the co-existence of the Swaroopam units, it is also seen that a Swaroopam could engage in productive activities in the Temple without the presence of an active muppu for the Temple/Threppappur. Such activities were squarely within what the aachaaram prescribed. Even when Swaroopams were expected to have their respective muppus, the contrary situation was also equally possible; that is, the perpetuation of the identity of that Swaroopam as well as collaboration and collective action by different Swaroopams was possible. This shows beyond doubt that the direct equation between 'the absence of the muppu for a Swaroopam' or 'the absence of a ruler/king for a territory/kingdom" and chaos does not hold well. There were moments in the history of Swaroopams when the inevitability of a Swaroopam-muppu could be forgotten temporarily.

Along with the display of high esteem towards the aachaaram and a near perfect adherence to it, the reconsideration and alteration of aachaaram could also take place. Aachaaram can get problematised even when there is a strong bond among the social units, because there is a situation or context in which reconsideration of the event could be consistent with the aachaaram that necessitates the convergence of the sabha and muppus. The situation that we are going to talk about, in the following paragraphs, is an instance of reconsideration of the relationship between a muppu and the Temple sabha and the re-activation of a relation between the sabha and the muppu. Any intersection of the relationships between the three, which were in fact quite frequent, demanded coordinated action between the sabha and the muppu.

Compulsion and Aachaaram

With the completion of the Temple reconstruction, several ceremonies that had been discontinued during the interregnum were to be restarted, and the kalasham ceremony marked its beginning. That is, one can find the historical context of necessitating co-action between the sabha and the muppu. For this ceremony, the aachaaram had stipulated the physical presence of both the Threppappur and Chiravay muppu in the sabha. The aachaaram of jointly fixing and announcing the date of commencement of this ceremony by the Threppappur and Chiravay muppu had to be followed. Once announced, the decision was inscribed on the palm leaf (which was called anugnja) and issued to the Chief Thantri (high priest) of the Temple. The specific context and course of the reconsideration of the padiyettam and the repudiation of certain acts of Unnikerala Varma can be detailed now.

Ravi Varma, the Chiravay muppu who was the pivotal figure in the organisation of the Temple reconstruction, and Kerala Varma, the ilayathu (younger one) of Unni Kerala Varma (muppu of Threppappur and Deshinganadu according to the diagram) were present in the assembly of the sabha to initiate the procedures for kalashamatal and mulayidu. In the sabha, however, an objection against the adequacy of Kerala Varma to be the ilaya Threppappur-muppu and thus to be the representative of the Threppappur muppu was raised. The objection was not that the Threppappur muppu himself should be present and ilayathu cannot act on behalf of him for the occasion. The right of the Threppappur muppu to depute his brother as the ilaya Threppappurmuppu was also not questioned. The objection was that, only after Unnikerala Varma became the Threppappur muppu could his brother be the ilayathu capable of issuing anugnja on behalf of his elder brother. The objection was made while the aachaarakanakke (written account of aachaaram) was being read out in the sabha. This implies that, when the field of aachaaram that binds the muppu and the Temple is considered, once Unnikerala Varma performs the padiyettam, only then he would be recognised as the Threppappur muppu and only after that would his younger brother be the ilaya Threppappurmuppu as per the aachaarakanakke. So far as the former did not conduct the ceremony, he could be treated only as the Deshinganadu muppu. The muppu status was accorded by the diagram, and it was liable to be questioned in the assembly of the sabha on account of the respective aachaarams that the sabha and swaroopam mutually shared. The objection was raised especially because the issue at stake was an extraordinary ceremony in the Temple.

Even if one was a legitimate muppu of a swaroopam, the exercise of its full potential required the observance of certain aachaarams such as padiyettam, and this was independent of the order in the diagram. For example, there was an instance of a muppu designating his younger one in the mura as the *ilayamuppu* in order to give effect to the functions of the muppu position in the Temple[45] without any objection being raised against the act. He could do so because he had already conducted the padiyettam. Procedures like this defined the manner in which the muppu of a swaroopam was unquestionably recognised as the muppu of the Swaroopam. The legitimacy of this position in the Swaroopam was grounded in the aachaaram that defined the activity-relations among the muppu, swaroopam, sabha and Swaroopams. As far as Unnikerala Varma was concerned, he had been postponing the fulfillment of the 'obligation' while performing several other roles incumbent upon the Threppappur muppu; it was this practice that became objectionable.

As the objection was raised on the basis of the aachaarakanakke, Unnikerala Varma came from Kollam (Quilon) in Deshinganadu to the Temple and duly performed the padiyettam rite. After that, along with the Chiravay muppu he performed whatever was required of him. The reiteration of the aachaarakanakke was possible only within the proceedings of the sabha and under the specific conjuncture. It took place especially when the intertwining aachaarakramams of the swaroopam/muppu and sabha came to have a bearing upon each other.

The reiteration (recalling old palm leaf documents and reading it in the sabha)[46] of it itself was an aachaaram observed in the assembly of the sabha.

Both the Chiravay and Deshinganadu muppus were having interactive relations with the sabha and they also engaged in several activities of the Threppappur Swaroopam in different capacities, as per the aachaarams. During this entire period, no occasion had risen that required the reading of the aachaarakanakke pertaining to the non-performance of padiyettam. In other words, it was not only that Unnikerala Varma had been postponing the conduct of the rite but the sabha too, during the thirteen long years, had been postponing the deidentification of Unnikerala Varma as the Threppappur muppu. The way the aachaaram worked in determining inter - positional relations were extremely sensitive to the specific configuration of the unit-entities and the specific context of their interaction. It was the aachaarakanakke that gave force to the objection and compelled Unnikerala Varma to conduct the rite; there was a specific time and context, in which only the kanakke could be invoked. Neither the karanakkanakkan,[47] who reiterated aachaarakanakke, nor the dispositions of the sabha could be said to confer authority to the challenge.

To reiterate the recognition and derecognition of Unnikerala Varma as the Threppappur muppu was conditioned by the context, and the aachaaram determined the context in which aachaarakanakke could be invoked. Simultaneously, one was recognised as the Threppappur muppu irrespective of whether he had conducted the rite or not and the same person was also derecognised on account of the non-conduct of it. One possible explanation for such a situation could be that there were exceptionally important prerogatives of the Swaroopam muppu in the Temple that could be realised only after the padiyettam, as it would otherwise appear as an anaacharam, at least to the sabha. There were sets of activities in the Temple, the performance of which were conditional to the conduct of it and other activities that were free from any such conditional binding. If this was so, then the principles that made such a desegregation of the muppu vaazhcha possible became crucial.

A hypothesis that can be formulated now is that the differentiation was correlated to the intention of the agent in question, not the nature or type of activity or non-activity. The thirteen years lag in problematising the nonconduct of it is an indication of the validity of this hypothesis. When a muppu declared his intention to conduct some ritual in the Temple, with either spiritual or material purposes, then any anaachaaram that the muppu might have committed could be called to question by the sabha. This would be done in such a way that the intended activity would take place only after the termination of the anaachaaram or only after reparations for the anaachaaram had been performed. When the initiative for the co-action between the muppu and the sabha originate from the latter, the sabha can force the muppu to terminate his non-action/non-observance/non-performance. The conduct of padiyettam or the postponement and non-performance became a necessity for Unnikerala Varma, because it was in turn related to another necessity to follow his aachaarakramam that related him with the Temple as the muppu in the diagram and his subjectivity as a member of his swaroopam.

The Interface Between Compulsion, Acceptance and Self-Integration

The thirteen years respite culminating in the sudden reconsideration of the nonconduct of the padiyettam rite provides an instance wherein one can decipher the kind of interactive power relation that was possible between the muppu and the sabha. This relationship should not be considered stable over time and across specific interactive and co-active sites. There was reciprocity between the individual muppu position and the collective sabha. To both, the aachaaram of padiyettam was instrumental in determining their reciprocity. This aachaaram could, in different ways, be instrumental in the strategic relation between the two and their differing relations with the Temple.

For Unnikerala Varma, the purposive postponement of the rite was tantamount to the maintenance of a partial non-relation with the sabha. Several co-activities of them could be inactivated and certain supposed relations between them could be made dormant. Further, it was not so much the nonconduct of the rite[48] as such that was functionalised in the strategic move of the sabha. If it was so, then it would not have been necessary to separate permissible/conditional activities from nonpermissible/non-conditional activities of a muppu on the basis of whether he had conducted the rite or not. But the conduct of it as an aachaaram can be instrumental in the moves to alter or reset relationships between them. Any changed hierarchy between them had temporary effects on their interaction and co-action in the matters of the Temple. The important thing is that there had to be an aachaaram-based context and a proper co-action space wherein the 'nonconduct' could be functionalised to gain a relative advantage over the other. However, such contexts and spaces were few and took place far between, as in the thirteen years lag. The portrayal of their relations through 'static' or 'dynamic'[49] frameworks would thus amount to a mere mechanical reduction. This is especially so, for it is not just that their mutual-relations and relative positions varied over time but also that their identities differed across different sites of aachaaram bound activities.

When the question of the conduct of the extraordinary ceremonies at the instance of the completion of the renovation work of the Temple came up, it provided the context for the reading out the aachaarakanakke in the assembly of the sabha. The reading of it had to take place only as per the aachaaram that connected the muppu, sabha and the Temple. When 'nonconduct' was functionalised, it got implicated not only in the relationship between the sabha and the individual muppu, but also in the relation between the Temple and the muppu. The reconsideration took place within the aachaarakramam that related Unnikerala Varma with the Temple. The assembly of the sabha insisted was on the conduct of the rite in keeping with the aachaaram that was proper to the relation between the Temple and muppu. Thus, the sabha was only an aachaaram-bound mediating factor between the Temple and the muppu/swaroopam.

The sabha fashioned and presented itself as an aachaaram-observing subject in its relation with the Temple and the muppu. Invoking the aachaarakramam that defined the muppu and the Temple, it instructed Unnikerala Varma to terminate the anaachaaram. Rather than acting as an external force, it was found to operate by making every individuals internalise the aachaaram as something integral such that it in turn constituted their identities and inter-subjectivity. The preservation of one's identity thus became tantamount to the preservation of the aachaaram in which one's subjectivity was grounded. Such a subject position warranted the preservation of the sanctity of the muppu's relation to the Temple and also his worldly life in general; it was same with the members of the sabha also. It becomes most visible at the intersections of the activity-relations of different individual units and also in the relations that one maintains with one's own self. It operates in the field of inter-subjectivity of the individual units by entering into one's relation with others and with oneself.[50] Both the "technologies of self" and the "technologies of external persuasion and compulsion" were combined in the operation of it.

Exigency and Subjectivity

The event also provided an exemplar for the manner in which an exigency emerged and how it got formulated and later resolved. On account of this, the event is a window upon the 'reality' of the period in question. The sabha treated the postponement of padiyettam by Unnikerala Varma as an exigency in which both the sabha and muppu were implicated. Their respective positioning was governed by the mutually accepted and intersecting aachaarams. The event should be considered as the formulation of an exigency. The padiyettam as a pre-condition for the muppu vaazhcha is not to be taken as a reality that always mattered, but as something that acquired significance in the context of an exigency in the observance of the aachaaram. When conduct of it became imperative, Unnikerala Varma immediately ended his procrastination, although the 'nonconduct' was essentially intentional. His compliance with the instructions of the sabha for the non-compliance on his part could be construed as a disregard to the sabha and as such an anaachaaram in terms of his relation with the Temple. Basically, the reading of the aachaarakanakke only persuaded him to activate an aachaaram that he already knew about and the anaachaaram that he had been intentionally perpetrating.

As far as the relation between him and the sabha are concerned, after thirteen years his anaachaaram got foregrounded.

Another critical aspect to be noted about the event is that the 'reiteration of aachaarakanakke' introduces a temporal disjunction in the relation that was maintained by Unnikerala Varma with the Temple and also the mutual-relations between him and the sabha. It separates the relations into two, namely the pre-reiteration and the post-reiteration period. The fact that the aachaarakanakke had already been reiterated in the assembly of the sabha was one that added to the intensity of the exigency. Had the reiteration been not done, the postponement would have continued. It was only in the 'postreiteration' situation that the alteration of the intersubjectivity of the muppu and the sabha emerged as a problem. The thirteen years of combined postponement of it or the 'nonconduct' of it amounting to anaachaaram got terminated and this anaachaaram would have become a duraachaaram if the postponement had continued in the post-reiteration period. The exigency was articulated by creating a context to transform the anaachaaram into a duraachaaram. The definitiveness of the possibility of this transformation brought forth an immediate reaction from Unnikerala Varma. The way the muppu and sabha alter and realign their mutual activity-relations within the network of aachaarams that intersect at the Temple space/activity is now quite visible. The reality and the truth attached to the aachaaram may be viewed from another vantage point of view also.

The mutual relationship between the Swaroopam and the sabha could be deciphered at the points where their co-actions become necessary as per the aachaaram that connected them with the Temple. That was the way in which the sabha and the swaroopam/muppu were aligned in the aachaarakramam, and it was derived from the manner in which the aachaaram connected each of them with the Temple. The existence of the intersection and the need for co-actions within the aachaarakramam were the contexts of the formulation of the exigency and the persuasion/compulsion on Unnikerala Varma to conduct it. Under the 'postreiteration situation', the conduct of it was the first step to face the exigency and to satisfy the general demand for the conduct of the extraordinary ceremonies in the Temple. Here the relation and inter-action between the sabha and the muppu got reinstated. The aachaaram becomes active at such intersections among different groups rather than in the moments of conflict and independence.

In terms of subjectivity, the exigency seems to have been more severely felt by the "unaccomplished muppu" Unnikerala Varma than by the sabha, particularly during the post-reiteration period. As far as the sabha was concerned it was more a question of procedure and it was its functionalisation at the appropriate time that was important, while Unnikerala Varma's predicament was primarily ethical. Unnikerala Varma had to posit himself as an ethical subject within the internalised framework of the aachaaram that linked him to the Temple and therefore with the sabha. For thirteen years, he had maintained a rather indifferent relationship with the sabha, may be due to reasons specific to history (here, I am not entering into this history at all), and the aachaaram that linked them never demanded more than that. Perhaps this indifferent relation between Unnikerala Varma and the sabha explains the postponement of the rite, and it is the spiritual bond, which was rather strong, between Unnikerala Varma and the Temple that explains the termination of postponement that culminated in the compulsive act (compulsive, at least, as far as Unnikerala Varma was concerned).

Therefore, as a subject posited within the aachaarakram which shaped his subjectivity in Threppappur Swaroopam and the Temple, Unnikerala Varma had to be in a norm-bound relation with the Temple, it was beyond a problem of relating oneself with the sabha. It was one's relation with the prevalent aachaarakramam and one's subject position as a responsible muppu and devotee of the Temple that made possible the convergence of the sabha and muppu as in the exigency. Similar problems of subjectivity were involved in the relationship that was obtained between the members of the sabha, both as individuals and as a collective body, and the Temple.

Further, the sabha, swaroopams and Swaroopams should not be treated as homogeneous unit-entities, especially because there are differentiations within each of them. For example, in the event in question, there were two muppus, they could be treated as having the same relation with the sabha or with the Temple or the swaroopams. Like this, there can be differential self-interests among the members of the sabha;[51] however, this issue is not the direct concern of the present exercise. The aachaaram was invariant to the existent relation between the two muppus even though it implied differential effects on them and both of them were equally liable to conduct the rites. In the particular exemplar, Unnikerala Varma felt the aachaaram to be compelling, while both Ravi Varma (the muppu of Chiravay) and the sabha found this 'compulsion' both necessary and positive.

However one muppu was not placing the other under an obligation, as both were equally implicated in their shared aachaara-kramam and were impelled by it. The aachaaram did not emanate from either of them nor was it conceived as originating from any of the external bodies like people (naattaar) or the sabha.

The differentiation between the muppu vaazhcha of Deshinganadu, Threppappur and Chiravay Swaroopams took place within the shared aachaaram and their combined responsibility to the Temple. Although Ravi Varma wanted the compulsive act to take place, the aachaaram functioned in such a way that this compulsion had its origin in neither on him nor on the sabha. The body of the sabha did not insist on padiyettam and neither did Ravi Varma, but the sabha only articulated or reiterated the aachaarakramam and the reconsideration of the 'nonconduct' became a problem only when an aachaaram-governed context arose. In spite of this, the functionalisation of the aachaaram helped Ravi Varma celebrate his glorious deed, that is, the large-scale reconstruction of the Temple. Here the exigency was functionalised by Ravi Varma for his advantage.

Power and Persuasion

Unnikerala Varma had been reluctant to take up the Threppappur muppu position although this would have enhanced his claims to power. Focusing again on the subjectivity of Unnikerala Varma, what one can see is that he recognised the 'privileges and rights of Threppappur muppu' as obligatory, and he reluctantly participated in the 'opportunity' that he got to be the dual muppu. Even during the auspicious occasion of restarting the Temple affairs after a long discontinuity, he did not intend to be a participant in the occasion. The deputation of his younger brother was a derivative of this mind set. At the same time, he recognised that the delay in the reinstallation of the suspended ceremonies in the Temple should not be caused solely by his duraachaaram. This realisation persuaded and compelled Unnikerala Varma to go against his intention.

Let us look at this reluctance to power or the postponement of the sequential succession enabling dualisation by combining Threppappur and Deshinganadu. Although Unnikerala Varma respected the diagram and avoided any possibility of committing an anaachaaram to the Temple, there was an interstice between him on the one hand, and the sabha, Threppappur and Chiravay on the other. This was made visible by the force of the aachaaram because first, it got reiterated in the assembly of the sabha in the format of a kanakke (account) and second, this procedure itself got inscribed as a document with effects of power. The symbolic real gains of the Temple ceremonies at that time were to be accrued not so much by Deshinganadu or its muppu but by Ravi Varma of Chiravay who was in the forefront of the reconstruction of the Temple. The relative accrual of the benefits needs to be viewed not in terms of material gains or the authority over the people of Threppappur, but rather as symbolic and ritual gains; because the symbolism and rituals were perceived as more real than anything else in the inter-subjective relations[52] of those days. But then, the question remains regarding why Unnikerala Varma would want to take account of the relative gains. This takes us to see a trend in the interrelations among Deshinganadu, Threppappur and Chiravay.

It should be noted that in the process of the reconstruction of the Temple, both sabha and the Threppappur Swaroopam in general collaborated with Ravi Varma, who was simultaneously the Kulashekhara Perumaal of the Temple as he was the ilaya-Threppappur muppu and the muppu of Chiravay Swaroopam as well. This alludes to the unity (however momentary and flexible they might have been) that existed among them in the collaborative efforts. That is, their co-action had been positive as far as Chiravay, Threppappur and the sabha were concerned. It can also be discerned from the historical accounts that there were rifts between Deshinganadu Swaroopam and Chiravay Swaroopam from mid-sixteenth century onwards.[53] From the seventeenth century, the dualising combined Threppappur and Chiravay Swaroopams more frequently. There was friction between Threppappur and Chiravay on the one hand and Kunnummel Swaroopam on the other[54]. There were schisms between Deshinganadu and Kunnummel Swaroopams, as the latter did not recognize Unnikerala Varma's claim for the muppu position in Kunnummel. Deshinganadu attempted to appropriate land at a place known now as Kottarakara in the Kunnummel Swaroopam by the use of force, although the attempt to justify it by invoking the aachaarakramam in the year 1608 was not a success.[55] Unnikerala Varma, the Deshinganadu muppu, wanted to get dualised through a sequential succession to the Kunnummel Swaroopam in spite of resistance from it.

What is intriguing about this is that the same Unnikerala Varma had been reluctant to accept the muppu position in Threppappur even though there was unanimous consent about it. It is evident that there was no hesitancy on Unnikerala Varma's part in becoming a dual muppu in general, but there was a postponement of dualising by becoming the muppu of Deshinganadu and Threppappur. A realignment of Swaroopams could be found in this instance. Unnikerala Varma was to succeed to the muppu position of the Kunnummel Swaroopam, but this was prevented by the master plan hatched by the Chiravay and Threppappur Swaroopams. Perhaps Unnikerala Varma refused the 'privileges' of being the muppu of Threppappur as a gesture of resentment, and thus the postponement of the padiyettam and his non-participation in the 'major' events in the Swaroopam. Remember that the large scale reconstruction of the Temple took place with the initiative of the Chiravay muppu. This shows a unique kind of power relationship between the two muppu positions and between the Swaroopams within the possibility of dualisation.

In the documented proceedings that we have been contemplating, there is no suggestion of any compulsion for the continuous presence/ participation of the Threppappur muppu in the Temple activities, as even important deeds like the Temple reconstruction could take place in the pre-reiteration period.[56] But still, when there is an active muppu, his involvement could be seen even in the decisions concerned with routine things. In the muppu vaazhcha of the Temple, there was an interlocking of Threppappur and Chiravay as two distinct Swaroopams and this necessitated a co-activity of their muppus. The copresence of the sabha and both the muppus (Threppappur and Chiravay) was inevitable for several functions in the Temple. Without being the muppu of Threppappur, Ravi Varma, who was the Chiravay muppu and the Kulashekhara Perumal of Threppappur simultaneously, could involve in the affairs of the Temple[57]. It was he and his ancestors in Chiravay who were decisive in the reconstruction of the Temple and in settling other Temple- related problems including the dispute among the members in the assembly of the sabha. Finally, Ravi Varma announced the intention to conduct kalashamaatal to mark the reregularisation of the Temple affairs after the historical reconstruction of the Temple. But then, although as the Chiravay muppu his presence was inevitable to restart the Temple ceremonies, he alone could not initiate it. Such functions could take place only in the co-presence of both muppus. This was so for the aachaaram of the Swaroopams, especially because the diagrammatic order did not accept Ravi Varma as the Threppappur muppu at that point of time (it was this Ravi Varma who succeeded Unnikerala Varma in Threppappur). Had Ravi Varma ignored the aachaaram that linked the Swaroopams by overlooking the order, there after it would have amounted to duraachaaram. The Aachaaram allowed both Ravi Varma and Unnikerala Varma (even prior to his padiyettam) to perform certain acts in the Temple independently and it made certain another set of activities conditional and interlocked.

Now there is one more aspect with regard to the interlocking of the muppu vaazhcha in Threppappur; it was the co-activity of several Swaroopams in the Temple and the inter-locking of the Swaroopams in the matters of the Temple that gave distinctness/vitality to the Temple and the Threppappur Swaroopam. The preservation of this interlocking system corresponds to the perpetuation of the existent interrelations among the Swaroopams and swaroopams, however differently it may have benefitted them.

The transient nature of the compulsion that the sabha could inflict upon Unnikerala Varma or the supposed Threppappur muppu can be described now. This also brings out the way compulsions that were activated on the muppu by the sabha were made possible by the aachaarams that related them mutually. Elsewhere, we have seen the way the aachaaram-bound relation between the muppu and the Temple were functionalised in order to compel Unnikerala Varma to conduct the padiyettam. After that or after reinstating the relation between him and the sabha, Unnikerala Varma as the Threppappur muppu remained passive in the activities of the Temple. This shows that even after the conduct of the rite, his relationship with the Temple and his indifference to the sabha remained more or less the same; his degree of affinity with the other muppu named Ravi Varma also remained more or less the same.

Since the conduct of the rite in 1620, there had been a long time gap before his re-appearance in the activities in Threppappur. Only after twelve years did Unnikerala Varma come into the picture of the Temple and Threppappur. Once again, it was the inter-locking of the Swaroopams in the muppu vaazhcha of the Temple that necessitated and made possible the compulsion on Unnikerala Varma by reiterating the aachaarakanakku by the sabha. As a response to the suggestion that was put forward by the members of the sabha, both the muppus came together in the sabha and issued the requisite neettu that was demanded by the sabha[58]. The event of 1632 shows that, even after he was recognised as the Threppappur/Temple muppu by the sabha, during the post-reiteration period, he showed reluctance in paying serious attention to the functions that were proper to the Threppappur muppu. That is, the compulsion and persuasion that the sabha could effect on the muppu had been transient and it could not be exerted according to the 'free-will' of the sabha. Thus, any argument that presumes a more or less overarching and continuous hierarchy between them cannot be accepted. As we have already seen, the argument that the sabha had an upper hand over the muppu need not be so always. We also know that the appointment of the swamiyar in the sabha takes place according to the choice of muppu and the consent of the sabha. There is a document evidencing it.[59] We have evidences of the muppu removing one Pushpanjali Swamiyar from the position and bringing in another one as the swamiyar. This swamiyar held the highest position in the decision making in the sabha.[60] But yet, the removal of him could be executed by the decision of the muppu.

The re-convergence of both the Threppappur and Chiravay muppus in the sabha as it took place in 1632 can be viewed from a different perspective. To reiterate, when the Threppappur and Chiravay muppus came together at the Temple with the sabha to conduct the mulayidu, the sabha insisted that the proceedings should begin only after they together agreed to expedite certain procedures necessary for the regular conduct of the Temple affairs that were in accordance with the aachaaram.[61] Once the sabha insisted that the two muppus should jointly give word of assurance—which was getting postponed—the muppus, before their departure from Thiruvananthapuram (the seat of the Temple), made the orders to regularise the required rituals in the Temple. In spite of the skirmishes between the two Swaroopams at least since 1607, they came together within the field of the aachaaram as the members of the same set sharing something in common about the Temple. More than the power of individual will, what is apparent is the power functional in the aachaaram-bound collectivity.

The aachaaram worked in such a way that it differentiated and integrated the muppus and posited them equally within its myriad folds. Even if there were skirmishes between them, the collaborative performances took place when the compulsions of the aachaaram got activated and this in turn encoded the mutual relations among the muppus of the Swaroopams.[62] Such a 'conditional position' and 'conditioned patterns of relating' of the muppus within the folds of the aachaarakramam proves beyond doubt that the situation cannot be explained in terms of the strong-willed intention of the 'warlords', 'bandit kings', or strategic operators[63]. Strategic operations, an infliction of violence, or acts that alter the 'coexistence of Swaroopams' etc., could take place only within the aachaarakramam or within the justifying narratives of the aachaaram.

Even though there had been a realignment of inter-Swaroopam ties from the mid-sixteenth century, as we have noted above, the reality of the diagram and the truth of the aachaaram were quite tactile in the activity-relations. Now the question is, if Unnikerala Varma did not intend to be the muppu, then why did Ravi Varma, or someone else from the diagram, 'not' become the muppu of Threppappur; this is especially so since discontinuance and de-succession were normal. Was the diagram such a crucial matter among swaroopams that even when 'under' the condition in which the senior-most was unwilling to be the muppu, no one else could occupy the position, not even the Kulashekhara Perumal? Whatever be the answer to this question, it can be said that the reality of diagram and aachaaram encompassed every one. The operations by which the identities were mutually differentiated and the way the space for intersections among their activities was constituted within aachaarakramam may, however, differ. The effect of their interaction was distributed among the actors differently; the working of the aachaaram may have lead to hierarchy, domination or equivalence among the entities involved. Once any one was recognised to be within the fold of a specific aachaaram, then any indifference and breach of it could lead to several outcomes including the introduction of a new aachaaram (under certain conditions, which were rare). The Aachaarakramam and Pravrethikramam (order of activity, occupation or business) were immanent in one's being in the world, one's relation with others as well as with oneself. Further, mutual relations among the muppu, sabha and Ettuveettil Pillamar could be smoothened or made worse only by appealing to the aachaaram.

So far we have been concentrating on a rather short period wherein an instance of reading the aachaarakanakke took place in the sabha, which in turn was catalytic in the mutual-distancing between the sabha and muppu, and the point of reinstating—momentarily or not—the relations between them along with several other correlative relations. This reading or reiteration of the aachaarakanakke had been critical in terminating the persistent agent-based options. The act of reiterating it has bearing on the importance of the relation between the aachaaram, its written forms, its reading/recalling, and the way the positions and agents involved in the muppu vaazhcha interacted with one another. This event of reiteration leads us to the aachaaram that privileges writing and inscribing and how they were made to perpetuate and effect deviations from it.

From the first quarter of eighteenth century onwards, the conditions for the co-existence of the Swaroopams began to wane. Along with this, the self-identity of each of the Swaroopams were also waning for different reasons, such as reasons related to the organisation of the muppu vaazhcha and due to changes in trade with European countries and also with the British. What is more important for us to underscore is that the aachaarakramam that had been followed till then also got flayed. By 1750s, the Swaroopams and their co-existence became something of the past. Swaroopams were merged through war especially wars with Deshinganadu and Kunnummel Ilayetam. The wars of Thiruvithamkur with territories which never belonged to the four Swaroopams, about which we have been talking about, were also taking place, thereby extending the territorial expands of it. All these together bid farewell to Swaroopams and their co-existence. Moreover, the continued aachaarams got rewritten and reconstituted in tune with the fury of the guns of the king of Thiruvithamkur and the swords of the 'new satellite elites'. What was considered as anaachaaram during the time of the co-existence of Swaroopam with its own identity was metamorphosed as a new aachaaram.

The next chapter takes up a detailed analysis of the relationship between the aachaaram and writing and representation of the past. This shows the way in which the sabha, those of the swaroopam involved in the muppu vaazhcha and others (who were directly or indirectly mentioned in the documents) recognised the need for recording and hence developed a mass of material documents with which they were in turn inextricably linked. This would show how the aachaaram, once activated, was indispensably linked to itself through the processes of writing, preservation of the written-documents and in the recall of past through it. Some of the conclusions of that chapter would question the general belief that the medieval 'Orient' had custom and not law[64] and also the notion that it had been far removed from any kind of 'writing cultures'.

Notes

1. Here the term custom does not mean unwritten law, but a set of normative principles that bind human relations and their relations with the corporeal and other worldly worlds.
2. For the structure and composition of this brahminical institution which had right to administer the day-to-day as well as ceremonial matters of the Temple, see Maheshwaran Nair, (1975).
3. (Lakshmi Bhai, 1998)
4. For details about the *sabha* and *ettarayogam*, see Shivashankaran Nair. K, 1993.
5. *Ettuveettil Pillamar* belonged to eight houses namely Marthanda-matham, Ramanamatham, Kulathur, Kalakkattam, Venganur, Chempazhanthi, Kutaman and Pallichal. These were not only the names of their houses alone but the villages to which they belonged.
6. Nagam Aiya. V, Vol I, (1906:304).
7. T. K. Velu Pillai, Vol II, (1940, 1996:207).
8. T.K. Velu Pillai, Vol I, (1940, 1996:206).
9. Gundert, H, (1872:75).
10. M.I. Warrier, E.P. Narayana Bhattathiry and K. Radhakrishna Warrier, 1999, 2011, *Malayalam-English Dictionary*, D.C. Books, Kottayam.
11. Gandert, H, (1872:75).
12. B. C Balakrishnan, (1974) *C. V. Vyakhyaanakoosham*, Vol. I, C.V. Ramanpillai National Foundation, Thiruvananthapuram, (pp. 380-82).
13. Ramalingam Pillai, (1956, 2010) *English-English-Malayalam Dictionary*, D.C Books, Kottayam.
14. Gundert, H, (1872:794).
15. For an example of *chaithikkanakke*, see M.Doc. CLXXXVI. Velu Pillai. T.K, (1940).
16. B. C. Balakrishnan, *C. V. Vyakhyaanakoosham*, Vol. I, (1994), C, V. Ramanpillai National Foundation, Thiruvananthapuram, (pp. 380-82)
17. A universe of heterogeneity.
18. In the general instances where the term *aachaaram* appears, it is used along with the term *maryaada* also, that is, it commonly appears together as *aachaara-maryaada*.
19. For example, when a *muppu* deviates from the way he was supposed to behave in the matters that related him with the *sabha* and the temple, then it is called a *sanketham azhikkal* which was considered as a deed that should be later reprinted; see Rajaraja Varma, M, (S.8:1931:97).

20. The word 'constellation' should be understood in its difference from those conceptualisations that are grounded in the antinomy between the 'total' and 'parts'. This phrase is chosen because everything is related to everything else, similar to the way a star is independent of others as it has its own orbit and powers to be 'effective', while at the same time every star is mutually related. The mutual relations among them do not negate any 'one's' existence.
21. For several documents on the pronouncements of Threppappur *muppu* on the matters of removals and appointments of not only higher positions but also lower level positions in the temple; for details, see Maheshwaran Nair, K, (1975). It contains evidence that cover the period 1490 to 1568. All these suggest that there was no distinction between the important and unimportant matters of the Temple from the point of view of the copresence of the *muppu* as well as the *sabha* in issuing the relevant *neettus*.
22. Maheshwaran Nair, K, (1975:9091).
23. M. Doc. VIII, Velu Pillai, T.K., Vol. II, (1940: appendix).
24. Document No. 2, Parameshwara Iyer, S, (1962).
25. Document Nos. 19, 20, 25 and 30 Parameshwara Iyer. S, (1962).
26. Document No.14, Parameshwara Iyer, S, (1962).
27. Document. Nos. 9,10, and 237, Parameshwara Iyer, S, (1962).
28. Document Nos. 38, 44 and 68, Parameshwara Iyer, S, and Document No. 1, Maheshwaran Nair, K, Vol. I, (1974).
29. Document Nos. 1, 8 and 72, Parameshwara Iyer, S, (1962).
30. Rajaraja Varma, M, (1931:9798). Also see for a contemporary reconfirmation of the same argument made in the above reference, Ganesh, K.N, (1990:1920).
31. The literal meaning of the word *paditharam* is 'rule', 'custom' etc., Gundert, H, (1872:598).
32. The term 'complex' is used here to suggest the 'pantheon' structure of the temples and the pantheistic form of devotion and worship.
33. Here after Sri Padmanabha Swamy temple would be denoted with the word 'Temple'.
34. For example, see, Rajaraja Varma, M, (1928 & 1930) and Parameshwara Iyer, S, (1961).
35. For details, see Rajaraja Varma, (S. 8, 1931:98).
36. Henceforth, the terms Temple and *sabha* would denote Sri Padmanabha Swamy temple in Thiruvananthapuram and its *sabha* known as the *thiruvaananthapurathu sabha* respectively.

37. For details about the structure and composition of the *sabha* of the Temple see Maheshwaran Nair, K, (1970).
38. This point will be exemplified later on.
39. For Rajaraja Varma, M, (S.8, 1931:97) *padiyettam* is tantamount to the "grant of freedom" to the sovereign over the Temple centered *sanketham*. For a contemporary historian, the conduct of *padiyettam* "was an essential prerequisite for the eldership of Threppappur"; see Ganesh, K.N, (1990:20).
40. Document Nos. 231 and 232, (both refer to the year 1613); Document Nos. 234 and 235 referencing to the year 1618, Parameshwara Iyer. S, (1961). Also see Document No. 22, Maheshwaran Nair. K, Vol. 1 (1970).
41. This event is constructed and discussed about with the help of the Document No. XV, Rajaraja Varma Raja M, (1928).
42. Document. XV, Rajaraja Varma, (S. 1, 1928:21).
43. Shivashankaran Nair, K, (1993:112).
44. For details, see Shivashankaran Nair, K, (1993:114-125).
45. Document No. XI, Rajaraja Varma, M, (S. 1, 1928:19).
46. Such recalls and reading it in the *sabha* will be taken up in the next chapter.
47. The particular *karanakanakkan*, namely Ayyappan Ananthan, who read the *karanakkanakke* in the *sabha* and declared the criterion for the treatment of Unnikerala Varma's brother as the *ilaya*-Threppappur *muppu*, was appointed by Unnikerala Varma himself two years prior to the event in question. For details, see Document No. 234, Parameshwara Iyer, S, (1961:269). As the reading of *karanakkanakke* being an *aachaaram*, the question of loyalty of the *karanakanakkan* towards the person who nominated him would not arise at all.
48. For thirteen years the *padiyettam* had nothing to do with Unnikerala Varma's *muppu vaazhcha* in Threppappur.
49. The categories, static and dynamic, are concepts of mechanics.
50. The relation that one constitutes with oneself should not be read as the one that gets constituted in and through 'knowledge', but as a subject who gets posited and posits himself in and through *aachaarakramam*.
51. Document No. XV, Rajaraja Varma Raja (S1, 1928:21).
52. For an analysis of the way signs, narratives and truth were discursively combined and the way it worked in the Kerala society, see Raju, S, (1991).
53. Shivashankaran Nair, K, (1993:9292) and Nagam Aiya, V, (1906:301), also see a poetic version in *Anchuthampuran pattu*.

54. Ravi Varma goes to Madurai and buys forty horses in the year 1607 and in the next year he goes to fight against the Kunnummel *Swaroopam* near Quilon; see Document Nos. 217 and 220, Parameshwara Iyer, S. (1961).
55. Shivashankaran, Nair, K, (1993: 97).
56. The fact that the Chiravay *Swaroopam* could conduct the construction activities in the Temple, which is the family temple of the Threppappur *Swaroopam*, testifies either that it could legitimately be done by the Chiravay *muppu* as he was the same family member (if membership in the family mattered in such instances) or that such differences did not matter in expending wealth on such institutions. An expenditure of such kind always elevated the relative position of the donor. For instance, during 154551 there were disputes between the Deshinganad and Chiravay *muppu* that resulted in activities that violated the prevalent *aachaaram* of resolving conflicts. Later, both of them, as a gesture of atonement, expended wealth on the Temple. (Nagam Aiya, V. (1906:301).
57. M.Doc. CX, Velu Pillai, T. K, (1940:78) and Document no. 226, Parameshwara Iyer, S, (1961: 261).
58. For example, see Document Nos. 236, 242, 243 and 144, Parameshwara Iyer, S, (1961), Document No. 3, Maheshwaran Nair, Vol. 1, (1970), and M. Doc. CXVIII, Velu Pillai, (1940:84-85).
59. Document No. 78, Ulloor S Parameshwara Iyer, (1941, 1961:100-102).
60. Document No. 47, Ulloor S Parameshwara, Iyer (1941, 1961: 71-72).
61. M.Doc. CXX, Velu Pillai, T.K, (1940:86-90).
62. There is an argument that the *sabha* had the power to bring different *Swaroopams* into a unity, and this should be corrected by noting that it is not so much of the capacity or power of the *sabha* but the fact that in the domain of the Temple there are several mutually accepted *aachaarams* and *aachaaram* bound activity relations like the interlocking of the *muppu vaazhcha* in the Temple which structure and restructure the inter-*Swaroopam* relations.
63. As Unnikerala Varma was showing reluctance to be the Threppappur *muppu* in any significant way, it could have been justifiable, counter factually, for Ravi Varma to conduct the *padiyettam* and to be the *muppu* of Threppapur. But that option was never chosen nor exercised. Even if Unnikerala Varma showed such reluctance, it is also true that he could not desucceed from the position.
64. A differentiation is achieved by differentiating social orders in terms of 'writing'; one is written and the other is not.

Chapter - 7

The Custom of Archivalisation: Writing and Right to Rule

In the previous chapter, I had explicated that the customary power play involved in the organisation of Swaroopams and their co-existence was closely related to documentation or to written documents. This chapter focuses on this relation by elaborating on the intricate practices involved in writing documents, their modes of classification and highlights the instances of recalling them even at a much later stage. The documents are recalled at a future time and therefore they are retained in the 'archive' for repeated recalls; therefore, retention is a key concept in this process of documentation besides recall. Such documents in general are known as Mathilakam Grandhavari (this refers to those cadjan leaf records related to the Padmanabha Swamy Temple). I am referring only to the Mathilakam Grandhavari of the Padmanabha Swamy Temple although there were many other institutions and 'houses' where such documents were written and maintained. "... the autonomous temples and temple-states wrote and preserved all the records in respect of the lands and men under their sway. In addition to this, there were some villages ... exercising power independent of the king. They too developed their own system of record-keeping with a view to improving the efficiency of their working."[1] However, I will confine my attention exclusively on the Mathilakam Grandhavari of the Padmanabha Swamy Temple[2]. Among other reasons, one of the attractions for me to choose it is that I have consulted this document set. Over and above this, the "Padmanabhaswamy Temple constitutes the largest and the most fabulous native record-hoard ever discovered in Kerala. These records have singular importance from many points of view, historical, linguistic, palaeographic and archival."[3] In short, what is intended here is to elaborate on the classification of documents, those who maintained them, and how centuries old documents were repeatedly recalled at different points in time. Such recalls always had a crucial role in resolving issues related to various types of power relations prevalent at the time of such recalls.

Such documents have been conserved at least since 1304[4] and the total number of them amounts to about three millions even after the decay and relegation of thousands of them over time. "The temple abounds in riches of all descriptions, but the richest assets are the countless charunas of records heaped up there. In this respect the Padmanabhaswami temple is quite unrivalled by any other in stitution of the kind in the whole of India."[5] Additional efforts were made in 1425CE to procure more documents and preserve them (Thekkumbhagam, Mohan, 2011:70). There are documents dating back to 840 AD. This temple is mentioned in some of the extant texts well known as Sangam literature (500 BC to 300 AD).

Such a splendid wealth of records/documents should be read along with the fact that this Temple is well known as one of the wealthiest temples in the world which retained fathomless treasures. In the year 2011, different vaults of the Temple were opened following the instructions of the Supreme Court of India and a conservative estimation of the treasure at market price was close to 1.2 lakh crore rupees (about one trillion US dollars). It should be noted that this estimate does not include the antique and cultural values. This treasure includes gold coins and artefacts from the Chera, Pandya, Thiruvithamkur, Kolathiris, Mesopotamian, Greek and Roman kingdoms.[6] All these indicate that both in terms of the stock of historical documents/records and historically inherited treasure, this Temple has immense importance. However, in this chapter my concern is solely on the treasure of the documents and not on the treasure of material wealth.

These documents were not preserved or archived not to be passive but to be recalled to substantiate decisions "in the present" at least till the first half of the nineteenth century. These documents, especially these cadjan leaf documents, were not mere written materials stacked at the remote corners of archives; it was substances which become vehemently vocal with authority whenever they were recalled. They were recalled to make sense of the present events of importance or disputes or to decide what needed to be continued and discontinued. In short, they were recalled to make judgements about the present in terms of the past. That is how the aachaarams became a perpetuation. The writing of the present events and proceedings, and the preservation of them to be recalled in future can be termed as a process of 'archivalisation'. These processes were indispensable to those who were in the worlds of ruling or writing. In other words, the comprehensive (although elusive) term used in this chapter to capture the different dimensions of documentation and their circulation with effects of power is archivalisation. The concern here is to explore how one can discern the ways in which these 'cadjan documents' were embedded in the acts of ruling oneself as well as others. Some variety of Orientalism argued that there was no culture and history of writing every day matters in this part of the globe; but this chapter undermines such arguments. To illustrate, in the year 1811, there was an instance of the recall of old documents which traced events from 1335. We will return to such empirical details as we progress with our depiction.

The attempt here is not so much to refer to the content of the documents but to delineate the manner in which the documents and rulers were mutually related. The 'everyday life of the archivalised documents' touched the common man as well as the rulers with their proclamations, revenues-expenditure, rituals and so on. Those involved in the muppu vaazhcha recognised written palm leaf accounts as self-evident authority and generated a mass of written documents with which they were in turn inextricably entangled. It is possible to argue that even those who were directly or indirectly referred in them also got placed within its orbit. That is, this archive related the past with the present; they were active forces revealing the past for the present. And perhaps they were influential in coursing future historical choices as well. The extent as well as the complex ways of documentation will also be brought forth here by examining the events of recall of the past with the aid of such documents; the importance of writing in perpetuating and constituting a prevalent 'order' in this world will also be touched upon.

Before getting into the historical details however, mention could be made about the kanakkupura where these records were kept. It is important to underscore that the kanakkupura was not only the house where the records were retained and preserved but also a place where the records/documents were written as well. kanakkupura can be divided as kanakku + pura. The term kanakku lexically means account, but it has wider denotations "... it includes all sorts of records like sale deeds, proceedings, instruments, royal edicts, proclamations, circulars, memoranda etc."[7] Pura literally means building, house, room etc. Therefore, Kanakkupura means "house or room of accounts". It was important that its location was a part of the Temple complex, that is, at the south-west corner of the Temple. Its location changed over time as renovations and reconstructions of the kanakkupura took place. In this chapter, Kanakkupura and archive are used as if they are interchangeable, while clearly being aware that such a translation has all the problems inherent in any translation. But towards the end of this chapter I will show that Kanakkupura is not tantamount to archive.

Besides the Kanakkupura, there was another edifice known as the Karuvelappura Malika, possibly constructed by Marthanda Varma which stored the revenue records collected from the land endowed for meeting the Karuvelamkulam Chilavu.[8] This implies that the kanakkapura was not the sole store house of records/documents. There were record rooms in the palaces of Threppappur, Chiravay, Deshinganadu and Kunnummel Ilayetam etc. At this juncture, let me turn towards the details about the classification and the category complex of the archive, especially the kanakkupura.

Scheming: Classification and Categories

To get to know an archive, it is pertinent to look at the ways of listing, arranging, classifying and the classification of the classifiers.

I have detailed the ways of punctiliousness involved in classifications to unravel the importance attached to archivalisation. I have carried this out by invoking different terminological complexes and referring to the terms of classifications. However, I do not provide the meaning for them as what is important for us is not so much the meaning of them but the abundance and variety of them. That is, the intention is to highlight the enormity of the terminologies to illustrate the punctiliousness.

The Vyavaharamala, one of the law texts, classifies archives into three broad groups. They are Rajalekhya, Sthanalekhya and Svahastalikhita.[9] Once again, whatever may be their meanings, for our purpose it is sufficient to know the intricate classification in order to bring forward the conscientiousness involved in the maintenance of the archives. Now, the documents in these three types are sub-classified into ten. A few of them are the following: the *Danalekhya* recorded the permanent grant of land to an individual, but this land could neither be appropriated, nor it could be dispensed under any circumstances. The *Simalekhya* was a document executed at the time when boundary disputes were settled. The *Karayalekhya* has correspondence with the present day sale-deed. The realisation of the Samihitarth' records the achievement of the desired object. The Uddampatra resembles a promissory note. The verdict pronounced on a controversy was called Jayapatra. The Sandhipatra was an instrument of mutual agreement signed by both the parties after burying the hatchet (Maheswaran Nair, K, AAAT). Another text known as *Keralakshitiratnamana* speaks of a six-fold classification of records.[10]

The text *Lekhapaddhati* or *Lekhapanchasika* which deals with the science of archives refers to 40 main classes of records[11] and 52 types of archives. In another text, we read archive classified into three sub-divisions. The text *Prasastiratnakara* or *Dalapatriya* divides the archives into three sub-groups. They are: *Sandesatmaka* which refers to communication (yet it indicates action, judgement, refusal, pleasure, grief etc. as well), *Vyavaharatmaka* which are files of official business and branches of agreements and *Nidesatmaka* which are executive orders issued by the muppu and nearby authorities. Similarly the

Chirika type of archive is classified into 31 types by Kshemendra. What is interesting here is to note the intricacies involved in archive maintenance and different classificatory schemes which in turn reveals the importance attached to written documents and their retention. For timely recall, the classification and arranging the documents are extremely important if not indispensible.

The *Lokaprakasa* of *Kshemendra* classifies *Hundika* (giving and taking of money for the convenience of traders) into five types[12].

Now let us move on to the content of a certain type of record, known as *adhara* which means "record in evidence of a transaction or deed". It is stipulated that it should have the following particulars: the year, kind of the instrument, tenant's name, amount of consideration, description of the land, nature of title, amount of tax, possession, time of disposal enjoyment, time of purchase, name of the buyer, names of witnesses and name of the document writer.[13]

So far we were dealing with the texts in which the archives and documents/records are classified, taking care of minute specificities with meticulousness. The archive of Travancore has a long list of 76 categories; although the list is labyrinthine, I have purposefully invoked them in the main text without leaving them in the footnotes with a view to emphasise the conscientiousness, meticulousness and precision that went into the classification and categorisation of documents in the archive. It might have helped the timely and quick recall of them at the spur of the moment of need. This classification is made on the basis of subject matter. I am listing the categories in detail, although it is cumbersome, to intimate the readers that punctiliousness and conscientiousness are quite amazing; not only amazing but flabbergasting. The list of the categories in terms of the content is the following[14]: *Vilangipper, Oluku, Thirattu, Anuvu, Grandhavari, Variyola, Divisavariyola, Sankada Variyola, Ayakkettu Variyola, Ayakkettu, Ayakkettu Thirattu, Pramanam, Danapramanam, Udakapurva Dharmadana Pramanam, Ninavu, Pathivu, Chatta Variyola, Neettu, Samuahti Neettu, Sadhanam, Pattola, Masantha Pattola, Thrumukham, Kaicheettu, Sannathu, Kalpana, Vilambaram, Eradavu, Hukkumnama, Thavamudakkam, Thiruveluththu Vilambaram, Kankanikkankku, Karanam, Thiruvadayula Karanam,*

Ekaththuka Thirattu, Thuka Thirattu, Kuri, Kurimanam, Chettu, Parru Chettu, Pathivucheettu, Tharaku, Adayola oradamannola, Chattola, Panampola, Moli Ola, Valivattola, Ola, Orri Ola, Nila Orri Ola, Chora Orri Ola, Vilayola, Munnorri Ola, Chirrorri Ola, Mun Ola, Palaya Ola, Pidipadu, Pokkuvaravu, Sammatha Pathram, Thavanakkanakku, Thandapper, Thavana Thirattu, Theeroha Peredu, Vattavari, Cheruththirumukham, Sakatimukham, Irayill Ola, Melkankani Kanakku, Sri Pandarakkanakku, Karanakkanakku, Arulichchapadi Neetu, Danasadhanam, Adharam, Thiruvullachcheettu, Kayitham and Pidipadu Ninavu.[15]

Whatever be the meaning of each of the categories, what is important is to note the enormity of the categories and the subtle differences among them. To repeat, all this reveals or bring forth the energy that might have gone into the archive maintenance and the significance given to the documents. It also reveals the close nexus between document and the exercise of power. For the authorities to rule according to custom there should be a custom of maintaining an archive staked with documents that have authority. Now let us move on to look at who were the authorities of drafting and writing these records to glean an idea of the subtle differences among them and the conscientiousness involved in classifying the classifiers.

The Mathilakam documents were also classified into different series such as *pandaarakkanakke, chaithikkanakke, karanakkanakke, naalvariyoola, aachaarakanakke, chattavariyoola* with each of them entrusted with *kanakkans* (I will be elaborating the meaning and significance of kanakkans later; for the time being let us consider that they were those who document and were entrusted with documents). To begin with, the kanakkans had specialisations such as *karuvelamkanakkan, pandaarakkanakkan, acharakanakkan* and *karanakkanakkan* etc. This specialisation without the erosion of subtle differences alone is capable of suggesting the existed erudition, meticulousness and energy that went into the arrangement of the archive. Besides, the desegregated responsibility reveals the purposiveness involved in an easier and timely recall of the documents whenever the need arose. The *karanakkanakkan* was not merely a scribe or an accountant of events, material exchanges etc., more than that he was the accountant of the documents and the one who read the documents when and where the aachaaram required him to do so; he reiterated before the sabha what was pertinent in the documents. In fact, close affinal relatives and confidantes of those in the muppu vaazhcha form of rule occupied these positions. The aachaarakanakke was a basis of the actions and reactions between the various positions in the sabha and those who came under the referential field of the activities of the Temple. It can be proposed at this juncture that the material documentation was a formalised operation with stratified kanakkans and classified documents on the basis of the content.

There were different types of kanakkars (those engaged with drafting and writing the records, chroniclers, those who minute, etc.) who had a prominent place in the organisation of the Swaroopam and the conduct of the Temple. These chroniclers were not merely scribes, but ones who had authority in the matters of the Temple and they may have had kinship relations with the Swaroopam, that is, they might have been one of the swaroopikal. As mentioned earlier, there were four types of kanakkar of the Temple, they were the karanakkanakkan, pandarakkanakkan, acharakkanakkan and the kilkanakkan. In addition, there were the Karuvelathukanakkan and the Karuvukarakkanakkan. One finds another position known as the Sri Pandarakkakku in the Temple.[16] Yet another kanakkan was the paniarakkanakku.[17] On and above, there were a corpus of subordinate kanakkans. The kanakkans were at the same time drafters, writers, signatories, custodians and retrievers/re-callers of Karanams or documents/instruments. They did all these functions within the kanakkupura; of course as we will see later, the recalled documents were read out in the sabha.

The karanakkanakkan had a special and distinctive function as he was the one who wrote and wrote and maintained the proceedings and transactions of the Ettarayogam. "Moreover, a good number of records say that the communications to the Yogam were at least placed under the custody of the karanakkanakkan and that the previous records relating to the temple were under his custody.")[18] The term karanam means document, instrument etc. The semantics of the usage of the karanakkanakkan clearly brings forth that he is the custodian, and the one who drafts, writes, maintains and retrieves the documents pertaining to the present and past.

In one of the texts on the archival administration in ancient Travancore, the author concludes that:

> ... we have to think that in times of yore in Travancore certain well-established principles and well accepted procedure were adopted in the appointment of an accountants. This was in view of the serious nature of the functionary who handled the temple archive which played a vital role in the administration and routine affairs of the Padmanabhaswamy Temple. (Maheswaran Nair, K, AAAT, p. 55)

Given the importance of the documents or records and their drafters, it is important to examine how the documents used to appear in the sabha or in decision making. The six categories of kanakkans correspond to six types of documents that each of them was the writer, signatory and custodian of. Let me pay attention to one of the aachaarakanakke to show the circulation of the documents and its activation.

The Passages of Documents

The kanakku or records, especially the aachaarakanakke (the enunciated custom) inscribed by the aachaarakanakkan, preserves the ways in which people inter-acted with each other and related with the material, institutional and religious worlds. Extensive documentation in turn generated new documents that refer to the manner in which people related with the old and new documents. Documentation as a process generates new documents that have referential relations with pre-existing documents and their recalls. Documents, in short, generate documents about themselves also, which I refer to as inter-documentation. Such practice was an integral force in archivalisation.

The processes involved in archivalisation can be classified into six, they are the following:

1. Documentation of contemporary events and regularities (however selective and prejudiced they are) with a view to preserve those documented facts.

2. Re-inscription of them from time to time to prevent them from decay.
3. Documenting the events of recall of the documents belonging to the past to judge the present, and it is likely that they are centuries old.
4. Documentation of what had been recalled from the old documents by way of inter-document relation.
5. Documentation of what all had been recalled in the past recalls.
6. Documentation about how they were classified and who were responsible for the different types of them. This implies that each documentation of the present anticipated or expected its recall in the future and thus its entry into power relations. We will return to these categories of archivalisation as we analytically progress with this concept.

The object of the aachaaram in general had been "ways of being of the highly differentiated and distinguished groups of people", limiting and permitting certain acts, and coding the ways of relating and positioning in relation to others. Within the broad rubric of the aachaaram, there was one important aspect which is archivalisation. In fact, it is possible to discern close nexuses and niches among writing, remembering and formulating/reformulating the present and future. That is, the power effects of archivalisation and the repeated invocation of earlier documented events are not innocent of the effects of power. Such power effects were closely related to the way people related to themselves through writing and the anticipation about the recall of the written in the future. The truth that was in the written material conferred the status of a temporality to the 'document'.

The way the aachaaram got reiterated in the assembly of the sabha as presented in a document[19], may provide a good start. In general, the documents that describe the act of 'reiteration or reading of the aachaarakanakke' in the sabha helps us to distinguish two stages involved in the process of archivalisation. First, the observance of aachaarams and instances of their non-observance were written or documented as they came up repeatedly for discussion. In the second stage of documentation, the events of recalling documents and what were reiterated to judge or appraise some contemporary issues are once again documented (inter-documentation). That is, the present was judged and prescriptions were made on the basis of what was recalled from the earlier documents as aachaaram, which established the continuity between the earlier "documented events" and what was taking place at that present.

Recall and Documenting the Content of the Document

Instances of documenting the recall of old documents and their content can be found in several documents, and a well-known among them is presented here:-

> The younger brother of Unnikkerala Varma, Kerala Varma is present in the assembly. The karanakkanakkan, Ayappan Ananthan, **as he was reading the aachaarakanakke**; also **read** that, only after the temple muppu become Threppappur muppu, should the younger one be the muppu. Thereafter Unnikkerala Varma came to Raamana Madham and succeeded to the Threppappur muppu vaazhcha. (Document XV, Rajaraja Varma, M, 1928, emphasis added).

In this excerpt, the reading of the aachaarakanakke (another document that belonged to the past) by Ananthan Ayappan, the karanakkanakkan (a person of distinction, and responsible to inscribe, oversee and recall the documents) could be seen. The excerpt presented below is only a fraction of a document, which reiterates the past events relating to the reconstruction of the Temple of the tutelary deity, and the document is recalled for the present need. The critical act that got documented was the "recall of the aachaarakanakke", as there was a deviation in the continued course of affairs. As and when the precondition for Unnikerala Varma and his younger brother to be treated as Threppappur muppu and ilayathu respectively was pronounced, there appeared a need for the realignment in the inter-subjective relations between Unnikerala Varma and the sabha. More than challenging the postponement of the padiyettam (succession to the throne) by him, it stated "how things used to take place" and suggested "how it should have been". No overt legitimisation was provided to substantiate the truth values of the aachaarakanakke as if it is unwarranted; it stated that only after Unnikerala Varma, the Temple muppu, become the Threppappur muppu could his brother become the representative of his elder brother and become the Threppappur ilayathu.

The need for this recall and its rendering would not have raised if no demand for the physical co-presence of both the muppus in the sabha to issue the anugnja (order), as per the aachaaram had risen. There was no statement in the recalled document stipulating that Unnikkerala Varma should conduct the rite, and no judgment of his action was made in it. But still, the reading alone could act upon his subjectivity and influence him to comply with the aachaaram. Such was the true effect of aachaaram. The compulsion felt by him was thus closely linked with and followed by this act of recall and reading the "written document" in the sabha. He had no other way but to comply with what was read in the sabha. On the whole, we are persuaded to examine the documents as effects of truth and something that affect truths. I will be reiterating this point in the subsequent sections.

Such events of recalling document and reading it itself was something that demanded documentation and such documentation by itself becomes the subject matter for another document. It becomes a subject matter as other documents are derived from the documented readings. For instance, the document cited above gets abbreviated and re-inscribed in the next year of its inscription, i.e., 1621. This shows the effects of power involved in documentation, its recall and reading in the sabha, or, in general, archivalisation.

Such archivalisation is one thing that was persistent, such that it itself has been an aachaaram. Archivalisation and the way in which the aachaaram worked on the behaviour of people were closely linked. This link became extremely intense when it came to Temple matters, as the aachaaram of documentation was most severe in this case. That is why even the instances that appeared extremely mundane or parochial would be documented when they took place in the Temple sabha. The object of archivalisation had been the behaviour of the people and their interactions. The power effects of archivalisation on the manner in which people of distinction modulated their own behaviour are clear. Now let us move on to the terminological apparatus of archivalisation before entering into the other processes involved in it.

Karanam in the Archive

Let us begin this section by dwelling with its lexical meaning. In its noun form, the term karanam means the scribe who takes into account what happens and inscribes it on palm leaves. The term karanam also denotes the organ, instrument, faculties, deed or documents etc[20]; here the instrument is the 'written document' or the inscribed palm leaves with the sign of the inscriber. There was an individual position in the sabha, which was known as Shreekaranam. Apart from this position, there was yet another one called karanakkanakkan, who was designated as one who had a permanent place in the assembly of the sabha. Here, karanam also means activity[21]. This term means the accountant who records the Temple activities (both worldly and spiritual). When the term karanam signifies document, the terms like karanakkanakke and karanakkanakkan gains another meaning. This latter term means the accountant, the record keeper, the inscriber of documents and the one who recalls and reads the documents, all rolled into one. The former term means 'the documented accounts' as well as the "account of the accounts". It can be said that the activities in the Temple were not only accounted in documents, but these documents were also classified and accounted for; in other words, not only were there accountants for writing the accounts, but there was a separate accountant for classifying and recalling the documented accounts belonging to the past. Some were at the sabha and some were at the kanakkapura. To be precise, there were separate accountants, those who objectified the activities in the Temple and those who objectified the documents.

Reading What Was Written Long Ago

The material and procedural processes that enable such 'reading' or 'reiteration' with power-effects and the hierarchy of relations immanent in it can be schematised. At first some or other documents had to made, and as the number and variety went on increasing, they had to be classified and preserved to enable timely retrieval of them when needed. This documenting was important because they were inextricably linked with the encoding of one's (ruling people) behaviour as well as with the appraisal of one's way of being in the world and perhaps to judge the present in terms of the past. The first stage, therefore, involved the actual process of writing down the daily accounts of what happened (*naalvazhioola),* special orders made by the sabha or those in the ruling positions (*chattavarioola)*, and proceedings of the sabha etc. With this emphasis given to the documentation of everyday events and other exchanges and the exalted position of the documents in them, the aachaarams that were otherwise memorised through oral tradition were given another medium to perpetuate the memory, namely the written document. The written document freezes the past for future and thereby language that represented the past warranted fixity. Fixity in inscription and the past that it presents were integral to the authority of the written cadjan leaves with antecedents of inscriptions on copper plates, rocks, granite slabs, clay etc. The act of writing and its relation to fixity affirms a certain truth-value to the documents or *karanams.*

In the beginning of the sixteenth century, the documents, which were stored till then in the Temple, were shifted to an exclusive building[22] (*granthapura* or archive) at the premises of the Temple. Perhaps, exclusivity was provided to them with the intention of preserving/retaining for recalling them in future. Probably, the sporadic conflagrations that took place in the Temple could have prompted the concerned people to anticipate incidents of such events to recur and in turn to take steps to guard this highly inflammable substance in its own right elsewhere. At the time of shifting there were about three lakhs of documents and they referred to events that occurred since the mid-fourteenth century. The documents that were stored in the Temple compound thus came to acquire a singular existence in the *kanakkappura* (house of accounts/documents) with exclusive functionaries. Some of them had a permanent place in the transactions of the sabha. All these show the energy that was expended on documentation and the relation that they had with life and memory.

The documents were not only made, but they were also preserved to transcend amnesia and time. The culture of inscribing the present (although in a limited way) and the display of will to preserve the inscription 'as long as the sun and the stars exist' dates back to a period prior to the duration under consideration, that is prior to the fourteenth century. From ancient times inscriptions were made with the intention that what is stated in it has to be prevalent till the sun and moon existed in this world and this intention was also given presence through drawing them.[23]

The *modus operandi* employed for storing the documents had been quite evolved and extensive during the late medieval period. The house of accounts/documents was not merely a space to stack the documents; over and above, it was also the site of perpetual re-inscription of the documents. Thus, the second process in the practice of archivalisation involved the preservation of the documents through 're-inscription'. The re-inscription (reproduction) as it took place here should be highlighted in order to understand how the inscribed statements were central and intrinsic to the contemporary concerns and sense of making out reality and truth.

There were two types of re-inscriptions of documents. One kind of re-inscription recurrently re-generated the true copies of the original solely with the motive of preservation. This was only to overcome the natural degradation of cadjan leaves, the material substance on which the statements were written. In difference to this verbatim reproduction, the second type of re-inscription selectively abridged and edited several accounts/documented events and they, in turn, were inscribed as different documents.[24] This process of re-inscription generated a different continuum of events within the newly generated documents.[25] Obviously, the effects of such re-inscription were not simply the preservation of the documents but events revisited. Whatever might have been the intention behind such a selection in re-inscribing, it constituted new historical continuums for the present and past.

Besides creating a temporal continuity between present and past, it constituted a continuum between present and future as these documents were expected to be recalled for judging the 'present' in the future. These inscriptions were at once authentic and authenticating without an original document. With the authenticity (truth/power effects), it reproduced the existent modality and the way of relating the present with the past for the future. In short, a process of innovating a 'selective tradition' and perpetuating the past in the present and future in and through such re-inscriptions (including the way people related with the documents) has to be recognised in the history of documentation.

The way the re-inscription of documents gave birth to new documents, or the reconstitutive nature of the re-inscription could be deciphered in this second process, particularly in the second type of re-inscription. Now, whether the first type of re-inscription covered all perishable documents without omitting any of them is not known. If some of the documents were not re-inscribed and others were chosen, then one can say that the selective tradition enters in the first stage of re-inscription as well. Any such screening of the documents involves the application of a criteria that enabled the inclusion of some documents and the omission of others. If that is so, it can be said that both the processes of re-inscription had effects over and above preservation.

Let us elaborate the second type of re-inscription; there was a clear and overt selection and it differentiated between what events were relevant for the present and future and what could be overlooked or set aside. The chosen or the 'relevant' documents or statements were in turn divided and distributed into a series to produce new documents. These re-inscriptions, apart from reproducing certain historical facts and truths, also constituted an inter-document relationship on which the continuity and unity of the new documents depended. Let me proceed to explicate some of the documents of this sort. Once again, I am selectively invoking them not because they are the only ones, but on the basis of convenience of exposition with brevity.

These re-inscriptions produced several subsequent series and continuums. For example, a summary of events that took place in the Temple and the successions to the muppu that took place in Chiravay between 1544 and 1677 were re-inscribed in the year 1721.[26] Here, it is easy to find the thematic continuity that is achieved by such a serialisation. At the first level, continuity gets formed between 1544 and 1677 in terms of successions and the deeds that the ancestors had done. This continuity, as we have seen in the previous section and here, was maintained through the inextricable linkage between the recall and reading, and their power effects in the present.

At the second level, a much longer temporal continuity gets constituted between 1544 and 1721 with a termination at 1677. The first level of continuity invoked into the present was the period between 1544 and 1677 as the events that were recalled were made known as they were found to be relevant even at the time of the selective re-inscription in the year 1721. Another example of re-inscription is the one in which documents that recalled the historical instances of the adoptees becoming the Swaroopam muppu got inscribed;[27] in fact, there were several such re-inscriptions.

There was an interesting re-inscription of selectively chosen documents from the past, one which provides significant political information to us, made in the year 1673.[28] What was otherwise remained as disparate was implicated into a continuous narrative and a temporal continuum between past and present with the effects of authority conferred by the 'written' status of the 'document' was achieved. The primary characteristic of a document, even as we understand it today, is the 'written' or 'printed' nature of it[29]. The norms employed to determine what was to be re-inscribed and what needed to be excluded is not known, but this process of exclusion and inclusion should have been influenced by the contemporary mentality, requirements and the ideas involved in archivalisation.

Such abstracts might have had political implications. One thing that is known is that such summarisation or selective re-inscription and construction of historical series, which engender continuities directly, enter into historical chronicles as empirical facts. For example, in the first historical accounts of Thiruvithamkur written by Pachumuthathu[30] in the nineteenth century, he 'claims' that a great part of his description of the medieval period is nothing but a verbatim reproduction of one of the re-inscriptions (second type).[31] This document was re-inscribed in 1625. That is, such summaries had indisputable authenticity and truth effects. It was the supposed authenticity and attributed authority of them that, in turn, lend whatever historicity his writing had come to possess.

The retention of documents was not merely to know what happened in the past but to know or to make sense of what is happening in the present as well. This necessitates the timely recall of old documents which is a part of archivalisation. Such recalls of previously written documents were quite frequent and phenomenal during the late medieval period. The reading of the aachaarakanakke in the year 1620, which was discussed at length in the previous paper and in this one, illustrate the manner in which the old documents were recalled for contemporary purposes, another effect that archivalisation had. Such occurrence of recall necessitated another process in the archivalisation, which may be classified as the third process.

Documents that were four centuries old, that is, those made since the mid-fourteenth century were recalled in the sabha in the year 1711. In that year, the kanakke and grandhavari that contain the aachaaram pertaining to dathetukkal and padiyettam were recalled.[32] It should also be remembered that the classificatory system was so evolved that any document could have been recalled even at the spur of the moment.

When we look at the history of the recall of the old documents for the re-inscription of them as well as the event of the recall and reading, we find that events that took place since the mid-fourteenth century were repeatedly recalled and reiterated in the assembly of the sabha. Thus, the beginnings of documentation of the present events along with its continuous preservation can be located at this period. In the years 1588 and 1632 there were recalls of events since the mid-fourteenth century in order to verify whether there existed any dues to be paid to the Temple by the previous Swaroopam muppus.[33] After the perusal of the documents by the sabha, the respective muppus of the years 1588 and 1632 promptly cleared all the dues. This exemplifies the truth effects that the recall and reading had. The truth value of the documents had a general effect and acceptability, especially to the sabha and the muppus, and to the Swaroopam in general.

Another process involved in archivalisation is the documentation of the event of the recall of older documents, what was recalled and the effects that it caused. This was another type of inscription and establishment of the series. For example, one of the documents presents the act of retrieval and review of the "documents of past" in which the documents made since 1346 onwards got recalled. It was made when the recall took place in the year 1736.[34] There is another document of such a recall inscribed in the year 1632, which included the documents from the year 1384.[35] There are several such documents that reveal instances of such re-inscriptions of the recall of a shorter duration. For example, there were retrievals that covered the period between 1729-1755[36], 1673-1685[37] and 1480-1483[38]. All of them were documented at the terminal year of the respective temporal coverage.

The fact that a document was recalled and read itself becomes the subject matter of another document which demonstrates its centrality in the position that was rendered to them, the relation that people maintained with them, its functionality in inter-subjective relations and in judging the present for the future. This stage of archivalisation is indicative of the possible power effects that they had on the individual subjects and agency.

Apart from describing what was there in the recalled documents and how the present was judged, the prescriptive statements issued were also written down. Here a temporal translocation of the past takes place, and the past and present become historically conjoined in the circulation of the aachaaram. In this fourth process, the political implications of archivalisation are clearer. For one had only to recall the archivelised document, without mentioning what needed to be done (without prescriptive statement) to bring conformity with the aachaaram and to achieve the desired response from the agents. Therefore, this kind of inscription of the act of recall/reiteration and what was read should be differentiated from the other kinds of re-inscription and documentation. Thus, this kind of inscription shows us more than anything else the importance that was attached to the event of recall of the 'past' in the muppu vaazhcha.

There are several documents where we can observe the depiction of such retrieval. These documents provide us with instances of such reviews of old kanakke. The documents or kanakke, whenever retrieved, had uniqueness and they became part of a new series of events in the history of documentation and recall. As mentioned earlier, those recalled and re-inscribed aachaarams could date back to even more than three hundred years from the time of the retrieval. The series of events that got constituted in the documents that depict the recall did not have any common year of beginning. In general, it can be proposed that the karanam referring to an event of the mid-fourteenth century seems to be the earliest one that was recalled.

A trend that can be observed from some of these documents is that certain events that took place since the mid-fourteenth century never fell to disuse as they were made to be revisited again and again. The documents were bearers of authenticity, and had the power to effect and also to get affected (especially when documents become an element in a strategic manoeuvre). The sites of re-visitations of the aachaarakanakke either affirmed an ongoing continuity or indicated alteration, discontinuity or shift. Therefore, such visitations were in turn inscribed even during the beginning of nineteenth century, thus constituting the four hundred years history (known) of archivalisation.

Repeated Recalls and the Present

The inscribed past was never left to the remote interiority of the racks of the past, that is, it had gained repeatable materiality in the present. As a part of the present, it was also given life and movement in the life-world by attributing to it a genealogical continuity achieved through the re-inscriptions. (Here re-inscription refers to both the third and fourth processes of archivalisation). Archivalisation was central in perpetuating the aachaaram that related the Swaroopams with one another and with the Temple. There was obviously a selection involved in all the inscriptions and re-inscriptions, but hermeneutic issues are not found to have been raised in the process of the 'reading'; the aachaarakanakke was so influential to the extent that it is taken for granted. But this was so at most till 1811, when a turn in the history of archivalisation had taken place and we find hermeneutic issues surfacing while 'reading'. I shall comeback to these issues soon.

Two different historical trends in archivalisation can be discerned.[39] When chronologically looked at, from the second half of the fourteenth century onwards, there was a great deal of continuous accumulation of the documents contemporaneously inscribed and such production gained added impetus by the beginning of the sixteenth century. Thus, in the history of archivalisation, the mid-fourteenth century can be said to be a turning point. That is, the beginnings of the first processes of archivalisation stretch back at least to the mid-fourteenth century. It is not that prior to it inscriptions did not exist.

It can be hypothesized that the second process, namely re-inscription, might have been prevalent during those days. However, it is not clear whether this process also started during that period or not. The second trend in the history of documentation begins from the mid-fifteenth century onwards, when we begin to see a retrieval and reading of them and their re-documentation or re-inscription. That is, the third and fourth process of archivalisation becomes evident only by the mid-fifteenth century. Within a hundred years of the history of material documentation, there took place an alteration in the status of the archive. The archive has become indispensable to the present. The documents became the objects of archivalisation and the aachaaram.

How were the past documents implicated in the 'present' as in the archivalisation of the aachaaram? As old karanams got recurrently employed in the present, it simultaneously constituted a temporal continuum among the unities of events, among documents and between them. The ways in which the documents, thus accumulated, were recognised in the present could be seen in the repeated recall and in the inscription of this act of recall. This fourth process of archivalisation shows the extent and intensity of the need felt for recording and developing material documents with which they got bound. This process shows how the aachaaram, once activated, was intricately linked to itself through archivalisation.

In the case of the history of such an aachaaram of documentation, by the mid-fourteenth century its articulation took the format of a kanakke and the written form of karanam. But then, the possibility of recall was limited by its beginning; the availability of karanams limited the possibility to extend the historical limit of the aachaaram into the remotest past so that its truth-effect was all the more potent. However, these documents function as if it is a-temporal. The recognition of the aachaaram in the documented account, its "documentary articulation" and the documentation of articulation etc, have close correspondence with the written law. We will return to it later. Here, the point is the close link between writing, the aachaaram, archivalisation and the present.

The medium, the aachaarakanakke, with its truth-value-effect, seems to be independent of the truth of what was orally transmitted. This is so despite the fact that it was also a time when the "word of mouth" was also inerasable because "words uttered" had an ethical value. In fact, there are several orally transmitted stories in which the answer to the question "don't you value your words" becomes their moral. There are also statements to ridicule others, by telling the targeted person that "there is no point in having a moustache unless you value your words" itself could put that person into shame. These observations suggest, once again, that archivalisation was directed more by future than the present, or it was carried out with the idea of perpetuation/retention. However, it should be underscored that there seems to be no observable prioritisation of the written over the oral in terms of their procedures of effecting truth, although they circulated within different socialities.

Along with archivalisation, there was another process in which legal texts began to get formulated and gained proliferation, and one of them is the *Vyavahaaramaala* (garland of customs and usages)[40]. It had circulation among, at least, the Malayalam and Sanskrit-speaking communities and the texts that were recovered to be reproduced in print dates back to the sixteenth century. It consists of a sequence of selectively chosen statements translated from other legal texts in Sanskrit. This information prompted one to enquire how this archivalisation coexisted with or was distanced from such legalisation.

This system of perpetuation of the aachaaram through its archivalisation and its effects of power has to be distinguished from the textualisation of legal idiom as in the Vyavahaaramaala that had taken place within the metaunity of the discursive formation of brahmasutra[41]. There is no need to suspect that these legal texts were written and read during the period under examination, although they do not get invoked in any of the documents in the archive we have been familiar with so far.[42] With these two types of administration of the aachaaram, namely through the reiteration of the aachaarakanakke and the textualisation of it as in the Vyavahaaramaala, the aachaaram became a locus of judgement about oneself, what one should be, what one had been, what one could be etc, and more importantly what one should not become.

These two written forms could be differentiated in terms of their respective modalities of circulation, site of application and the way the aachaaram got stated in them etc. While the object of the former was the documents themselves, which objectified different activities of sets of people at different contexts, in legal texts, the aachaarams were abstracted and made into a generalised code of conduct. While the aachaarakanakke articulated how the aachaaram have been, the emphasis of the legal texts was only about what ought to be. The new aachaarakanakke was anchored on earlier ones and in turn perpetually generated others that led to the creation of inter-document concerns, whereas the legal texts engaged in hermeneutical procedures and tried to give eternal fixity to what they contained in them. Thus, aachaarakanakke or aachaarakramam supplemented with 'texts' together made aachaaram well-founded and gave it both a general and particular applicability at the same time.

The propositions in this paragraph need to be substantiated further; however, this remains outside the purview of the present efforts. Still, certain peculiarities of the relationship between the way the aachaaram circulates and the process of archivalisation, and textualisation may be appropriate. This will give us an idea about the way in which the aachaaram circulated through the aachaarakanakke along with the legal texts, but with a difference. I am making these distinctions because there is a conviction that there were no legal texts in this part of the world, India in general, and a tendency to distinguish custom and law on the basis of 'the written status'.

The 'reading' involved no statement of opinion nor did it involve any interpretation of what was 'read', be whether the document read was old or new. A statement such as "the fact that this is the aachaaram as in the document" itself was sufficient to effect truth. In short, the aachaaram worked through the concomitant process of its archivalisation. The kanakke of any type never appeared as a trace or as a sign that alluded or referred to something that was not intrinsic to itself, but as something 'transparent' and 'at the surface'. Whenever they got recalled, it was not done in order to interpret it (the status of documents in the eyes of the modern craft of historiography), rather it had been stated as truth in itself. There was no arriving at a truth in archivalisation as it is already inscribed forever. These karanams were not treated merely as traces that were left by the past, but as a reality in the present.

The aachaarakanakke was the active memory and the aachaaram maintained its coherence by linking itself inextricably with this practice of documentation and by permanently reinstating the truth of them through circulating them. The content of the kanakkappura was not de-linked from the present in terms of its reality or truth, as the documents of the past centuries actively partook in the continuing reality, be it in the fifteenth, seventeenth or eighteenth century. Wherever its field of coverage extended, it was constitutive of the present and in turn the present perpetuated it with a fixed significance, free of hermeneutic-queries. When this aachaarakanakke, devoid of interpretation, was contemporarily recalled, its reality got well grounded without the aid of any other process of legitimisation or any metanarratives.

Unlike the 'files' in the modern archive, the karanams were not re-examined to glean the past, but to make sense of the present and judge it without the aid of any other textualised law, which might have gained circulation. As far as the inclusion of the documents was concerned, the documents were not stratified as old and new (contemporary documents) as it would be in a modern achieve, for as an aachaaram it had to include documents that refer to contemporary matters also. Antiquity did not render any extra power to the files; nor that there was any parallel between oldness and authenticity.

The documents maintained in the kanakkappura not only got preserved, but the possibility of recalling the oldest available document rendered judgemental authority - unlike the files. The documents thus generated, also became part of the kanakkappura; for convenience, this property of it can be termed as the self-generativity of the kanakkappura.

Aachaaram always necessitated constant retrieval and functionalisation of some preserved past in warding off duraachaarams that were defined in terms of the kanakke. Such visitations of the past in the kanakke, formalised the aachaaram and gave repeatable materiality to it in the present. This maintained the continuity in the determination of how an event should take place with respect to time and space of its occurrence. The aachaarakramam reproduced itself in the pravrithikramam that directly appealed to the way one conducted some or other acts and how one was expected to conduct them.

The aachaaram thus archivelised, among many others, ordered the relationship between the swaroopam, sabha and the Temple. The archivalisation of their interrelationship was an aachaaram in itself. This archival practice exemplified the procedure-bound activities and the position-bound interindividual relationships implicated in such activities and relations. The knowledge of the way aachaarakanakke can be recalled to achieve definite ends were imminent in the force-relations both between the Swaroopams and the sabha and among them also, whenever they were united by aachaaram/anaacharam.

One of the last instances of this kind of archival practice was the one that took place in 1810-1811 about which I made a passing mention.[43] I am elaborating this particular instance which may be one among many others as they reveal different patterns. Such events introduced scientific factuality and juridico-political diction into the reasons of the state. Correspondingly, one can trace the relegation of the document as part of the Swaroopams and not of the kingdom. A relegation of those statements that does not fit into their truth/political regime can be discerned from them. The power effects of archivalisation diminished with the shift from the Swaroopam to the kingdom and what became more conspicuous were the facts, proofs, justifications etc. The distinction between Swaroopam and kingdom could be read about in this particular event about which I referred to in the beginning of this paragraph. Let us move on.

There surfaced a predicament to decide upon a successor to the throne of Travancore. The British Resident in this State was involved in the acts of resolving the disputes by following the terms of the aachaaram. The question was, in the absence of a male member to succeed as the Travancore king, could an adopted male member be a legitimate successor? In fact in many princely states, succession disputes were productive situations to extend their resource exploitation through dominating the rulers of such states. Although a detailed examination of the historical conditions for such a problematisation of the impending succession is relevant, it is not attempted here.

Instead, we will confine ourselves to show the way the retrieval of past documents became functional in the strategies of those ruling members who were aligned with the British in Travancore and the Company. The distinguished positions, especially the position of the king of Travancore, had been by then the site of several centrifugal intersecting force-relations including the fraction led by Veluthampi Dalava who was assassinated by the Paramount-palace combine in a military encounter.[44] Therefore, the question as to who should become the next king was extremely significant in terms of strategy and future achievements of the stakeholders, especially the British. Since some traces from the past were completely relegatable, any legitimate decision on the dispute had to be founded on the aachaarakramam; and hence an old aachaarakanakke was recalled and consulted to arrive at a judgement.

A series of past karanams were recalled,[45] and a review had to be done to examine whether in the past any of the adoptees had become the muppu of Threppappur or the king of Travancore. The karanams that belonged to the year 1336 onwards were invoked and reviewed with purpose of resolving a succession dispute. But the last of the reviews[46] (there are several documents of the reviews on the same issue conducted during the short span of a few months) concluded that facts could be found only in those documents drafted before the year 1748 and those drafted that year were incredulous. As no adoptee since 1748 became the Travancore king, a new continuity with a new base year got formulated which gained persistence.

Whether the conclusion contained in the document just referred to is true or not, and whatever had been its historical contexts and consequences, it is to be noted that with this recall of the karanams, the continuum in the history of archivalisation got discontinued and a new continuum got affirmed. Had the review taken into account of the karanams prior to that particular year, then the conclusion would have been different.

That is, by the time this retrieval of the aachaarakanakke occurred, the confirmed truth-content of the documents that maintained the temporal continuity (from the early medieval days to the turn of the Swaroopam-epoch) had been broken and a new continuity, beginning with the mid-eighteenth century, had been fabricated to justify the contingent need (that is of 1811) of positing a "pre-matured lady" as the legitimate successor.[47] If an adoptee was not to become the king, then the female-infant could be foisted on the throne. The temporally restricted and selective recall of the aachaarakanakke and the functionalisation of the archivelised kanakke accomplished a continuity that marked its beginnings in 1748; this in turn rendered the legitimacy for the female infant's succession and acceptance of British Paramountcy.

The members of the sabha who were to derive conclusions and judgements might have also felt a sense of uncertainty about their own actions, as they were in the process of constructing something new and undermining the existent aachaarakanakke. The hermeneutical issues were raised along with the reading of the documents, which was not required till then. It could be because of this enigmatic dimension of the period that, for the first time, we find in the proceedings of the sabha a reference to the 'Hindu maryaada' legitimised by the legal text, Dharmashastra.[48] For legitimacy and to establish truth claims about the sabha's conclusion, over and above the aachaarakanakke, the invocation of this legal text had become necessary. That is, under the uncertain and the changed condition, a reference to the text had become more forceful as an authority for legitimisation than the recall. And further, it legitimised its own claims to truth by explicitly stating that they had followed the codes of the Manu Vignaana Shaastram. One should note that, within the archivalised observance of the aachaarakramam and the aachaaram of archivalisation, there had never been any need for any such mode of legitimisation. The need to resort to the 'book' had entered into the relation between men and the kanakke/karanam.

Another male member would have become the successor, had this new continuity and forms of authorisation not been constituted, and that would have been contrary to the wishes of the British who were striving for Paramountcy over Travancore.[49] That is, the aachaaram of recalling the aachaarakanakke of the past had become a part of the project of colonising the Travancore kingdom. With this event of the recall, the aachaaram of recalling the past as represented in the documents and their unquestioned legitimacy were undermined. The karanakkanakke had metamorphosed itself and became mere documents that waited for an interpretation and classification in terms of the 'norms' of the present.

With this new instrumental use of karanams, a new beginning was made in the archivalisation of the aachaaram. The observance of aachaaram and its archivalisation ceased to be a "truth game" with norms mutually accepted by both those who ensured its perpetuation and those who were obliged to observe it. The aachaarakramam was no more a taken-for-granted order. The archivalisation that was constitutive of and constituted by the aachaarakramam, had itself had given way to the English laws and regulations on the 'populace'.

Even though the kanakkappura and archive are used interchangeably, in the light of the above discussion it is possible to postulate that they are not one and the same in terms of the roles and functions that the kanakkupura performed. Besides, it was at the same time a place where documents were drafted, written, signed and preserved. New documents were generated from the existent documents and they were also clubbed together with the old documents. That is, the documents generated from the kanakkupura enriched it constantly at least in terms of number and content. It was not a static institution like the modern archive.

But then, one can state that with the transformations during the nineteenth century it became appropriate to translate it as archive. It became an archive, a modern one, the moment it began to be consulted to know the past imagined in distinction to the present, but before that it was consulted to recall what had happened in the past, un-separated from the present and future.

The archivalisation, which was imminent in the muppu vaazhcha, could become identifiable as monument, that is, the kanakkappura. With these transformations of the kanakkappura, instead of being an active site of the muppu vaazhcha, it had become just a monument differentiated from the present. In short, the events of 1810-11 marked the end of such an archival practice that had been intricately related to the muppu vaazhcha of the Swaroopams. No more could the archive provide a basis for distinguishing what was customary from non-customary; this authenticity was given to the Records, Library/Cellars and Verification.

Instead of the complex archivalisation, a generalised text began to be the final determining word in judging since the beginning of the mid-nineteenth century, and the archive became a frozen storehouse of mute palm-leaves bearing the relics of effective-documents/writing. Thus, the retrieval and recall of the aachaara-kanakke that occurred in 1810-11 could be seen as one of the last seductive breaths of the aachaaram of archivalisation and the archivelised aachaaram. The truth effects of documents legitimised both the aachaaram and the aachaaram of documentation. Both together linked ruling, challenging and effecting power. The Swaroopams had charunas and the kingdom had “files of reality”; the historical movement from the Swaroopam to kingdom can be read in such a grain of sand of changes and shifts in the genealogy of documentation.

Notes

1. Maheswaran Nair, K. (Archival Administration in Ancient Travancore, p. 68).
2. I will be extensively using the content of the unpublished and undated mimeograph of K. Maheswaran Nair, *Archival Administration in Ancient Travancore (From early times to 1798 A.D.)* in the following chapters

(hereafter AAAT). This text is there in Kerala University Library, Trivandrum, Accession Number: (1879/94).

3. Maheswaran Nair, K, (AAAT, p. 68).
4. Uma Maheshwari, S. (2018): 13.
5. Maheswaran Nair, K, Vol. 1, mimeographed, undated, p. 1.
6. According to confirmed news reports, some of the items found include:-
    - A 3.5-foot (1.1 m) tall golden idol of Mahavishnu, studded with diamonds and rubies and other precious stones.
    - A pure golden throne, studded with hundreds of diamonds and precious stones, meant for the 18-foot (5.5 m) idol of deity.
    - An 18-foot (5.5 m) long gold chain.
    - A gold sheaf weighing 500 kilograms (1,100 lb).
    - A 36-kilogram (79 lb) golden veil.
    - 1,200 *'Sarappolli'* gold coin-chains encrusted with precious stones.
    - Several sacks filled with golden artefacts, necklaces, diadems, rubies, sapphires, emeralds, gemstones, and objects made of other precious metals.
    - Ceremonial attire for adorning the deity in the form of 16-part gold *anki* weighing almost 30 kilograms (66 lb).
    - Gold coconut shells studded with rubies and emeralds.
    - Several 18th-century Napoleonic-era coins.
    - Hundreds of thousands of gold coins of the Roman Empire.
    - An 800-kilogram (1,800 lb) hoard of gold coins dating to around 200 BC.
    - According to varying reports, at least three, if not many more, solid gold crowns all studded with diamonds and other precious stones.
    - Hundreds of pure gold chains.
    - Thousands of gold pots and jars.
7. Maheswaran Nair, K, (AAAT, p. 36).
8. Maheswaran Nair, K, (AAAT, p. 36).
9. Maheswaran Nair, K, (AAAT, p. 26).
10. 1. *Anyadhabhodhanam*
    2. Sarparatipadam
    3. Prstam
    4. Ttathyadravyam
    5. Kevalam
    6. Sodakadanam

11. They are *Dinara Hundika, Dhanya-yava-godhuma-Hundika, Sevya Hundika, Kriyakara Hundika and Gotikanma Hundika*.
12. For details, see Maheswaran Nair K. Archival Administration in Ancient Travancore, Undated Mimeograph, unpublished. p. 29.
13. Maheswaran Nair, K, AAAT, pp. 29-30.
14. The *Lokaprakasa* of *Kshemendra* is another important work of immense utility to a student of the Archive Science of ancient India. I am purposefully referring to this to show that such classifications of documents of archive was not confined to Travancore alone. Speaking of the '*Loka Lokhakasikshacharita* Kshemendra refers to the following kinds of records:
    1. *Swadhayapatraka*
    2. *Prasadapatraka*
    3. *Dakshninapatraka*
    4. *Likhitalekhapatraka*
    5. *Parityagapatraka*
    6. *Arthipratyarthism*—vadapatrka
    7. *Purvottarapakshasm*—vadapatraka
    8. *Agachehayanamadhtastha*
    9. *Urdhamadhastha*
    10. *Vastavyamadhyastha*
    11. *Digijjadyalamadhyastha*
    12. *Lavanamadhyastha*
    13. *Kriyakaramadhyastha*
    14. *Laganamadhyastha*
    15. *Dhanushkamadhyastha*
    16. *Laganamadhyastha*
    17. *Vangalamadhyastha*
15. Maheswaran Nair, K, (AAAT:35).
16. Maheswaran Nair, K, (AAAT:50).
17. Maheswaran Nair, K, (AAAT:45).
18. Gundert, H, (1872:209).
19. Gundert, H, (1872:209).
20. Shivashankaran Nair, K, (1993:107).
21. From the ninth century onwards, there were several instances of 'writing' that was intended to be effective till the sun and moon exist. For a brief history of the "historical inscriptions", see Narayanan, M.G.S, (1997).
22. Document No. XVI, Rajaraja Varma Raja, (S. 1., 1928: 25-26)

23. For exemple, see Document, No. XVI, Rajaraja Varma Raja (1928 : 25-26).
24. Document, No.XVI, Rajaraja Varma Raja (1928:25-26).
25. Velu Pillai, T.K, M.Doc. CCII, (1940: 241-244).
26. Velu Pillai, T.K, M.Doc. CXXII, (1940: 91-100).
27. See Webster Comprehensive Dictionary, (Vol. 1, 1986: 374).
28. Paachumuthathu, (1867:14). The *karanam* that was used in this historical account got re-inscribed in the year (1786).
29. For example, Velu Pillai, T. K, (C.V.R. Doc. CXVI, Vol. 2, 1940: 82-83).
30. Velu Pillai, T.K, (M. Doc. CCIII, Vol. II, 1940: 244-248).
31. Shivashankaran Nair, K, (1993: 186).
32. Velu Pillai, T.K, (M.Doc. CXXIX, 1940: 106-114).
33. Velu Pillai, T.K, (M.Doc. CXX, 1940: 86-90).
34. Velu Pillai, T.K, (M.Doc. CXXX, 1940: 114-133).
35. Velu Pillai, T.K, (M.Doc. CXXII, 1940: 106-114).
36. Parameshwara Iyer, S, (Doc No. 22, 1962: 35-39).
37. This hypothesis is based on a primary analysis of the set of published *Mathilakam Grandhavari*.
38. (Parameshwara Aiyar, S, ed, (1925).
39. (For details, see Davis. Jr, Donald, R, (1999: 159-213).
40. (Parameshwara Aiyar, S, ed., 1925: ii).
41. (See Velu Pillai, T.K, (M. Docs. CC, CCI, CCII, CCIII, and CCIV, 1940).
42. (Velu Pillai, T.K, (M. Doc. CC, 1940 : 228-237).
43. (Velu Pillai, T.K, (M. Docs. CC, CCI, CCII, CCIII, and CCIV, 1940).
44. (Velu Pillai, T.K, (M. Doc. CCI, 1940: 237-241).
45. (Shivashankaran Nair, K, 1996: 173-181).
46. (Velu Pillai, T.K, (M.Doc. CCII, 1940: 241-244).
47. One Kerala Varma should have been the legitimate successor, but then, it was he who gave lead to the protest against the British in Travancore.

Chapter - 8

Postscript

We all know that the histories of the late-medieval period were overwhelmingly influenced by the metaphor of centralised state or its referential variants such as fragment, little, exceptional etc. This period was also characterised in the framework of 'expansionist' regimes. The framework adopted here did not have any referential relation to these ways of thinking; not even in terms of any of the variants of state. The patterns in history that we have presented in this book show a tendency towards non-centralisation, such that, there is a traceable tendency to resist it; although some historians maintain otherwise[1]. One could not find evidence for any attempts of expansionism as well. This tendency could be advertent or inadvertent. This tendency is not merely reducible to either structures that were prevalent during the period or the efficacy and intentions of the agents or their mutual interaction. Here resistance and power were not differentiable as much as structure and agent as they are evident by now.

There were designs enabling diagrammatic distribution of individuals in the distinguished positions and influenced the relations between them. There were diagrams of Swaroopams, of kinship relations and their improvisations, of subjectivities and inter-subjectivities and recurrent reactivation of the past through writing. There were diagrams of maneuvers, of functionalisation of strategies and counter-strategies, of actions and reactions and, of perpetuation of the past and devising it.

In short, if we think through the concepts such as culture and politics there were culture and politics were indistinguishably merged together; there were culture and politics of writing and written culture. Late-medieval period is shown to be more complex and enigmatic than what have been considered in the received views of them in which these two concepts are indispensable. The present study has found that they are dispensable and focused on the micro dimensions of the Swaroopams. Further, the continued and strategic use of select truths that were constituted within, and were constitutive of, the co-existence of the Swaroopams was examined. This has brought forth the complexities, minute differences, reciprocities and negotiations between different agents and structures of social organisation that were involved in the co-existence of Swaroopams and other socio-territorial unities such as naadu. Summarisation of the previous chapters may be tantamount to repetition; therefore this chapter explores trajectories to move forward from where we are at present.

The mode of analysis adopted could be referred as microscopic analysis or micro history. Aggregate and aggregating categories such as culture, politics, feudalism, society, domination, caste, class, state, and so on were sparingly employed. Here, in this last chapter, we shall consciously make use of these categories to come out with some inferences without, however, necessarily seeking to generalise these for South India. Simultaneously, this chapter will also raise certain questions of theoretical import, again without necessarily suggesting Universalist implications.

The use of western categories to represent a non-western context has been problematised.[2] Alternative modes of analysis and representation have also been consciously sought. Our own mode of inquiry, microscopic analysis/microhistory, has brought forth the complexities that had critical role in many processes, structures and structuration[3]. The aspects that are analysed in this book were the perpetuation of the Swaroopams over a few centuries and their co-existence. The complexities recurred quite frequently in the cultural, political, religious and symbolic practices in swaroopams and the muppu vaazcha. Nevertheless, these aspects, perhaps owing to their subtlety, remain dimly recognised in historical works. If discussed at all, they are considered as exogenous, deviations, retrogression, transition, fragmentation or decomposition of the general rule of Chera Kingdom. At variance with these, the present study took Swaroopam in its own right or as endogenous to the political and cultural practices of the time. They were even functional in the metamorphosis[4] of the Swaroopam into the kingdom of Thiruvithamkur (here after 'Travancore' to indicate the princely state). The narratives about the kingdom had been transacted through the abstract notion of the 'total'[5] with a spatial-Center[6]. Till the formation of the kingdom of Thiruvithamkur, political and cultural negotiations among the Swaroopams took place without these notions. This study has shown that the use of such conceptual/metaphysical binaries in the existing historical representations of late medieval period has created pitfalls in description and the historiography contain internal-incoherence. Swaroopams coexisted, but their relational milieu did not involve containment of one by another or mergers. Existence of the Swaroopams did not correspond to a simple Cartesian scheme of 'total' and the 'part'.

The micro-analysis of the minute and subtle aspects of the Swaroopam was carried out without presupposing either the existence of micro-units within any central/mega Swaroopam. Microscopic analysis is not the binary opposite of any imagined macroscopic analysis. Therefore, in terms of the object of analysis and methodology, the micro/macro antinomy is bracketed out. The mode of analysis excluded western antinomies like nomothetic/idiographic or value/fact and the concepts, categories and other terminological apparatuses based on any such antinomies.

The description and analysis of the Swaroopams as advanced in this book have implications for the prevailing thinking on the pre-colonial or the non-western political organisations. The study demonstrates this through its potential to trace some of the antecedents of a kingdom that in a short period got converted into a Princely State under the British Paramountcy. Apart from this direct implication, it has also a bearing on situating Thiruvithamkur kingdom. Further, an understanding of the Swaroopams also has the potential to shed new light on the conceptual issues in the prevailing representations inspired by Orientalist discourse.

The 'Marthanda Varma Period' (from 1729 to 1758) is often viewed as of a typical 'Hindu State', and as representing the 'traditional rule' in Kerala. Such a conception leads to the trend of characterising the society as a stationary[7], in the manner of the Orientalists[8]. Even those who study colonialism or spread of missionaries, merely counter-pose this erroneously conceived Hindu kingdom against the British or Missionaries in Travancore. Barring a few moments like "crushing the 'feudal' elements", or expanding the army to build an autocratic state[9] the history of this mid-eighteenth century kingdom is seen as a continuation from the past. This study shows that the culture of politics[10] of the pre-mid-eighteenth century was incomparably different from the political culture since the mid-eighteenth century. Delineation of select political and cultural processes during the period of the Swaroopams and their alterations during the shift (not transition or change) to kingdom has brought to light the rupture that took place in the mid-eighteenth century socio-political field.

The importance of altering the trend of Orientalist conceptualisation arises from the fact that most of the new scholarly inquiries have also floundered; the shadow of kingdom model has fallen over the Swaroopam and made it something other than it was. The outcome is non-acceptance of the specificities and unique patterns within the Swaroopam entity itself. The present book has sought to distance the Swaroopam from the kingdom. Such distancing becomes necessary for understanding the culture of politics of the Swaroopam and de-linking it from political culture of kingdom.

Imperial Strategies

New awareness of the late medieval period enables new visibility to the ways in which the agents of British imperialism and the Travancorians co-acted, interacted and contested under colonial conditions. This awareness also reveals how the claim over the knowledge about the past was part of the strategic moves within imperial condition. We shall exemplify the applicability of the new awareness about Swaroopam by focusing on an event in which the strategic move of both the British agents and the agents of Travancore kingdom are discernable. The event in question took place in 1800, after the revolt against the British Residency in Thiruvithamkur (one of the most important anti-British struggles of early nineteenth century) under the leadership of the Devan (who was a 'native administrative chief' next to the king and Resident in the hierarchy of authority).[11]

On the death of the king Rama Varma, there took place a succession dispute on whether an adopted member can be the legitimate successor or not. The colonial authorities orchestrated this contest among the members of the kuuru-mura order. As evident from the previous chapters, the succession disputes had been rare when the system of multiple-muppu vaazcha was prevailing; it became politically decisive and more frequent only by the turn of the eighteenth century. The British Resident at Thiruvananthapuram consulted the Brahmin elite at the capital of Travancore kingdom for their 'truthful' testimony on the contested question. In response to it, they referred the documents and verified whether any adopted male members had ever become the muppu of Threppappur or king of Travancore. Historically, the dispute entailed two possible outcomes, and they depended on the finding of the Brahmin elite. If an adopted member is found to have succeeded in the past, then senior-most (adopted in this case) male member will be the new successor; if the tradition has been otherwise, then an adolescent girl would be the successor.

The modalities of succession became a site of imperial intervention and a means to fabricate new structures of imperialism. The blurred boundary between the cultural and political spaces was amenable to the strategic manipulation. Before issuing the testimony, they verified the documented facts on successions that had taken place between the years 1336 and 1810. Unlike the archival practice of earlier days, this review did not reproduce the substances of karanams that were recalled, this marks a perceptible rupture in the aachaaram of archivalisation. The final conclusion was that there existed no document to affirm that an adopted member had become the muppu or king.[12] The agents, who gave the testimony, left clearly stated information in the documents on instances of the adopted members or *dathans* becoming muppu to auto-suggested amnesia. They stated that such practices never took place; in one of the previous chapters saw that number of dathans became muppu of Swaroopams.

The rightness of the testimony was taken for granted, and it became the legitimising instrument for the British Resident to preempt the succession of an adopted 'male member' to the throne. Instead of the legitimate successor, an adolescent girl was foisted on the throne.[13] Here the young girl on the throne was extremely opportune to the Resident as the existing eldest male member on the throne was found to be deterring British interests. It was an instance of "Hollow Crown".[14] Such concoction of the false statements and its investment was to the advantage of the British than anybody else. In this instance, what is more glaring is the functionalisation of the truths of the past by concealing and investment of tradition by the British and the Brahmin elite of Thiruvananthapuram.

There existed an adopted male member who was the senior-most male member in the kuuru-mura scheme. On this basis he along with a great majority of the swaroopam members asserted that he should succeed to the throne.[15] This was the aachaaram that prevailed. Reading of the old documents to find out precedents was also an aachaaram. In the case of the observance of the first aachaaram, 'culture of politics' was abided. When the second aachaaram was called for, 'political culture' played the game. The political culture won the game of deception.

The question of who should be the legitimate successor was not a problem to be sorted out by the Brahmanical sabha. It was kuuru-mura of the swaroopam was the basis to determine the order of succession. A redefinition of the functions of the agents who were involved in the administration and a new realignment of relations between the palace, the sabha and the British Residency got redefined in this episode. Now, one can identify beginnings of certain political manipulation camouflaged as the tradition/aachaaram and at the same time expose the metaphysics of continuity in the name of aachaaram.

By now, we know that the testimony that was furnished to the "Company government" was incorrect; the statement is contrary to the documented historical evidences. This study has brought out the long list of muppus who were dathans.[16] That is, even a new word such as dathan was evolved by the scribes of Mathilakam Grandhavari to denote those muppus who were adopted into the Swaroopam. The whole sequence of the consultation of the aachaarakanakku and production of the testimony and positioning of the adolescent girl as the *rane* or queen can be seen as a strategic move. An analysis of this gives insight to an understanding of how and on what the imperial forces operated. In the strategic moves of the British Residency as well as the Brahmin elites, seduction, deception, corruption, persuasion, concealment etc are clearly traceable. This is because the truth claim of the testimony stands suspected in the light of the knowledge about the Swaroopam organisation and archivalisation. This knowledge also clearly falsifies the statement in the testimony; the testimony was a historical lie and a marker in the history of imperialism of British in Thiruvithamkur. Without the knowledge about Swaroopam this lie would have remained buried. The dramatic sequence of the recalling the past documents, concoction of the testimony and placement of the girl as the queen etc were the enactments of mendacity.

It is right to mention that, colonialism spread through "dialogic production of a negotiated system of rules and institutions"[17]. Unlike the Portuguese and the Dutch, instead of military strategies, the British employed negotiation and manipulation to establish their authoritative power. It is also true that "the construction of what both British and local participants conceived of as the value of a former age formed an attempt to interactively generate answers to solve current pressing cultural and authorial problems.[18] However, such a production of negotiated system is only one of the aspects of imperial strategy; it included, apart from seductive and mendacious strategies, non-dialogical, coercive tactics as well. What we would like to add is that there was an invention and innovation of a 'fabricated past' in the interactive generation of legitimacy for the exercise of power during early nineteenth century onwards. The fact that some resolution was arrived at through the dialogic relation between British 'Company Government' and Travancorians need not be free of invention and investment of past and cunning strategy. To decipher such aspects of imperial conditions, an awareness of the genealogies of kingdom seems to be indispensible. That is why a study of Swaroopam.

The Culture of Politics

The important result of the previous chapters is the added clarity about the culture of politics during the period of Swroopams. The previous sections of this chapter have not only brought to the thought the indistinguishable political and cultural processes and sites of confrontation and strategic negotiations; it has also brought to the letters the negotiations between cultural and political activities, wherever they could be distinguished. The indistinguishability does not mean that political activities were not taking place; rather, the situation was such that, the political activities were well formulated to the extent that there was a 'political culture'.

The 'indistinguishable realms' of culture and politics became an object for historical analysis only after the rendezvous between history and anthropology; the methodological enhancement since Bernard Cohen and Annals School seem to have influenced several historical representations on South India in general.[19] The specific mode of the combining has been consciously or inadvertently influenced by the poststructuralist turn, particularly the type that was ignited by Michel Foucault. In this book the political and cultural co-action was build into the Swaroopam model.[20]

The rules and symbolic resources of the cultural sphere influenced the political activities through aachaaram. In other words, a given political activity will be permitted, enacted, evaluated and contested on the basis of the aachaara-maryada. The aachaara-maryada was coexistent with any political, cultural and even material and spiritual processes and occurrences. The co-existence had two sides; aachaaram existed either as something to be sincerely observed, as something persuade and prevent the political sphere. In the case of observance politics and culture are indistinguishable and in the rest of the instances they are distinguishable. Whenever aachaaram bound activities took place, as it used to be during the Swaroopam period, politics and culture were indistinguishably merged together. The culture of politics was such that the politics and culture including kinship were indistinguishably merged together and justifications for political practices were drawn from cultural basin. As one of the authors points out, the ritual and politics were closely bound together such that "ritual and political forms were fundamentally the same".[21]

It was shown that the performance of padiyettam, although a ritual in discipline bound academic language, it was a political gesture. In one of the chapters, we have seen that both the performance of padiyettam or succession rite by the legitimate successor to muppu vaazcha and the postponement of this performance become equally a matter to activate power relations. In the phenomena such as multiple-muppu vaazcha or dathetukkal or the kuuru-mura schematisation or the kind of archivalisation, the political and cultural negotiations were such that we can call it as the 'culture of politics' in distinction to 'political culture'. The latter phrase can be reserved to characterise the period just after that of the Swaroopams. During the latter period elements of the culture of politics were strategically functionalised as the reason of the kingdom. Since self-evident phenomena of an age is not graspable by another age or if a phenomena becomes what it was not or invisible, then we can separate that age from the age that preceded it. To repeat, the shift (not transition or change) from Swaroopam to kingdom is also a movement from the culture of politics to cultural politics; in cultural politics the culturally coded political practices and its justifications get functionally linked up with future and political/territorial gains of the present. The truths that were self evident to the Swaroopam organisation had become undecipherable, forgotten or left to oblivion by choice during the period of cultural politics that prevailed since first half of eighteenth century. Many truths of the culture of politics of the Swaroopam age became a bastion of cultural politics of the kingdom.

One of the aspects of the culture of politics is that there was no separation between administrative machinery and judicial institutions. The muppu and the Yogam along with the representatives of any given issue were parts of juridical judgments. These judgments took into account of both mariaatha and aachaaram. The former was context-sensitive, in the sense that the orders of judgment were context specific and context bound when they aimed at a particular social unit, including individuals, distributed across different social strata at a given time. The nature of the contest was determined to a great extent by the specificity of the configuration of the social agents involved in the pronouncement and who was judged. The aachaaram bound pronouncements was at the same time context-specific and 'precedent-bound'. The dependence of judgment on precedent was significant, and activities were explicitly judged on the basis of what had been permitted and expected in terms of the aachaarams. In most of the dispute settlements, 'rules and precedents of general applicability' had a critical role. As far as I know, the functionalisation of the truth effect of 'precedence' that stemmed from the early fourteenth century onwards were invoked and interpreted in the judicial practices in the Swaroopams. It has been proved beyond doubt that in the culture of politics of the Swaroopams 'decisions made in one context had, under certain conditions, automatic application in other contexts', even when the context got repeated after the lapse of centuries.

Because of the existence of precedent-boundedness in the legislative practice of the Swaroopam it is difficult to apply the distinction between administrative and legal functions. The muppu vaazcha of Swaroopams combined both the functions without making much distinction between them. In the case of muppu, he was not devoid of the office of the legislator. The muppu vaazcha had to combine both the practices of 'interpretation' and invoke 'precedence'. The existence of the Swaroopams was closely linked to 'generative rules and resources' that went into the definition, alteration and preservation of the social stratification. The rules and norms were not uniform across social strata. The generative rules were found to operate by clearly defining and focusing on the distribution of the differentiated social units with reference to the specific social strata (in terms of caste, religion, wealth, ritual status and so on). With all differentials, rules remained fixed however they differed with social strata.

Although the structures and human actions were socially coded and schematised by the past, as it appears in the example of kuuru-mura schema, human agency was not found to be passively receiving the compulsions of the structures. Agents altered structures and such alterations and by-passing of structures were the sites of political and cultural negotiations, sites of contests and compromises. For an example, recall the postponement of padiyettam during the first quarter of the seventeenth century.

The Self-evidences

There will be social stratification that make up the spatiality and temporality of any given society. There will be self-evidences unique to each stratum of activities, be it particular to the political, cultural, religious, symbolic, spiritual and economic spheres or combinations and permutations of them. The self-evidences were recognised without the aid of outside and inside of each of these spheres, although we bring in the 'specific variables and constants' for analytical advantage and conceptualisation. The specific historical themes that we have chosen for discussion are the phenomena that were unique and self-evident to the age of Swaroopams and the way their self-evidence got blurred, if not disappeared, after this age. This blurring of the visibility is evident in the emergence of a condition in which the problematisation of the succession and dathetukkal became necessary.

As already elaborated, the redefinition of dathetukkal, which was a self-evident phenomenon prior to redefinition of it as adoption, took place only by the turn of the first decade of the eighteenth century. Within few decades of the self-evidence about dathetukkal and positioning those within kuuru-mura got blurred and the 'tradition' of the dathetukkal with its variegated implications became indecisive. As a result, the confirmation about the criteria of succession became possible only after the contest, re-probing and production of special testimonies. The pragmatic context, the intentions, nature and relative distribution of the social agents etc had all changed, both the people involved in such matters and the system of dathetukkal and the system of succession that were clear to the age of the Swaroopams. When this age perpetuated the dathetukkal, multiple-muppu vaazcha (consisting of various types) and the aachaaram, what for us are only a vague and complex practice was for the Swaroopyes a set of clearly set-out practices.

The genealogical antecedents that emanated from Swaroopam to the kingdom of Thiruvithamkur are not to be considered as the same. They got altered in the kingdom in such a way that their significance and operative fields got redefined and relocated. For instance, the practice of dathetukkal was reduced to adoption. Threppappur Swaroopam had become the centre of Travancore and other Swaroopams became 'parts' of it. The historical truth of multiple-muppu vaazcha was self-evident, but soon after the formation of the kingdom it became redundant as the Swaroopam form itself was discarded. All these reveals time-irreversibility of history.

The blurring of the self-evidences took place to the extent that the meaning attributed to the human actions of the Swaroopam period and man-made social structures were getting beyond recognition. Those self-evident phenomena that have become beyond the grasp of the nineteenth and twentieth centuries had central importance in this study. What was extracted from the historical statements were self-evidences unique to the age of the Swaroopams, it is this theme that unites this book.

The blurred self-evidences could be simulated when the conditions that made the self-evidences are focused. Unless these 'conditions' are not analysed, as it is in the received view, many things will, including Swaroopam, have to be considered as exceptional, non-recurring, transitory period from Nadu to kingdom and so on. What we have today are the statements and things in the historical documents received from the past, but we have to simulate the conditions that opened them up and given self-evidence in the organisation of Swaroopam. The visibilities that are brought forth from the already interpreted 'documents' were not hidden ones, but they were none the less was not immediately visible. There were possibilities that perpetually sustained this self-evident visibility; it is this that we have tried to bring forth.

When we situate the present book among the existing histories of 'Travancore' then, the main difference is that many things that were treated as insignificant, unusual or abnormal (recall the 'co-kings' problem mentioned in the first chapter) turns out to be normal, regular and explicable. In fact, it is found that the things, at least some of the things that became exogenous in the existing histories are those self-evidences and truths of the Swaroopam age that had become part of the tacit ideology during the kingdom building. For instance multiple-muppu vaazcha became a convenient system for Marthanda Varma to amalgamate different Swaroopams. The self-evidences were part of the truth regime[22] of Swaroopam organisation, the society used to take them for granted and any expressed doubt about its rightness were taken into account.

For instance, Marthanda Varma claimed that he was the legitimate successor to the muppu of Deshinganad and Threppappur. He was accepting the rightness of the system of multiple-muppu vaazcha and the aachaaram of dathetukkal. He deployed the truth attached to the self-evident multiple-muppu vaazcha scheme in order to legitimize his activities that deviateed from the existent aachaaram. It is also known that Marthanda Varma prevented the multifarious dathetukkal to preempt a legitimate successor to Deshinganad so that he could become the successor. Failing such a strategy and after employing coercive force to amalgamate Deshinganad with his domain, he redefined dathetukkal in 1748 and the multifarious dathetukkal got incomparably altered to the extent that within few decades it became a non-self-evident phenomenon. Concomitant with the erasure of the co-existence of the Swaroopams, the scheme of multiple-muppu vaazcha also got relegated. The truth of the aachaaram had become part of the political culture and military strategy during the second quarter of the eighteenth century. In order to legitimize some acts that were deviations from the aachaaram, some other aachaaram was concocted and interpreted it to give justification and explanation for such deviations.

In all these examples, what is common is that, it was the already constituted and normalised truths of the Swaroopam age that become constitutive elements in the ideological armory of kingdom building. That is, the difference between the Swaroopam period and the kingdom period can be characterised as a shift/rupture not change or transformation. It appears that, it is apt to say that "power produces truth before it ideologises, abstracts or masks".[23]

Power and Subjectivity

An inference about methodology is that, in conceiving the culture of politics, the concept of 'relations of power'[24] is more advantageous when compared to the conceptualisation of the processes in terms of culture or political or economic relations. This is particularly so, in the study of the 'non-expansive' aspects of the political and cultural fields of operation and the inter-subjectivity[25] among the positions involved in the organisation of Swaroopams. A study of another Princely State in South India has come out with more or less the same conclusion.[26] It specifies the nature of relations between the processes identified in terms of caste, politics etc and 'relations of power'. To the author, the "caste structure, ritual form, and political processes were all dependent on relations of power".[27] In this conceptual formulation the political and other process are 'dependent' on power relations.

On the basis of the present study and theoretical understanding of the 'analytic of power', we specify the nature of the relation between the two on a different manner. The processes, particularly political processes, were not 'dependent on relations of power' but relations of power were inherent in all those processes. That is, these processes and relations of power are not distinct ones to have relations of dependence. Although the above argument and the one that is made by me are substantially different in terms of the conceptualisation of power and social processes, what is common in the arguments is the position that 'power relations' enable better understanding of the social processes of late-medieval South India. The non-coercive and "dialogic production of negotiated system of rules and institutions"[28] come under better visibility when analysed with the help of the poststructuralist notion of discursively constituted 'power relations'.

Another example, among several others, from the present study may be recalled. The multiple-muppu-vaazcha schemata cannot be understood in terms of juridico-political notion of power and domination; it has to be understood as a negotiated terrain of culture and politics as if it was a truth regime. The site of multiple-muppu vaazcha was also a realm of operation of inter-subjectivity. The scheme was at the same time woven through the inter-subjectivity of the participants and the commonly shared system as in the case of the kuuru-mura schemata which conditioned the subjectivity of the agents. When we say subjectivity, it is not that individuals were the bearers of structures and that they are subjected to others or one another. To explain the multiple-muppu vaazcha the 'enticing forms of power' implicit in it need to be traced. The kuuru-mura schemata does not bear the political reason, rather it bears the reasons of culture of politics in which elders were conceived as superior and need they need not be "efficient". Age as the criterion of determination of hierarchy among given set of individuals was definitely a discursively constituted one, but while it was fixed as the criteria, its operation was insensitive to changing discourses. The postponement of padiyettam, succession, reluctance to exercise additional authority that has taken place between the Swaroopams and within each of them etc reveal that the decisions of an individual or a group in the society depended on the inter-subjectivity that they maintained. The political or economic concepts will not help us to explicate the systems such as multiple-muppu vaazcha involving sequential and simultaneous succession to more than one Swaroopam, discontinuance and de-succession from one or more than one Swaroopam, and to explain the events like the postponement of Padiyettam, or the individualisation within kuuru-mura schemata etc.

One can say that the question of what legitimates one's relation to oneself and the way a soul is situated among others etc had been influencing the behaviour of those who were directly involved in the organisation of Swaroopam and those included in the kuuru-mura schemata. So they were found to be highly individualised[29] and placed in the matrix of power relations. A form of power relation that is blueprinted in the kuuru-mura, where everyone is considered as an independent individual but at the same time placed in the grid of inter-individual relationship. This individualisation of the swaroopikal (plural form of swaroopy) presupposes a hierarchy, which was based on the physiological age. Within the schemata what defined one's position and one's relation with the 'world' was always his place in the matrix of the distribution of individuals. The word 'individual' is not to be confused with either the 'modern Enlightened individual' or with a 'person', as we understand it today; the term individual can denote any social unit or agent. The inter-subjective relations among the positions were to a great extent guided by the aachaarakramam. The aachaarakramam specified how to place oneself and relate to oneself with others and with oneself; it also coded the relation that one ought to have with oneself. It was embedded in the technologies of self, or rather it was the audible form of the 'technologies of self' during the Swaroopam period. It gave self-evidence to what one can do and what one should not, the structures that determine the course of activities of each individual position and what each individual is.

The shift from Swaroopam to kingdom involved application of the coercive forms of exercise of power and this in turn effected physical and cultural violence. In this context the violence was justified with the help of anaachaaram (not duraachaaram), 'tradition' and through inventing 'tradition'. In general, legitimisation of kingdom or amalgamation of Swaroopamsas could be understood only by combining the juridico-political notion of 'power' and the notion of 'discursively constituted power relations'.

Possible Trajectories

A hypothesis can be formulated; in the shift from the co-existence of Swaroopams to the kingdom of Thiruvithamkur, the Yogam and Ettuveettil Pillamar had certain critical roles and functions. The alterations made in the constitution of them or eradication of them from their roles or redefinition of them were the sites of genealogical distancing that was the warranted condition for the making of kingdom instead of allowing the perpetuation of the co-existence of Swaroopams. These two agencies and strategic operations between them and Swaroopams were extremely significant during the period of Swaroopams and during the shift to kingdom, yet the depiction of their relations, non-relations and conflicts between them remains outside the limited scope of this book. The relation between the Yogam and Ettuveettil Pillamar, and the Swaroopam requires a study in itself.

The period under coverage is also a period which witnessed the European "monopoly mercantilism" making its presence felt in the organisation of Swaroopams. The Portuguese and Dutch were at the same time traders, religious activists and strategists of coercion and war. This kind of monopoly mercantilism was quite new to the Swaroopams. What was the kind of presence that this monopoly mercantilism emitted in the cost and spice-hills, and what were the repercussions that were effected by the trader-warriors? What were the actions and reactions of the Swaroopams that were generated as a result of their presence? How did monopoly mercantilism and culture of politics interacted? These are the questions that directly have direct implications on the important aspects of the organisation of Swaroopam; yet these questions remain unaddressed in this book. These questions are particularly important because, a cursory analysis reveals that their influence on the direction of movement of merchandise and on the life-world of the people dwelling in the coastal belts of the Swaroopams were substantial. The relation between the Europeans and the Swaroopams was mainly conflicting but at times mutually complimenting. It is also true that within the same Swaroopam there would be some who wanted to maintain trade relations with them and others who opposed it, and this resulted internal tension within the Swaroopams. There was no homogeneous relation between the Swaroopams and monopoly mercantilism. Therefore, their presence also influenced the specific inter-Swaroopam relations as well. How did the Swaroopam organisations co-acted with and reacted to these aliens? Did they appear as alien to the Swaroopams? This question is important because Swaroopams had been engaging in long distance maritime trade for centuries and centuries.

How the social boundaries which were blurred and shifting were mapped on to the geographical space? With the coming of the kingdom, the boundaries between Swaroopams got erased, although language united them. The inter-Swaroopam boundaries overlapped and intersected at several aspects. Members of a Swaroopam could hold land in another one. None of the rights over any given landed area was exclusive, exhaustive and absolute in the sense that the modern notion of 'property' was not in vogue and several rights converged on given space of land. The nature and implications of these rights, both inter-Swaroopam and intra-Swaroopam rights, would vary according to the social strata to which the holders of the right belonged. One hypothesis that can be framed is the following:

the right over land by any individual social unit depended to a great extent on that unit's social power relations with others not vice versa. Alternatively, one's relation with others was not determined by one's right over land alone.

The system of multiple rights converging on a given space of land was not friction free. There were several instances of disputes culminating in display of violence. What legitimated a muppu or swaroopam to exercise control over the landed area of the Swaroopams and what were the social spaces and objects on which a muppu could legitimately exercise authority are the questions that remain to be taken up.

The beginnings of a Swaroopam still remain non-deciphered; the description of the Swaroopam is partial. This book did not provide a general history either. Further, as we have projected certain select non-opened trajectories of inquiry, this study cannot be said to provide the complete picture of the Swaroopam although this is virtually impossible. But then, at a time when the histories of Truths are written, any claim to completeness is a longing and an enchanting fable of truth.

Notes

1. For instance, there is an assertion that *Swaroopams* attempted to expand their territory because of their trade-surplus. For an instance see, Raghava Varier, M. R. (2014, 2016: 215).
2. For instance, see, Tambiah, Stanly J. (1977).
3. The term 'structuration' is used here in Giddensian sense, for details, see, Giddens A. (1977).
4. I use the word 'metamorphosis' to stress that there is no presupposition about the cause for the process of change or shift; the process might have been caused by either external or internal factors.
5. For the theoretical implications of the concepts such as 'total' and 'centre', see, Derrida J. (1978).
6. Threppappur was the centre of the Travancore Kingdom since beginning of the second half of the eighteenth century.
7. Consider for instance one of the leading historian's statement on Travancore: "... a society which had survived fundamentally unchanged for 700 years". Robin Jeffrey (1976:249).

8. For example, see, Kawashima Koji. (1998:17).
9. For details, see, Shivashankaran Nair, K. (1993, 2005).
10. The culture of politics follow *aachaaram* and *maryada*, where as political culture considers culture as a field of strategic moves.
11. For details, see, Shivashankaran Nair, K. (1993, 2005).
12. M.Doc. CC II and CC III, Velu Pillai, T. K. Vol. II (1940).
13. M.Doc. CC III, Velu Pillai, T. K. Vol. II (1940).
14. Nicholas, B. Dirks, (1987).
15. For details, see, Shivashankaran Nair, K. (1993, 2005).
16. Rajaraja Varma Raja, M. (1930).
17. Eugene, F. Irschick (1969, 1994:7).
18. Eugene, F. Irschick (1969, 1994:7).
19. For instance, some of the works are the following: Nicholas B. Dirks (1987), Arjun Appadurai (1983), Eugene F. Irschick (1994:7), Kawashima Koji (1998) etc.
20. I have not suggested any *Swaroopam* model, yet select variables and constants that might go into such a model are delineated.
21. Nicholas, B. Dirks, (1987:5).
22. This idea of truth regime is influenced by the Foucauldian notion of power relations or strategic notion of power relations.
23. Deluze, G. (1988: 29).
24. Here the reference is to the discursively formed power relations, rather than the juridico-political conception of power. For details, see, Foucault, M (1981).
25. The term inter-subjectivity refers to the kind of relationship that one maintains with others (including corporeal, non-corporeal, and epi-phenomenal worlds) and with oneself. It also refers to the subjectivity of an individual in terms of one's relation to oneself that is mediated through the imagined/real gaze of the 'other'.
26. Nicholas, B. Dirks, (1987: 5).
27. Nicholas, B. Dirks, (1987: 7).
28. Eugene, F. Irschick, (1994: 7).
29. Here individual and individualised do not carry the contemporary meanings or modern meanings. They are not atomissed as well. It suggests a position in the hierarchy in the distribution of persons in terms of age.

References

Achutha Menon, A, (1911), *The Cochin State Manual,* Ernakulam: Cochin Government Press.

Achutha Menon, C, (ed), (1953), *Keralolpatti,* Madras: Madras University.

Aiyar, R, (1923), *Progressive Travancore,* Trivandrum: The Indian States Series.

Alcoff, L L, (1993), 'Foucault as Epistemologist', in *The Philosophical Forum,* Vol. XXV. 2, Winter.

Anderson, B, (1983), *Imagined Communities: Reflections on the Origin and Spread of Nationalism,* London: Verso.

Appadurai, Arjun, (1983), *Worship and Conflict under Colonial Rule: A South Indian Case,* New Delhi: Orient Longman.

Bailey, Benjamin, (1846), *A Dictionary of High and Colloquial Malayalam and English,* Kottayam: C.M.S Press.

Balakrishnan, B.C. (1994), *C.V. Vykhyana Kosam,* C. V. Raman Pillai National Foundation,Thiruvavanthapuram.

Barbosa, D, (1866), *A Description of the Coast of Africa and Malabar,* London: Hakluyt Society.

Barker, S G, (1919), *Report of the Industrial Survey of Travancore,* Trivandrum: Government Press.

Berkemer Georg, (2015), 'Little Kingdoms or Little Kingdoms', in Margret Frenz & Georg Berkemer, *Sharing Sovereignty: The Little Kingdom in South Asia*, Primus Books, Delhi.

Berkemer, Georg. (2015), *Sharing Sovereignty: The Little Kingdom in South Asia*, Primus Books, Delhi.

Bhandarkar, R.G, (1898), *Early History of Dekkan,* Calcutta.

Bloch, J, (1954), *Grammatical Structure of Dravidian Languages,* tr. by Ramakrishna Bourdillon, T F, (1893), *Report on the Forests of Travancore,* Trivandrum, Government Press, 1893.

Buchanan, A, (1807), *A Journey From Madras through Mysore, Canara and Malabar,* London.

Burke, K, (1969), *A Grammar of Motives,* Berkeley: University of California Press.

Caldwell Robert, (1856), *A Comparative Grammar of the Dravidian or South Indian Family of Languages,* Madras: University of Madras.

Chandu Menon, O, (1889), *Indulekha,* Kottayam: D.C. Books (1991).

Chattampiswamikal. (1914), *Pracheena Malayalam* (Malayalam), Kollam: Vidyathiraja Publications.

Colin Gordon M, (ed), (1980) *Power/Knowledge: Selected Interviews & Other Writings 1972-1977 by Michel Foucault* ed, Colin Gordon, New York: Pantheon Books.

Dancy, J, (1985), *Introduction to Contemporary Epistemology,* Oxford: Basil Blackwell. Deleuze G, (1988), *Foucault,* London: Athlone Press.

Deleuze, G, and Guattari, F. (1994), *What is Philosophy?* London:Verso.

Derrida, J, (1978), 'Structure, Sign, and Play in the Discourses of the Human Sciences' in *Writing and Difference,* London: Routledge.

Dillon, M, (1995), 'Sovereignty and Governmentality: From the Problematic of the "New World Order" to the Ethical Problematic of the World Order', in *Alternatives,* 20.

Dirks Nicholas, (1987), *The Hollow Crown: The Ethonohistory of an Indian Kingdom,* Cambridge: Cambridge University Press.

Einstein, Albert, (1953), 'Aphorisms for Leo Baeck' Reprinted in *Ideas and Opinions,* New York: Dell (1973).

Eugene, F. Irschick, Politics and Social Conflict in South India: The Non-Brahman Movement in Tamil Separatism, University of California Press (1969, 1994:7).

Fawcett, F, (1901), *Nayars of Malabar,* New Delhi: Asian Educational Services (1990).

Fernandez, J, (1986), *Persuasions and Performances: The Play of Tropes in Culture,* Bloomington, Indiana University Press.

Feyerabend, P, (1975), *Against Method: Outline of an Anarchistic Theory of Knowledge,* London: Verso.

Foucault, M, (1970), *The Order of Things,* London, Tevistock.

Foucault, M, (1972), *Archaeology of Knowledge,* New York: Pantheon Books.

Foucault, M, (1977), 'Nietzsche Genealogy History', in *Language Counter-memory, Practice: Selected Essays and Interviews,* ed, Bouchard, D.F. Ithaca: Cornell University Press.

Foucault, M, (1977), *Discipline and Punish, Birth of the Prison,* London: Penguin Books. Foucualt M, (1981), *History of Sexuality,* Vol. 1: *An Introduction,* New York: Pantheon.

Frenz Margret, (2015), 'Virtual Relations: Little Kings in Malabar', In Frenz Margret & Georg eds. (2015).

Galleti, A, (1911), *The Dutch in Malabar,* Madras.

Ganesh, K.N, (1990), 'The Process of State Formation in *Travancore*', in *Studies in History,* 6, 1, ns.

Ganesh, K.N., (1996), *Reflections on Pre Modern Kerala*, Cosmo Books, Thrissur.

Ganesh, K.N, (1996a), 'Polity and Society in Medieval Kerala: Preliminary Considerations' in Kump, K.K.N, (ed.), *New Dimension in South Indian History,* Calicut.

Gangadhara Menon M, (1998), 'Is there a Portuguese Period in Kerala History?' in *Samvada,* New Delhi: Institute of Social Sciences.

Giddens, A, (1977), *Studies in Social and Political Theory,* New York: Basic Books.

Gopal Panikkar, A. T, (1900), *Malabar and its Folk,* New Delhi: Asian Educational Services (1983).

Gopala Pillai, K.N, (1949), *Kerala-Maha Charithram,* (Malayalam, in two volumes), Trivandrum: Reddiar Pres.

Gopalakrishnan, N.R, (1998), 'Rev.Gundert: His Life in Kerala and his Contribution to Malayalam Literature' in *Samvada,* New Delhi: Institute of Social Sciences. Government of Travancore, *(1910-41), Travancore Archaeological Series,* 9, Vols, Trivandrum.

Govinda Pillai, P.G, (1881), *Malaya/a Bhaashaa Charitham,* (Malayalam) Trivandrum.

Gundert, H, (1868), *Kerala Pazhama (History of Malabar): From AD 1498-1531,* (Malayalam) Vidyarthi Mithram Press, Kottayam, (1983).

Gundert, H, (1843), *Keralolppathy,* Trivandrum: Balan Publishers (1961).

Gundert, H, (1848), *A Concise Dictionary of English and Malayalam,* Mangalapuram.

Gundert, H, (1869), *Malaya/a Rajyam: a Historical Geography,* Mangalore.

Gurukkal, R, (1991), *The Kerala Temple and Early Medieval Agrarian System,* Sukapuram: Vallathol Vidyapeetham.

Hacker, I.H, (1908), *A Hundred Years in Travancore 1806-1906: A History and Description of the Work done by the London Missionary Society in Travancore, South India during the Past Century,* London: H.R. Allenson Limited.

Homi K Bhabha, (ed), (1990), *Nation and Narration,* London: Routledge.

Ibrahim Kunju A.P, (1990), *Marthanda-Varma: Adhunika Thiruvithamkurinte Udayam,* Trivandrum: Government of Kerala.

Innes and Evans, (1951), *Malabar District Gazetteer,* Madras.

Irschick Eugene, F, (1994), *Dialogue and History: Constructing South India, 1795-1895,* Delhi: Oxford University Press.

Jeffrey Robin, (1976), *The Decline of Nayar Dominance: Society and Politics in Travancore, 1847-1908,* New Delhi: Vikas Publishing House.

Karashima, N, (1984), *South Indian History and Society: Studies from Inscriptions A.D 850-1800,* Oxford, Oxford University Press.

Karve, I, (1953), *Kinship Organisation in India,* Poona: Deccan College Monograph Series, no.11, Deccan College.

Kawashima Koji, (1998), *Missionaries and Hindu State: Travancore 1858-1936,* Delhi: Oxford University Press.

Kesavan, V, (1997), *Into the "Medieval" -And Out of It: Early South India in Transition,* Presidential Address, Section II, Indian History Congress.

Krishna Pillai. K, (1941), *Travancore and its Ruler,* Changanachery, Sudharma Publishing House.

Kuhn T, (1970), *The Structure of Scientific Revolution,* Chicago: University of Chicago Press.

Kunjan Pillai, S, (1946), *Lilathilakam: A Sanskrit Work or Manipravala,* Trivandrum.

Lakshmi Bai. G, (1995), *Sree Padmanabha Swamy Temple,* Bombay: Bharatiya Vidya Bhavan.

Leelavathi, M, (1985), *Malayala Kavitha Sahitya Charithram,* Trichur: Kerala Sahithya Academy.

Logan, W, (1887), *Malabar District Manual,* Madras.

Longman's Vernacular Series for Madras, (1916), *Longman's Brief History of Thiruvithamkur Charithra Samkshepam,* Kottayam: Green and Co.

Madhava Rao, T, (1873), *History of Travancore,* Trivandrurn (few chapters of this book was translated into Malayalam).

Mahadeva, Iyer, (1916), *Travancore Land Revenue Manual: Vol. V,* Trivandrurn.

Maheshwaran Nair K, (1974), *Chronicles of the Trivandrum Pagoda,* Vol. I, Trivandrum.

Maheshwaran Nair K, (1975), 'Ettara Yogathinte Ghatana', (Malayalam), in *Vignaanadeepika,* 6 (10).

Maheswari Uma S. (2018), *Mathilakam Rekhakal*, Akshara Offset, Thiruvananthapuram.

Martin Heidegger, (1947), 'Letter on Humanism', in Cahoone L.E, (ed.) *From Modernism to Postmodernism: An Anthology,*. Oxford: Blackwell Publishers (1996).

Mateer, S, (1871), *The Land of Charity:* a *Descriptive Account of Travancore and Its People with Especial Reference to Missionary Labour,* London: John Snow.

Mateer, S, (1883), *Native life in Travancore,* London.

McCloskey, D.N, (1985), *The Rhetoric of Economics,* Sussex: Harvester Press.

Menon, R, (1939), 'Medieval Kerala History', in *Bulletin of the Rama Varma Research Institute,* Vol. VII Part I. (1980).

Merquior, J.G, (1985), *Foucault,* London: Fontana.

Nagam Aiya, (1906), *The Travancore State Manual,* Trivandrurn: Government of Travancore.

Nair, P.M, (1932), *Otanad or Chiravay Rajaswaroopam,* (Malayalam): Prabhatham Book Series No. 8.

Nair, S.K, (1993), *Venadinte Parinamam,* (Malayalam) Trivandrum: Department of Cultural Publication.

Narayanan, M.G.S, (1972), *The Political and Social Conditions of Kerala Under the Kulasekhara Empire c. 800 A.D. -1124 A.D),* Doctoral Thesis submitted to the University of Kerala, Republished as *Perumals of Kerala,* Calicut (1996).

Narayanan, M.G.S. (1977), 'The Special Features of Cera Inscriptions from Kerala', Paper Presented at XXIII Annual Congress, Thanjavur: Epigraphically Society of India.

Nietzsche F, (1969), *On Genealogy of Morals,* New York: Vintage.

Pachumuthathu, (1868), *Thiruvithamkur Charithram,* (Malayalam) Trivandrum.

Padmanabha Menon, K.P, 'Aadikeralam', (Malayalam) *Mangalodayam,* 7.1, Vreschikam.

Padmanabha Menon, K.P, (1914), *Cochi Rajya Charithram,* Emakulam.

Padmanabha Menon, K.P, 1924, *History of Kerala: Written in the Form of Notes on Visscher's Letters from Malabar,* New Delhi: Asian Educational Foundation.

Panicker, K.M, (1957), *Kerala Swathanthrya Samaram,* Prabhatham Printing & Publishing Co.

Parameshwara Iyer, S, (1974), *Kera/a Sahithya Charithram,* Trivandrum: University of Kerala.

Parameshwara Iyer, S, (1941, 1961), *Important Mathilakam Records,* Trivandrum: Sree Chithrodaya Huzur Central Record *Granthavali* number 3, Sarkkar achukkodam.

Parameshwaran Nair, P.K, (1958), *Malayala Sahithya Charithram,* (Malayalam) New Delhi: Sahithya Academy.

Parameshwaran Pillai, V.R, (1963), *Praachinalighithamgal,* (Malayalam), Kottayam: NBS.

Pillai, I.K, (1955), *Leelathilakam: Manipravalalakshanam,* (Malayalam), Kottayam: N.B.S.

Price Pamela, G, (1996), *Kingship and Political Practice in Colonial India,* Cambridge: Cambridge University Press.

Prigogine, I and Stengers, I, (1984), *Order Out of Chaos: Man's New Dialogue with Nature,* New York: Bantam Books.

Probodhachandran Nair, V.R, (1984), 'Malayalam'- in George K.M, (ed.) *Comparative Indian Literature,* Trichur: Sahithya Academy.

Radcliffe-Brown, A.R, (1979), *Structure and Function in Primitive Society,* New York: R.K.P.

Raghava Varier, M.R. (2014, 2016) *Madhyakalakeralam*, National Book Stall, Kottaya.

Raja, P.K.S, (1953), *Medieval Kerala,* Annamalai: Annamalai University.

Rajaraja Varma, M, (1928-33), "Some Travancore Dynastic Records", Series I, II, III, and IV in *Kerala Society Papers,* Trivandrum: Series I (1928), III (1930), VI (1930a) and VIII (1931).

Rajaraja Varma Raja, M, (1941), *Shri Vanchi Rajya Charithram,* (Malayalam) Trivandrum: Kamalalaya Book depot.

Raju, S, (1990), Narratives, Signs and Social Order: Nagam and the People of Keralam, *Studies in History,* 7,1, n.s.

Raju, S, (1994), 'Excursus to Anticipated Futures in the Wor(l)ds of Nation and Wealth', Paper presented in the seminar on Modem India: Terms of Discourse, (23-27, May) at Indian Institute of Advanced Studies, Shimla.

Raman Pillai, C.V, (1891), *Marthanda* Varma, (Malayalam) Trivandrum.

Raman Pillai, C.V, (1912), *Dharma Raja,* (Malayalam) Trivandrum.

Raman Pillai, C.V, (1920-21), 'Videseeya Medhaavithwam' *Mithabhashi,* (Malayalam), Trivandrum: Government of Kerala (1994).

Ramanath Aiyar, (1923), *Progressive Travancore,* Trivandrum: The Indian States Series.

Rao, M. T, (1873), *History of Travancore,* (Malayalam) Trivandrum.

Rorty, R, (1979), *Philosophy and the Mirror of Nature,* Princeton: Princeton University Press.

Rorty, R, (1991), 'Solidarity or Objectivity?', in *Objectivity, Relativism, and Truth.*

Rorty R, (1982), *The Consequences of Pragmatism: Essays,* Minneapolis: University of Minnesota Press.

Said Edward, (1978), *Orientalism,* New York: Random House.

Sastri, M, (ed), *Keralacaritam,* Trivandrum: Travancore University.

Sastri N.K.A, (1966), A *History of South India: From Prehistoric Times to the Fall of Vijayanagar,* London: Oxford University Press.

Shangoony Menon, P. A, (1878), *History of Travancore from the Earliest Times,* Trivandrum: Government of Kerala, (1983).

Shanmugham, S.V, (1995), *Leelathilakam.Samoohika Bhaashashastra-dristiyil* (Malayalam translation) Trivandrum: Kerala Bhasha Institute.

Skoda Galey, 'On a Tribal Frontier' In *Sharing Sovereignty: The Little Kingdom in South Asia*, Primus Books, Delhi.

Smith, V.A, (1923), *Oxford History of India,* Oxford.

Soja Edward, (1989), *Postmodern Geographies: The Reassertion of Space in Critical Social Theory,* London: Verso.

Spate, O.H.K, (1954), *India and Pakistan: A General and Regional Geography,* London: Methuen & Co.

Sreedhara Menon, A, (1956), *Kerala Charithram,* (Malayalam) Kottayam: SPCS.

Stein B, (1980), *Peasant State and Society in Medieval South India,* Delhi: Oxford University Press, Delhi.

Stephen, T, (1958), *The Uses of Argument,* Cambridge: Cambridge University Press.

Stephen, T, (1982), 'The Construal of Reality: Criticism in Modern and Postmodern Science', *Critical Inquiry,* 9, Autumn.

Sundaram Pillai, S, (1894), *Some Early Sovereigns of Travancore,* Tinnevelly: The Saiva Siddhanta Workers Publishing Society.

Tambiah Stanley, J, (1977), 'The Galanctic Polity: The Structure of Traditional Kingdoms in Southeast Asia, Anthropology and the Climate of Opinion', M. Freed (ed.). *Annals of the New York Academy of Sciences 293.*

Toulmin Stephen, (1958), *The Uses of Argument,* Cambridge: Cambridge University Press.

Toulmin Stephen, (1982), "The Construal of Reality: Criticism in Modern and Postmodern Science," *Critical Inquiry,* 9,(Autumn).

Trautman, T.R. (1981), *Dravidian kinship,* New Delhi: Vistaar Publications.

Ulakamthara, M, *Arnos Padri,* (Malayalam) Ernakulam: Kerala History Association.

Velu Pillai, T.K, (1940), *The Travancore State Manual,* Trivandrum: Government Press.

Wallerstein, I (1996), 'History in Search of Science', *Review,* Volume. XIX, Number 1, Winter.

Wallerstein, I, et al, (1997), *Open the Social Sciences: Report of the Gulbenkian Commission on the Restructuring of the Social Sciences,* New Delhi: Vistaar Publications.

Williams Raymond, (1980), 'Base and Superstructure in Marxist Cultural Theory' in *Problem in Materialism and Culture,* London: Verso.

Williams, G (ed), (1969), *The Third Book of Horace's Odes,* Oxford: Oxford University Press.

Wittgenstein, L., (1958), *Philosophical Investigations,* Anscombe, G. E.M. and Rhees, R. (ed.), Oxford: Blackwell.

Index

T